IMAGES
of America

LEBANON

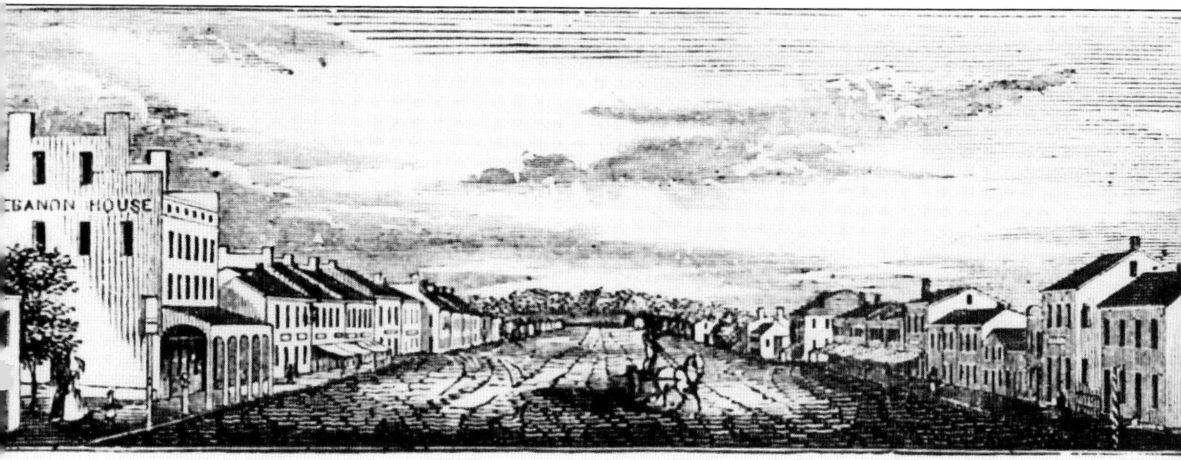

Drawn by Henry Howe in 1846.

CENTRAL VIEW, LEBANON.

This early illustration of downtown Lebanon was first published in *Howe's History of Ohio* in 1844. This expansive view, drawn from the base of Broadway Street, depicts many buildings that are still standing today.

ON THE COVER: This is the freshmen class of Lebanon High School in 1898. Taken in front of the Romanesque-style Pleasant Street School, those pictured include (in no particular order) Earnest Koogler, Willie Williams, Frank Miller, Raymond Corwin, Raymond Blust, Robert Blair, Fred Pauley, Margaret Wolcott, Hatie Dunkle, Miss Hall, Margaret McClain, Marie Thompson, Verdie Nixon, Mary Stockton, Ethel Melman, Alice Woodyard, Florence Keough, Helen Smith, Agnes Brown, Marie Hutchinson, Mildred Baldwin, Jacob Reid, and Evan Bone.

IMAGES
of America

LEBANON

Fred Compton

ARCADIA
PUBLISHING

ISBN 978-0-7385-8360-0

Published by Arcadia Publishing
Charleston, South Carolina

Printed in the United States of America

Library of Congress Control Number: 2010934173

For all general information, please contact Arcadia Publishing:
Telephone 843-853-2070
Fax 843-853-0044
E-mail sales@arcadiapublishing.com
For customer service and orders:
Toll-Free 1-888-313-2665

Visit us on the Internet at www.arcadiapublishing.com

To Ally, Marisa, Michael, and Susan, who spent too many weekends alone while I was out trying to make history.

CONTENTS

Acknowledgments

My first thank you has to go to my longtime friend Sally Foster of Cincinnati, Ohio. Sallie's ever-expanding collection of Lebanon ephemera, including postcards, photographs, and advertisements, formed the basis for this book, and her collection is featured throughout in almost every section. My thanks must also go to Traci and Scott Gallagher who are painstakingly uncovering Lebanon's history one glass negative at a time.

I also need to recognize the staff of the Warren County History Center for their help and assistance in gathering materials and images for the book. Making the project a lot easier was museum director Vicki Van Harlinsen, who gave me access to the museum's extensive archives; curator Mary Klei, who could put her finger on anything in the museum's collection in a matter of minutes; and alphabetically last, but certainly not least, museum historian and education director John Zimkus, whose search engine–like knowledge of Lebanon history needs to be put down in writing as soon as possible. Lebanon, as well as all of Warren County, is fortunate to have such experienced, knowledgeable, and caring individuals working daily to preserve their history for future generations.

INTRODUCTION

In the spring of 1975, a rather well-known traveler parked his motor home in front of Lebanon's landmark hotel, the Golden Lamb Inn. Inside the car was famous author, broadcaster, and writer Charles Kurault. The famed broadcaster was on assignment from CBS News filming a series of television programs titled *On The Road To '76*, highlighting what Kurault thought were the most historic spots in each of the 50 states.

He had planned to film the Ohio segment in Chillicothe, the site of the Battle of Fallen Timbers, which had opened up most of the Northwest Territory to settlement. But while in Chillicothe, someone mentioned to Kurault that he should take a ride over to Lebanon, Ohio. "Got a lot of history over there," someone told him, "and a real old hotel that's still standing."

Kurault parked his motor home on Broadway Street, got out, and started exploring the then 173-year-old town. Within a few hours, he had forgotten all about Chillicothe and the Indian battle of long ago. Kurault had indeed found, in Lebanon, the most historic spot in the state of Ohio.

In a broadcast that aired later in the year, Kurault would say, "If a man could have only lived long enough he could have sat in the lobby of the old Golden Lamb and watched the entire history of the state of Ohio pass by." In that one sentence, Charles Kurault distilled the history and tradition of Lebanon, Ohio; a small town that sat patiently and quietly by the side of the road while the world came to it.

Lebanon was formally platted in September 1802 by Ichabod Halsey. There were 100 lots carved out of a primitive forest thick with elm, sycamore, and white oak. In 1802, Lebanon was a little more than four blocks long and three blocks wide. The main thoroughfare through the newly platted village, Broadway Street, was "six poles wide" or approximately 100 feet from side to side. A wide street was needed so stagecoaches could make a complete turn without stopping. The other streets were a mere "four poles wide" or about 65 feet. The original city limits were Silver Street to the north, South Street to the south, Water Street to the west, and East Street to the east.

Tucked in the middle of these primitive boundaries was a town square made up of land donated by its owners Ichabod Corwin, Ephraim Hathaway, Silas Hurin, and Samuel Manning. Located at the intersection of Main and Broadway Streets, "the four corners," as they are known today, were set aside to be used only for the public good. Lebanon, Ohio, had green space a good 170 years before anyone even thought of the term.

Located exactly one-day's ride from Cincinnati, Lebanon became a popular stopping point for stagecoaches throughout most of the 19th century. Most weary travelers stopping in Lebanon after an eight-hour trip from Cincinnati were on their way north to Zanesville, Ohio, to pick up the National Road, the major east-west route across the Appalachian Mountains. Famous legislative firebrand Henry Clay spent many nights in Lebanon as he traveled back and forth to Washington, D.C., from Kentucky, shaping the political futures of the 19th century. Mark Twain passed through as did author Charles Dickens, Harriet Beecher Stowe, Daniel Webster, and 12 U.S. presidents.

Starting in the 19th century, the sleepy village of Lebanon grew, though not as much as its neighbors to the north and south, Dayton and Cincinnati. In February 1805, Lebanon became the seat of government for Warren County having been declared the county seat by a special act of the Ohio Legislature. Just five years later, in 1810, Lebanon was incorporated.

In March 1805, strange tales began to circulate through the town of three missionaries who had walked 1,000 miles through the dead of winter from New Lebanon, New York, and were now preaching at the old church at Beedle's Station 4 miles west of Lebanon. From these three individuals would spring a large, orderly, and prosperous community of over 500 individuals, which would leave its mark not only on Lebanon but on the surrounding area as well. The United Society of Believers in Christ's Second Appearing established Union Village in the area of what is now Routes 63 and 741 and continues to be a major part of Lebanon's history long after the village dissolved in the 1920s. The residents of Lebanon, like most Americans at the time, did not bother with the long official name of the group; they simply called them Shakers.

Throughout the 19th and early 20th centuries, dusty, old Broadway Street with its six-pole width began to take shape. With the advent of the railroads in 1881, a fine station was established at the base of Broadway along South Street. In time, one of the original Carnegie Libraries would occupy one of the four corners, while the Lebanon Opera House, called the finest building in the county, would sit opposite until its fiery demise in 1932; it was replaced by the current city building a year later. The landmark Golden Lamb would expand from a simple log cabin in 1803, to a two-story brick tavern in 1815, to a three-story hotel in the 1840s, and to its current four stories in 1874. Along the way, J. W. Lingo built his hardware store at the corner of Main and Broadway Streets, where it still stands today. Alfred Holbrook established a college or "Normal School," which lasted for 62 years and had over 80,000 graduates—all without even $1 of government funding.

The history of Lebanon has expanded far beyond the three-block stretch that was so carefully platted by Ichabod Halsey in 1802, and fortunately the history has survived.

One

An Occasion for Keen Regret

National Normal University

One of the few pieces of Lebanon history that has not survived is Lebanon's National Normal University. A small stone marker in Gazebo Park, at the corner of Main and Broadway Streets, is the only reminder of what was one of the greatest teachers colleges in the Midwest. Few people realize, including Lebanon residents, that from 1855 until 1917 Lebanon, Ohio, was home to a prolific and well-respected institution whose sole purpose was to train teachers.

Beginning with only 90 students and three teachers in November 1855, National Normal would soon grow to an enrollment of 930 students from 13 different states by 1870. The school quickly outgrew the Lebanon Academy building and would eventually encompass a 12-building campus, including a dormitory in the northwest section of Lebanon. All of those buildings, save the original academy building on New Street, are gone.

Through most of its storied existence, National Normal University was overseen by one of Lebanon's great educators, Alfred Holbrook. A part of the early college was funded with Holbrook's own money, and he began the library with his own books. With a salary of $392 a year, Holbrook served the dual function of administrator and instructor. National Normal University never was a self-sustaining institution and always carried debt. But throughout the college's lifetime, Holbrook never accepted $1 of aid, endowments, or subsidy. By 1895, Holbrook had resigned as principal of the university and was merely a salaried president of the school he founded. Because of failing health at age 81, Holbrook resigned from the position.

In 1917, strapped by debt and faced with dwindling enrollments, National Normal University was merged with Wilmington College in Wilmington, Ohio. The property and buildings were sold piecemeal to pay off outstanding debt, and current students were offered the opportunity to transfer to Wilmington or continue their education elsewhere.

In writing of the university closing one person remarked, "The passing of the university is the occasion for keen regret, not only in Lebanon but throughout the country."

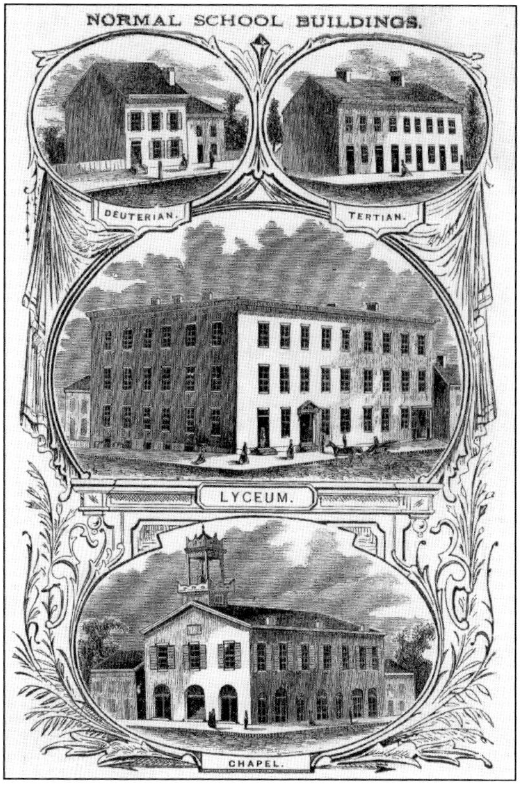

This mid-19th-century illustration of National Normal University shows four buildings, including the expansive Lyceum Building, which stood on the corner of Silver and East Streets. The structure was eventually turned into apartments and was razed in 1977 to become a parking lot for the Lebanon Presbyterian Church. (Courtesy of WCHS Museum.)

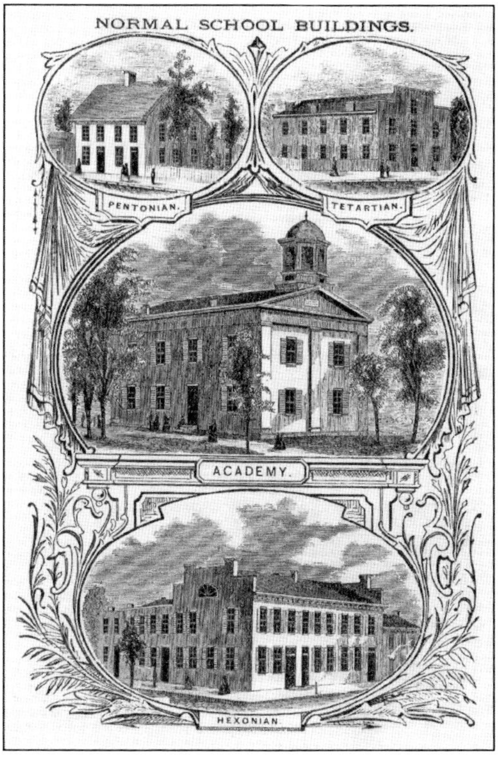

Centered in this early illustration is the Academy Building, the original home of National Normal. Located on New Street it is the only building still standing from the National Normal campus. After the closing of the university in 1917, it was used at various times by the Lebanon school system and now houses a local food pantry. (Courtesy of WCHS Museum.)

This illustration highlights several of the dormitory buildings purchased by Alfred Holbrook and used by National Normal University, including the Enditian and the Duodecian. Holbrook himself conferred these fanciful Greek names on the buildings. (Courtesy of WCHS Museum.)

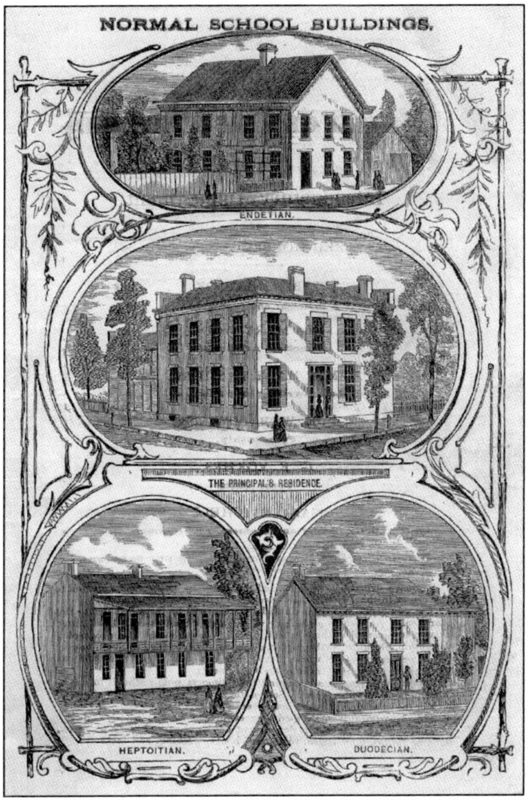

This early photograph shows a drawing class at National Normal. Pictured here (in no particular order) are F. W. Willhouse, E. S. Clark, Herman Hirsch, A. H. Kohli, L. E. Gray, D. E. Stephan, V. D. Watkins, L. M. Scofield, Martin Remp, W. H. Leffler, Paul Scullin, J. H. Synott, P. A. Tarr, Martha B. Campbell, F. W. Watkins, and their teacher Professor Withers. (Courtesy of WCHS Museum.)

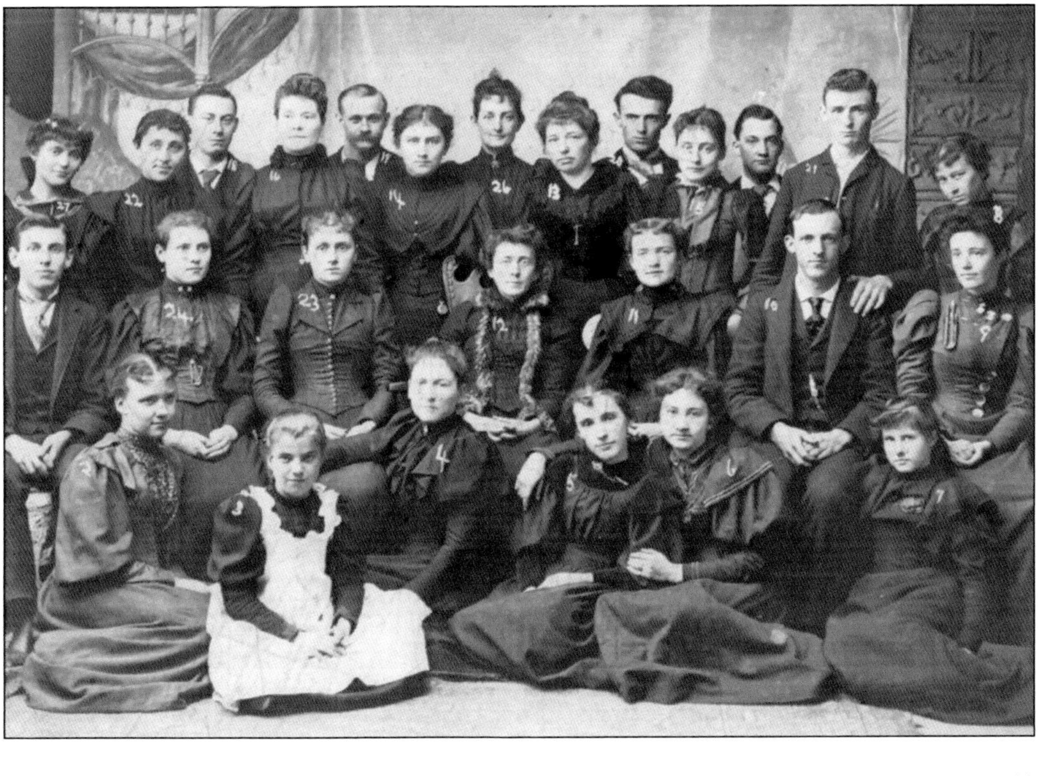

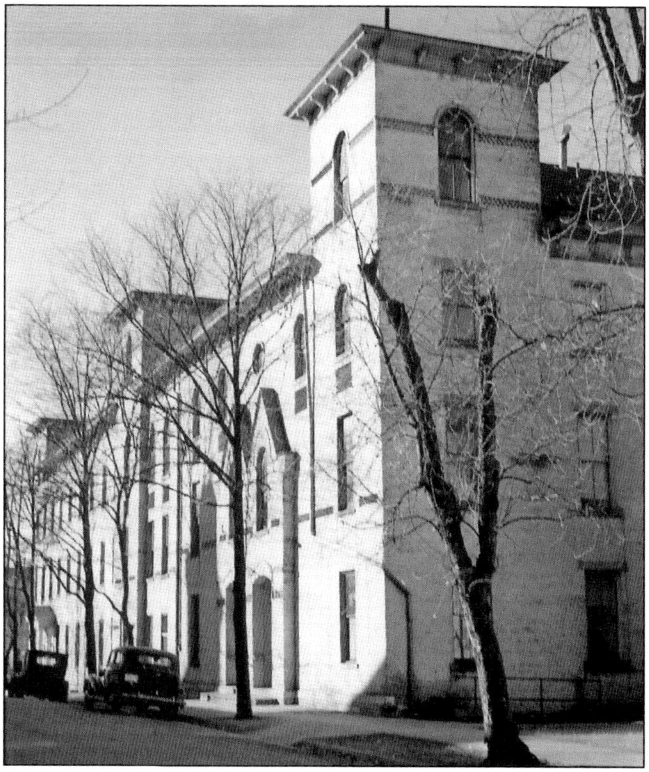

This c. 1930 photograph of the Lyceum Building was taken well after the university had closed. After the university's merging with Wilmington College in 1917, the building was purchased by private interests and was eventually razed in the 1970s for a parking lot. (Courtesy of the Sally Foster collection.)

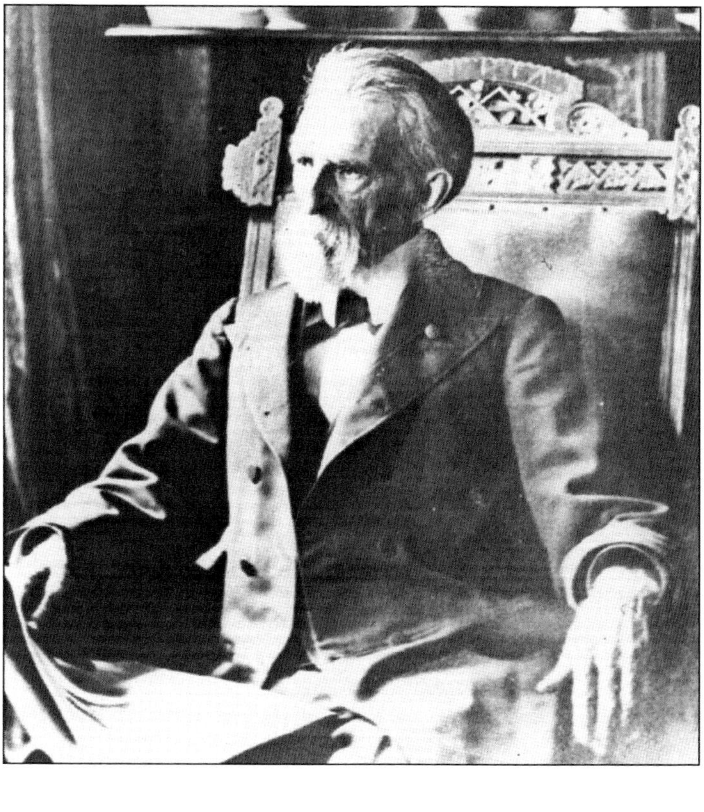

This image is of Alfred Holbrook in his latter years. By 1895, the university had such enormous debt that Holbrook resigned as administrator and became merely a paid president of the college he founded. Seven years later, at age 81, he resigned from the university entirely. (Courtesy of WCHS Museum.)

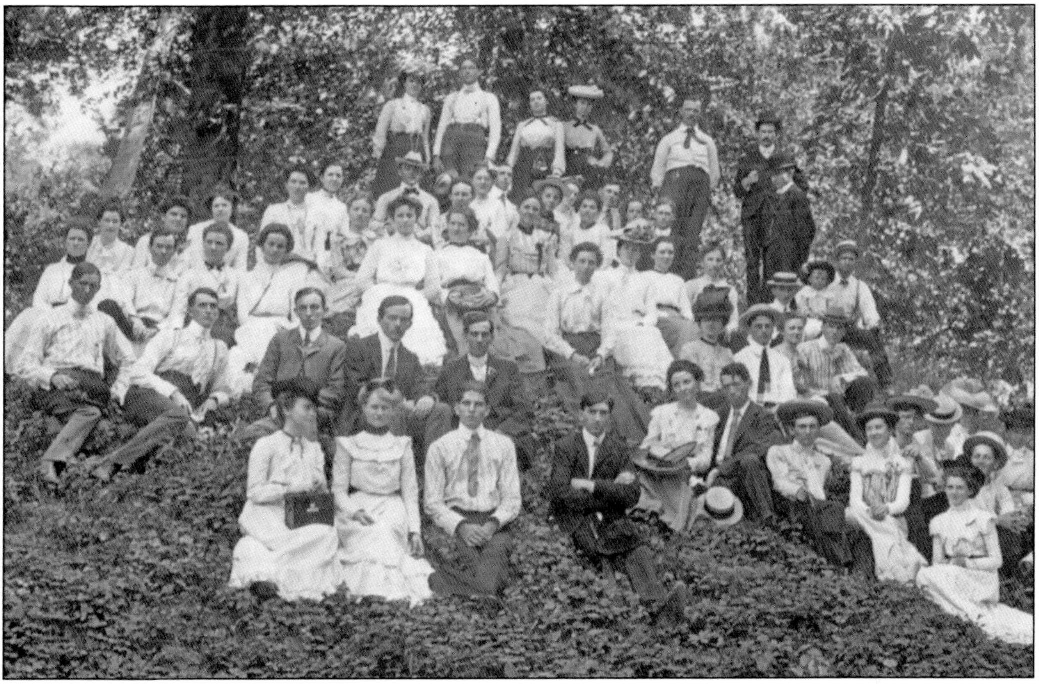

This early-1900s image is of a group of National Normal University students attending a picnic at a local park. Though the school term at National Normal sometimes extended throughout the summer months, students were encouraged to take time off from their studies to explore and enjoy the countryside of Warren County. (Courtesy of WCHS Museum.)

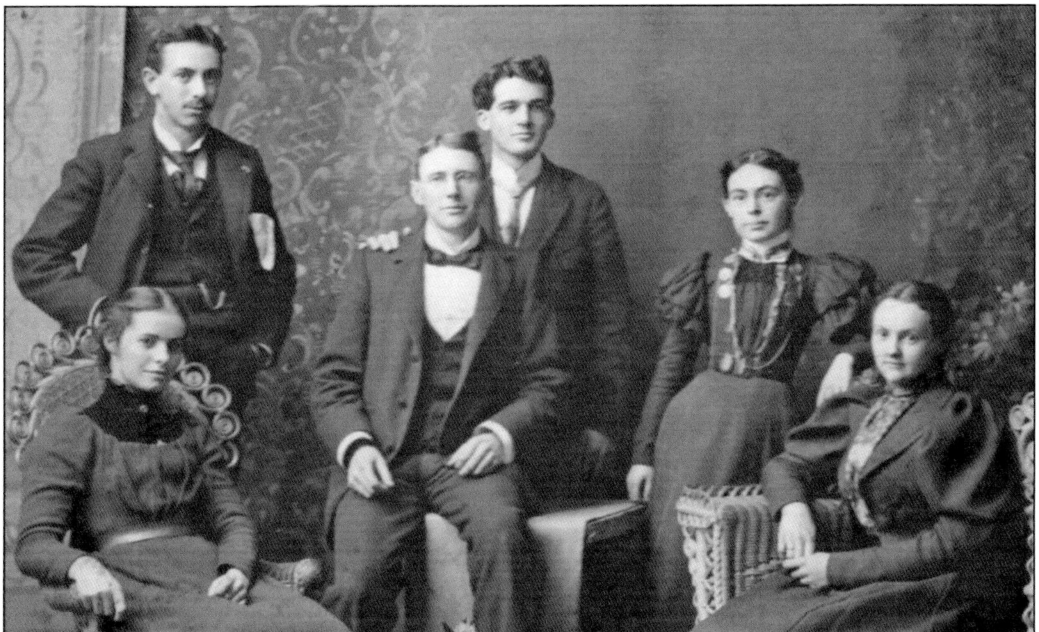

This early image of students at National Normal University highlights the early, and to some radical, coeducational aspect of the college. It was Holbrook's and the university's goal to provide education to all deserving students no matter what their gender. (Courtesy of WCHS Museum.)

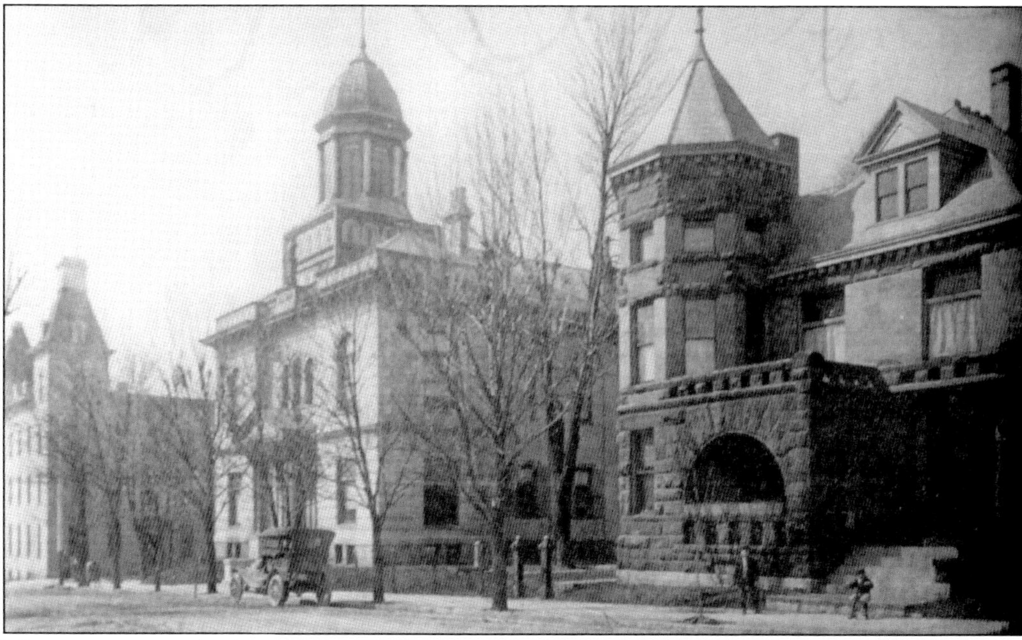

This unique view looking west on Silver Street vividly illustrates the massive architecture that was once a common occurrence in Lebanon. Nearest is the original Warren County Jail, next to that is the imposing Warren County Courthouse, and finally the crown jewel of National Normal University, the Lyceum Building. (Courtesy of WCHS Museum.)

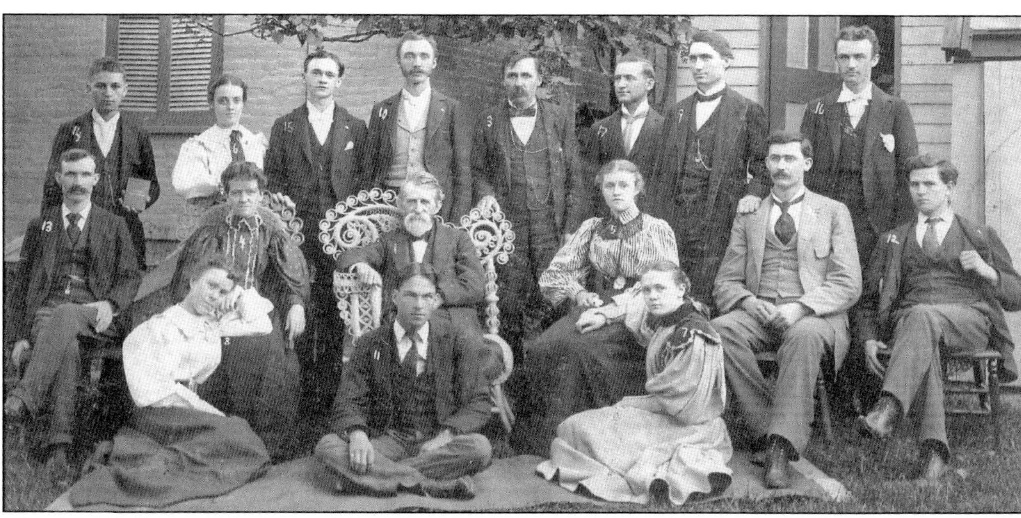

This late-19th-century image shows an aging Alfred Holbrook sitting amongst his students. At this point in his life, Holbrook had resigned his position as administrator of the university and served only as principal. (Courtesy of WCHS Museum.)

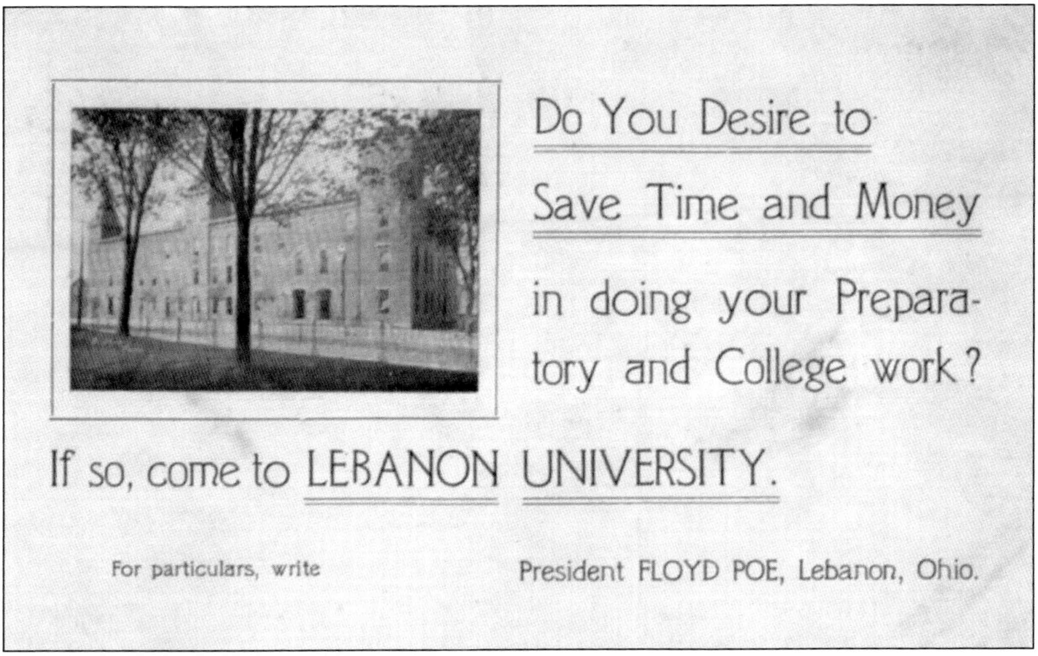

This advertisement for what was once National Normal University appeared at the turn of the early 20th century. The name National Normal University was changed to Lebanon University in April 1907. One year later, in 1908, all Lebanon high school students were given free tuition to the school. (Courtesy of the Sally Foster collection.)

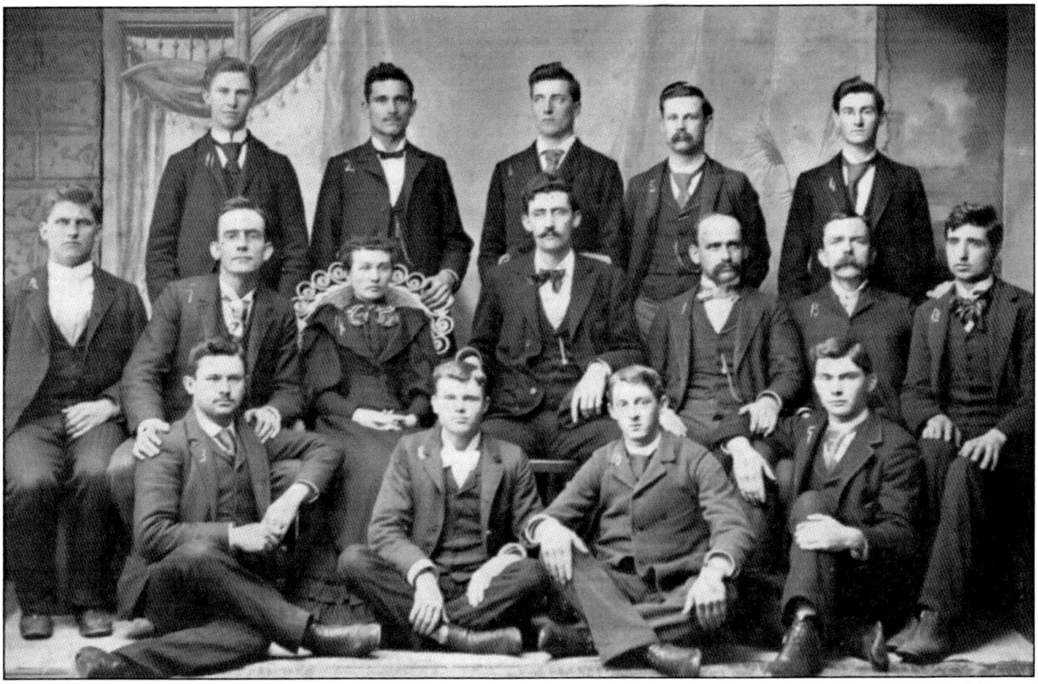

This image is of a 19th-century "Botanical Class" at National Normal University. In addition to the typical subjects of math, science, and English, the university also taught art, architecture, public speaking, and design to its students. (Courtesy of WCHS Museum.)

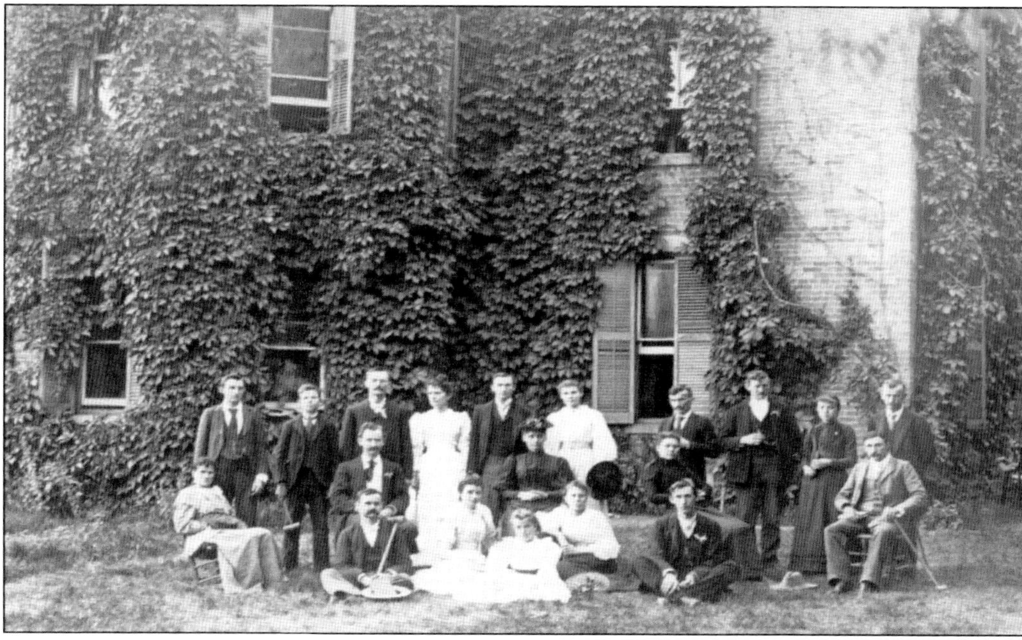

This 1900s image is simply marked "Residents of Angels Retreat" and was taken at the Holbrook home. No record exists of the purpose of the retreat, but it was known that Holbrook encouraged interaction with his students both inside and outside the classroom. (Courtesy of WCHS Museum.)

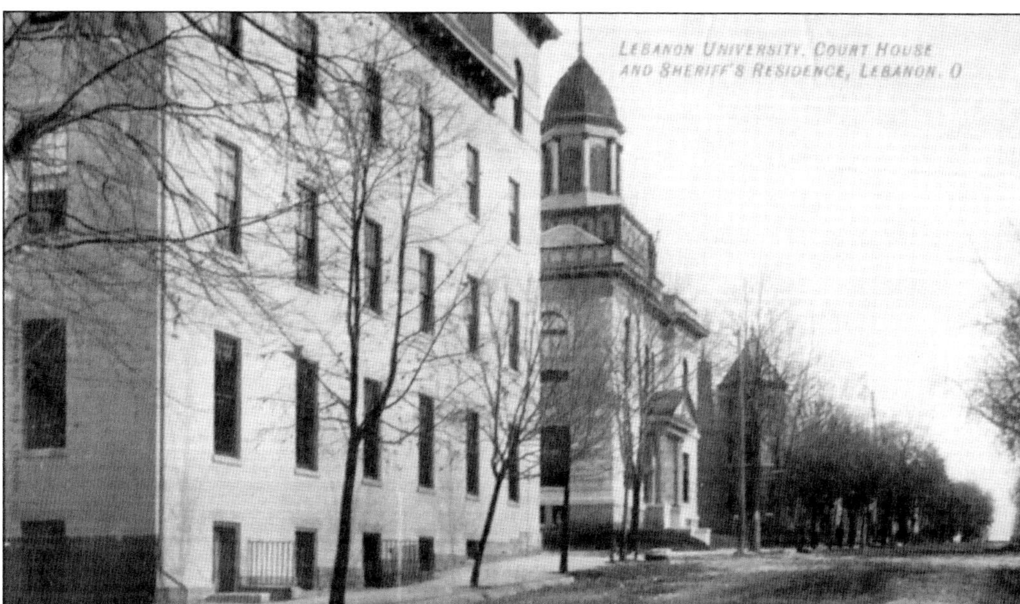

This c. 1910 image of what became Lebanon University shows its position to the county courthouse on Silver Street. After the school closed in 1918, this building, and much of the campus, was sold to local resident Solomon Fred for $4,400. (Courtesy of the Sally Foster collection.)

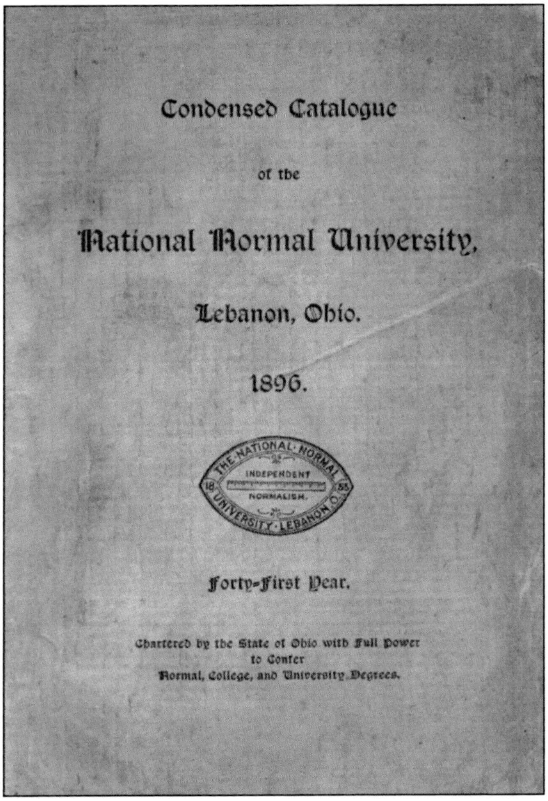

This cover of the National Normal University dates to 1895, a year after Alfred Holbrook resigned as president. By this time, the university was saddled with ever-increasing debt and had lost one of its major benefactors in President Holbrook. (Courtesy of the Sally Foster collection.)

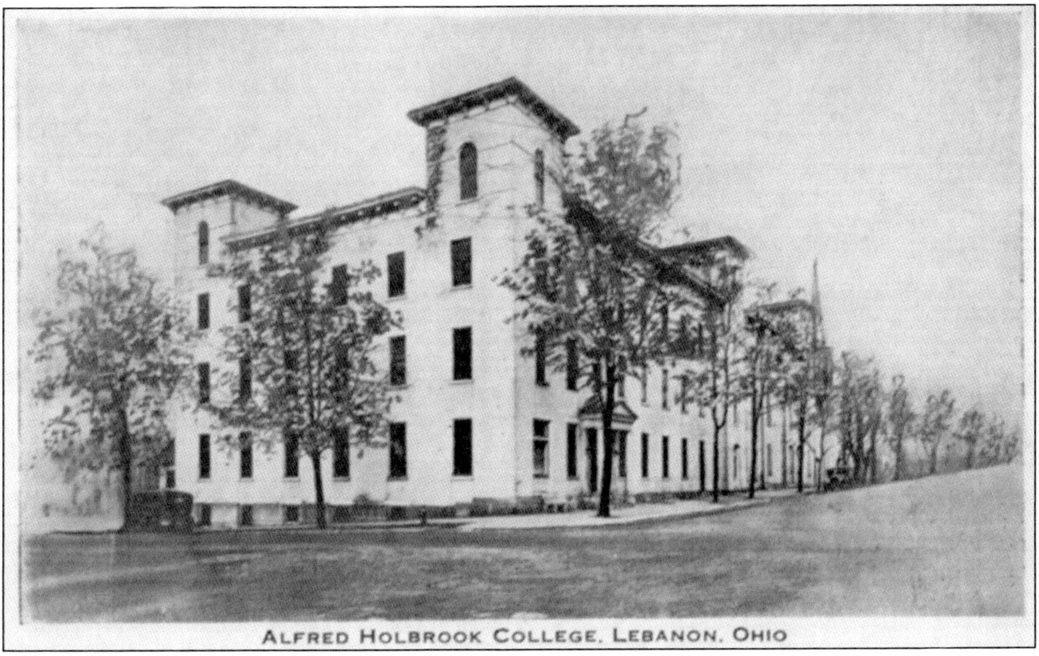

ALFRED HOLBROOK COLLEGE, LEBANON, OHIO

This early image of the Lyceum at National Normal was taken at the peak of the college's history. This photograph was probably taken prior to 1870 when the name was changed from Alfred Holbrook College to National Normal School. (Courtesy of the Sally Foster collection.)

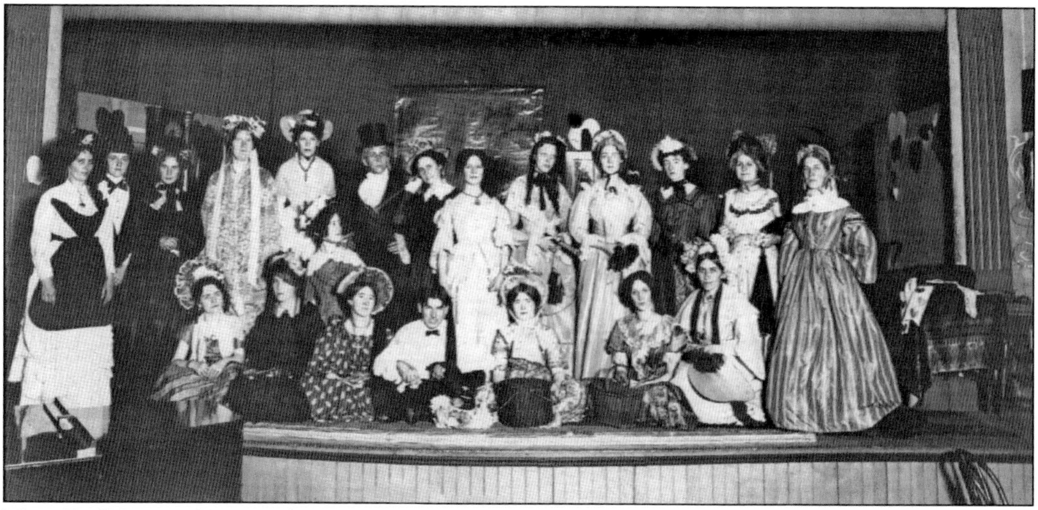

Not all of National Normal University was devoted to education. This early image of a theatrical production shows another side of National Normal. Entitled *The Old Maids Convention*, this play was put on by students of National Normal University under the direction of Professor Crane and Miss Mawhood. (Courtesy of WCHS Museum.)

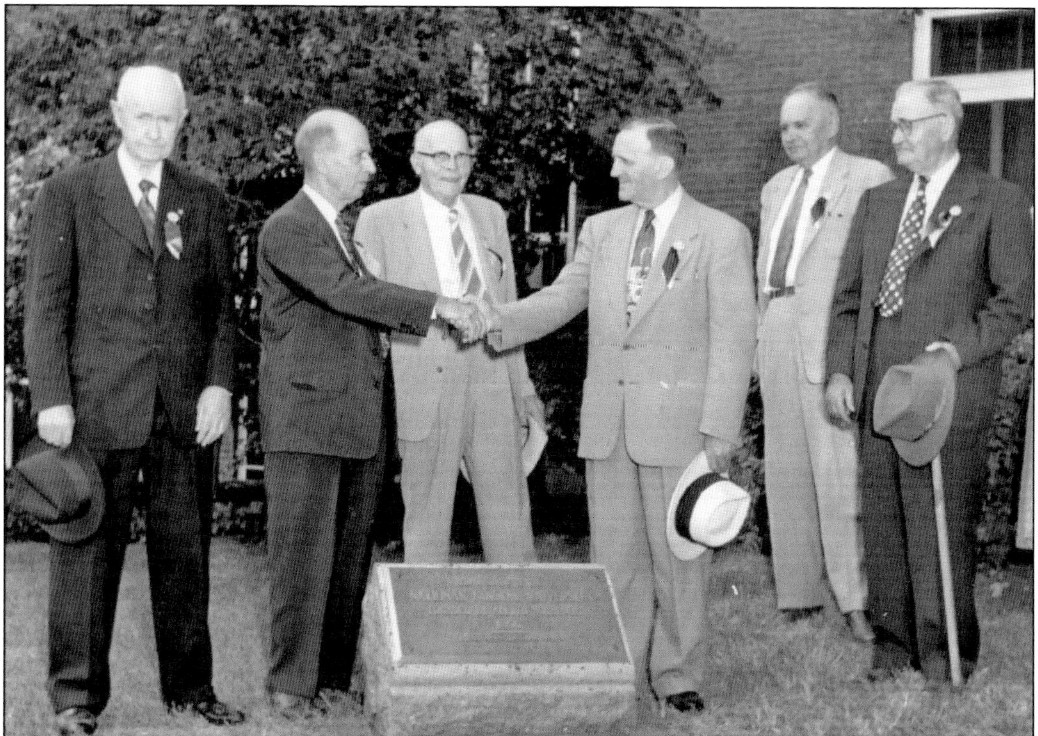

This 1950s image shows the dedication of the marker for National Normal University in downtown Lebanon. Since the campus of the university, in the northeast part of town, had all but disappeared by this time, it was decided to place the marker in what is now Gazebo Park, one of the original four corners deeded to the city in the 19th century. On the right, holding a white hat, is William Frasure, the mayor of Lebanon. (Courtesy of WCHS Museum.)

Two

J. W. Lingo and the New York Racket Store

Lebanon's Downtown Retail

Lebanon's first retail store began in a small spare room in Ephraim Hathaway's Black Horse Tavern on the east side of Broadway Street between Mulberry and Silver Streets. In the summer of 1803, fledgling shopkeeper John Huston laid in a small supply of goods and began an auspicious, although short, career as Lebanon's first downtown merchant.

The two mainstays of Lebanon's downtown retail area were family-owned businesses, both started before the early 20th century. Abraham Kaufman came to Lebanon in 1897 and founded a clothing and dry goods store that would last for 86 years. With the ambitious name of the New York Racket Store, Abe Kaufman rented a single room on South Broadway Street and stocked clothing, dry goods, and pots and pans. The store was so successful in 1900 that he moved to much larger quarters in the Masonic Building on South Broadway. Thus began Kaufmans, a Lebanon landmark that would last for over eight decades in downtown.

Just up the street on the southwest corner of Broadway and Mulberry Streets, J. W. Lingo began his hardware store well before the early 20th century. Even up until the 1970s when it closed, customers could walk into Lingo's and purchase a scoop of nails, rope by the foot, or even a saddle. The merchandise on the top shelf might be a little dusty, but it was there.

No matter what merchandise they stocked or what services they offered, Lebanon's downtown merchants all had one thing in common: they proudly put their own name over the door just like the generations of shopkeepers before them. The name over the door not only gave an identity to the store but also to who was inside.

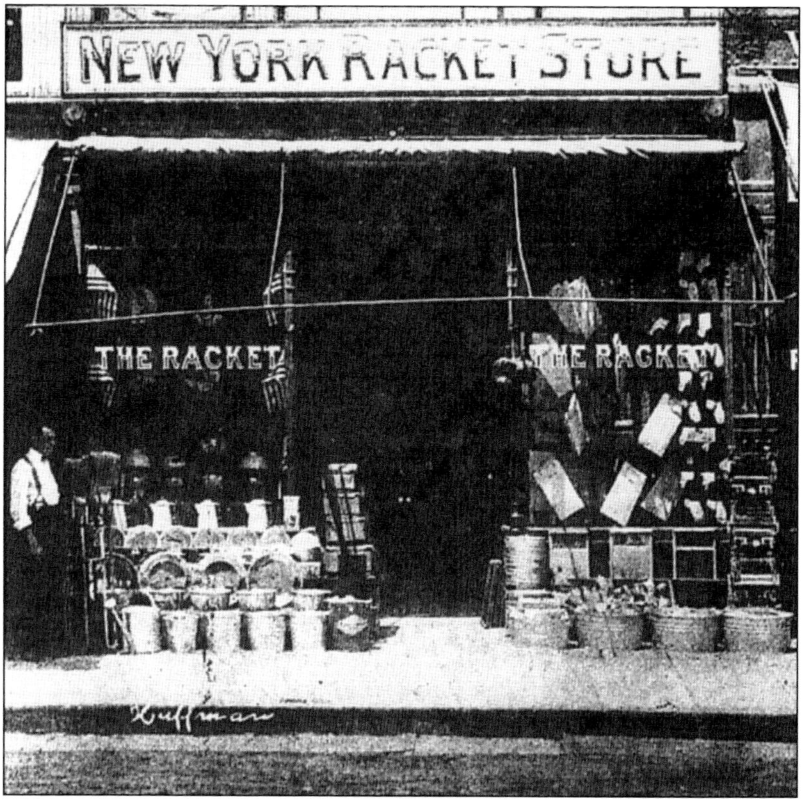

The New York Racket Store was started by A. B. "Abe" Kaufman in 1897. Beginning with a single, small storefront and an ambitious name, Kaufman's soon expanded and became a Lebanon retail institution for 86 years. (Courtesy of WCHS Museum.)

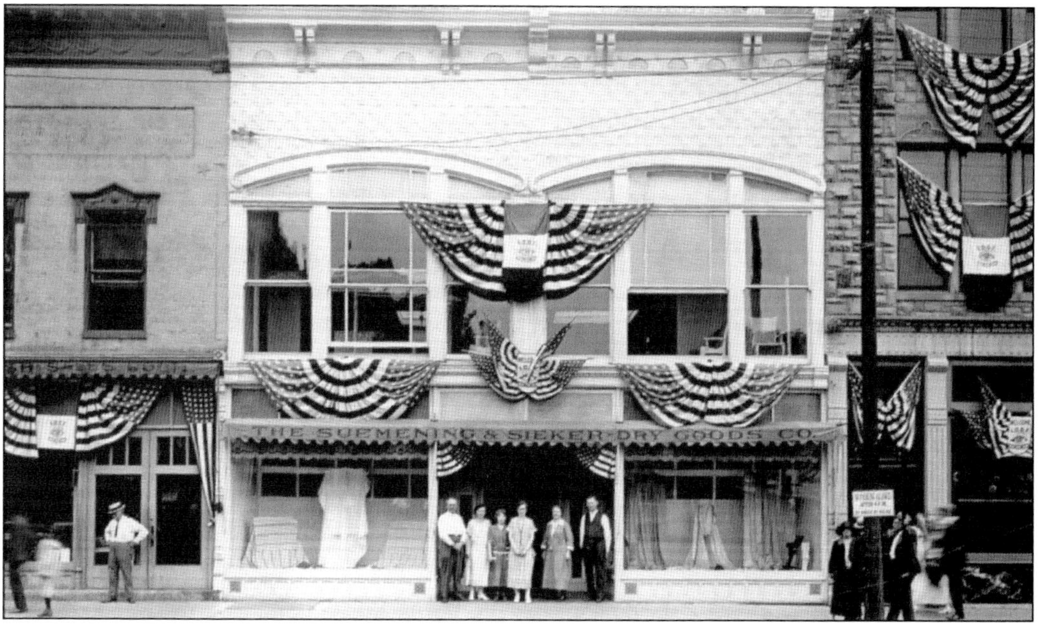

The Seuming and Sieker Dry Goods Store was another early Lebanon merchant located on the west side of Broadway Street. This storefront is now occupied by William and Mary and the Broadway Antique Mall. This picture was taken during a Fourth of July celebration around 1915. (Courtesy of WCHS Museum.)

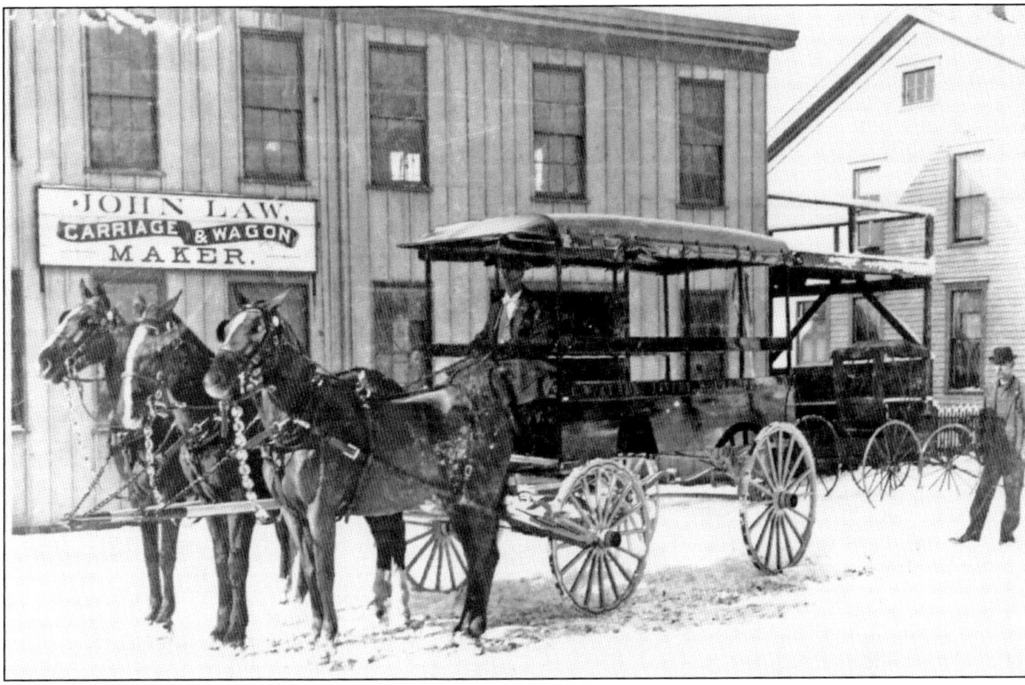

This *c.* 1880 winter image shows John Law standing behind a wagon in front of his business, which was located on East Street in Lebanon. Law was one of the numerous carriage makers that populated downtown until after the turn of the early 20th century. (Courtesy of WCHS Museum.)

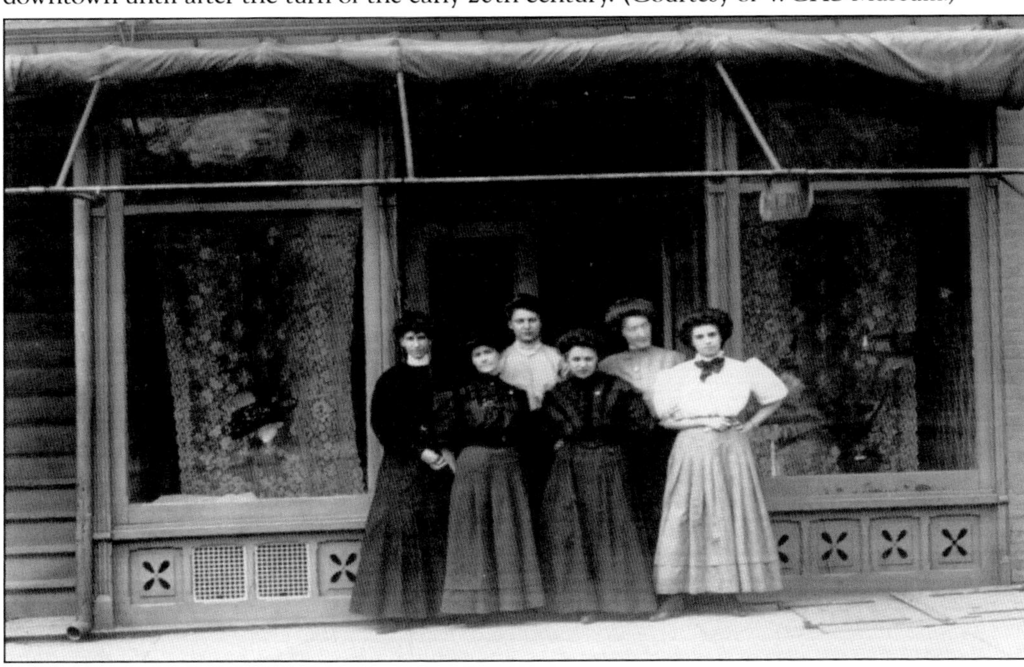

This 19th-century image is of Boyer's Millinery Store on east Mulberry Street in downtown. Termed one of the most fashionable stores in downtown, employees pictured here are (first row) Mabel Halderman, Mildred Conklin Coburn, and Hazel Lewis Brooks; (second row) Miss Potts, Madge Miller Simpkins, and Ethel Cheney. (Courtesy of WCHS Museum.)

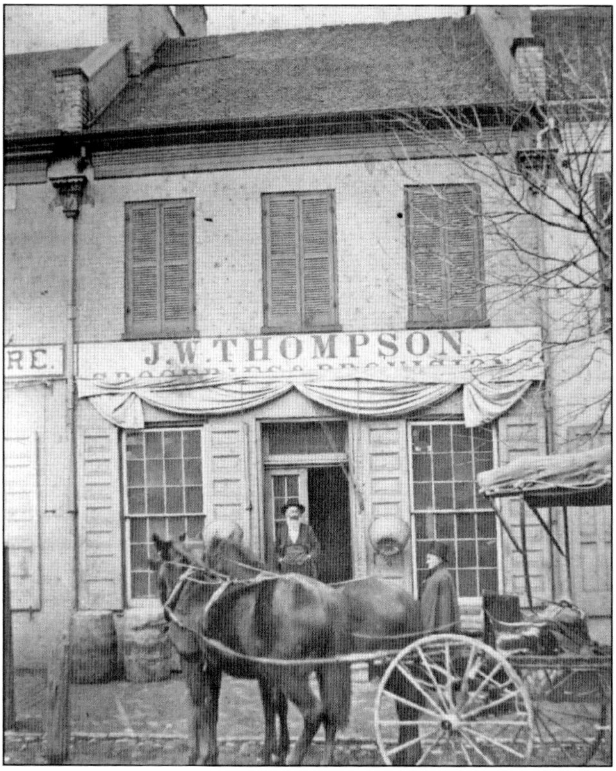

J. W. Thompson's Groceries and Provisions was in business until the turn of the century and was located on South Broadway Street on what was then known as the Maplewood Block. The block today runs north and south between Main and Mulberry Streets. Thompson's was only one of numerous grocery stores located in Lebanon's central business district until the mid-20th century. (Courtesy of WCHS Museum.)

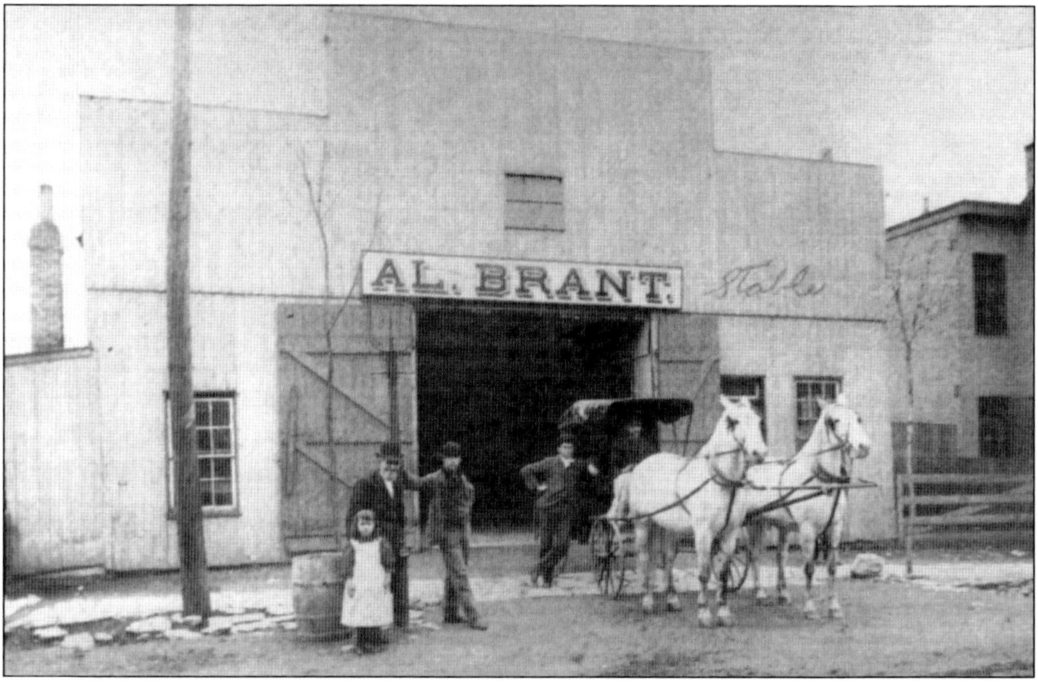

The Brant Livery Stables spawned a business that is still in existence. This 1880s image shows the original stables on South Mechanic Street. The expanded Brant's Hardware Store occupies the same location today. (Courtesy of WCHS Museum.)

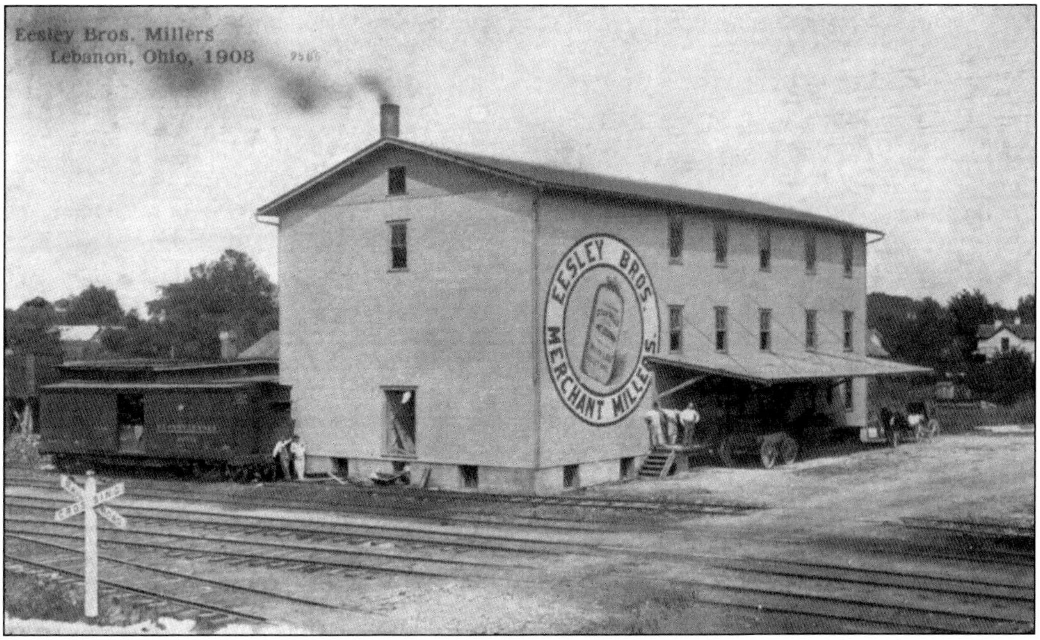

Eesley Brothers Mill was a major miller of flour in Lebanon, Ohio. Located in the southwest section of Lebanon, close to West Street, this mill was active in Lebanon well into the 20th century. (Courtesy of WCHS Museum.)

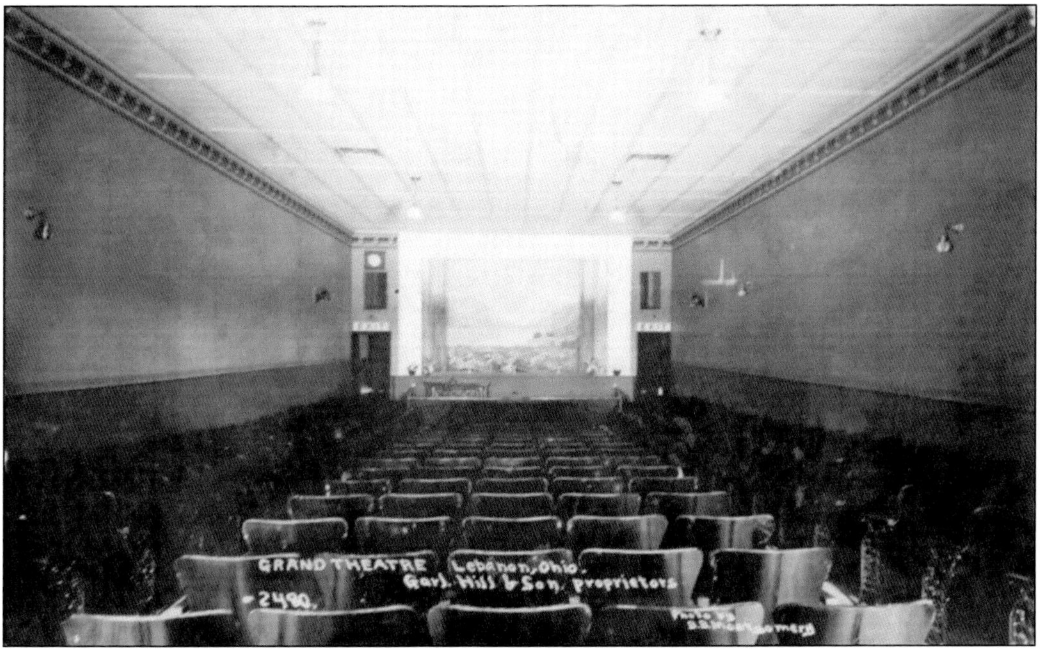

The Grand Theater was located on North Mulberry Street in the area now occupied by Knickerbocker Gallery. One of numerous theaters in Lebanon, its primary competition was the Law and Blair Town Hall theater located in Lebanon's city building on Broadway Street. (Courtesy of the Sally Foster collection.)

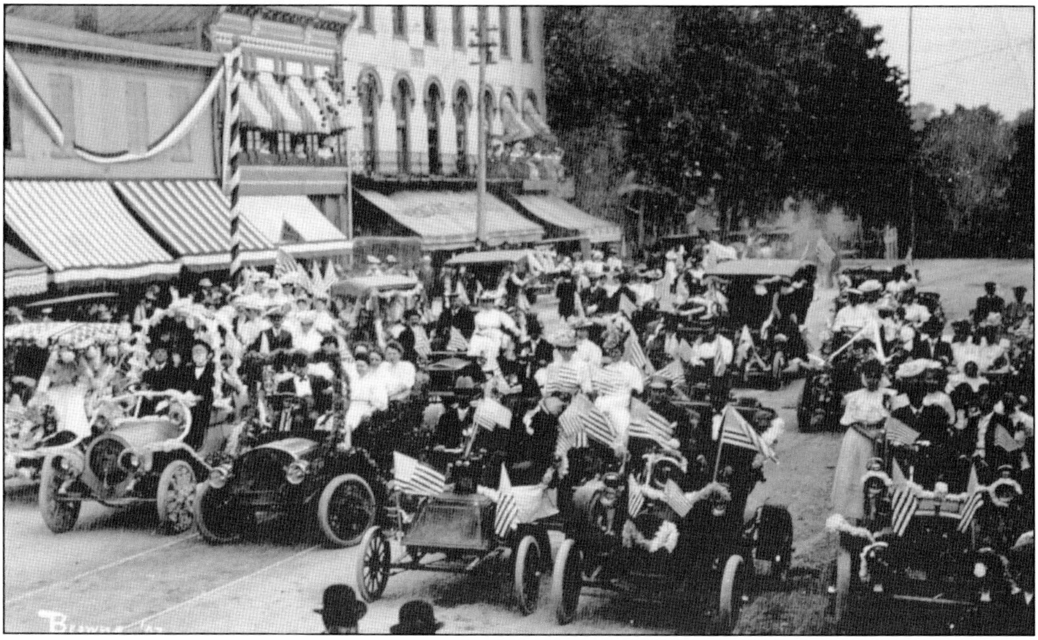

This 1907 image shows a crowded Broadway Street during a patriotic parade. With a view from the northwest corner of Mulberry Street, of particular note is the Masonic Temple (large building on the left). This rare photograph shows the original facade of the building, which was changed in the 1920s. (Courtesy of WCHS Museum.)

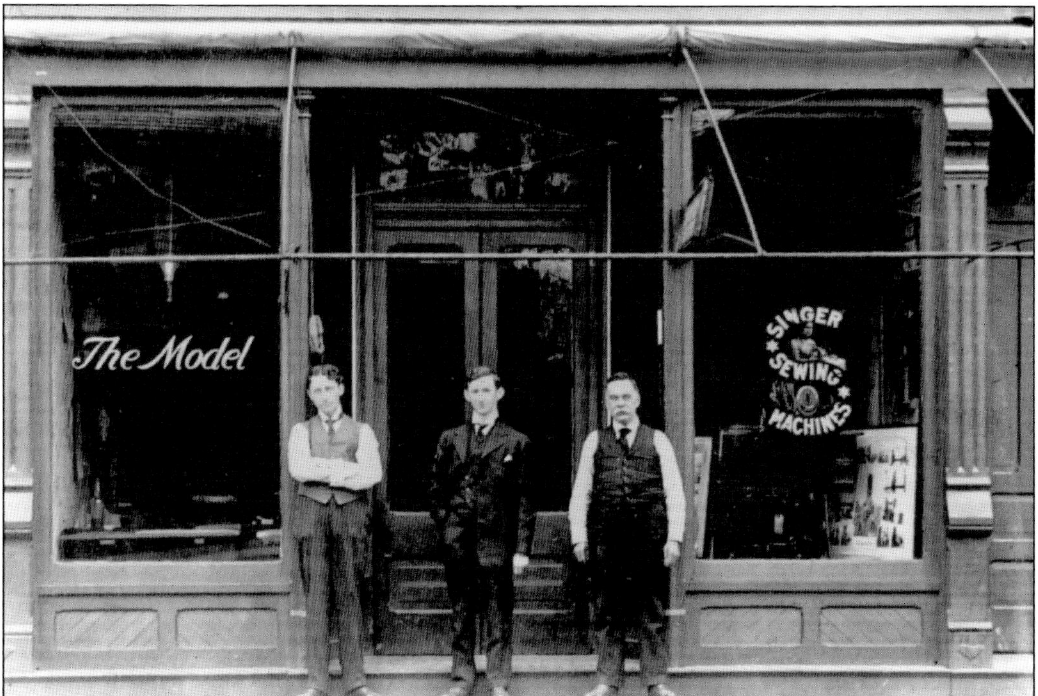

The Model Store was believed to have been located on the northwest side of Mulberry Street on the first block. (Courtesy of WCHS Museum.)

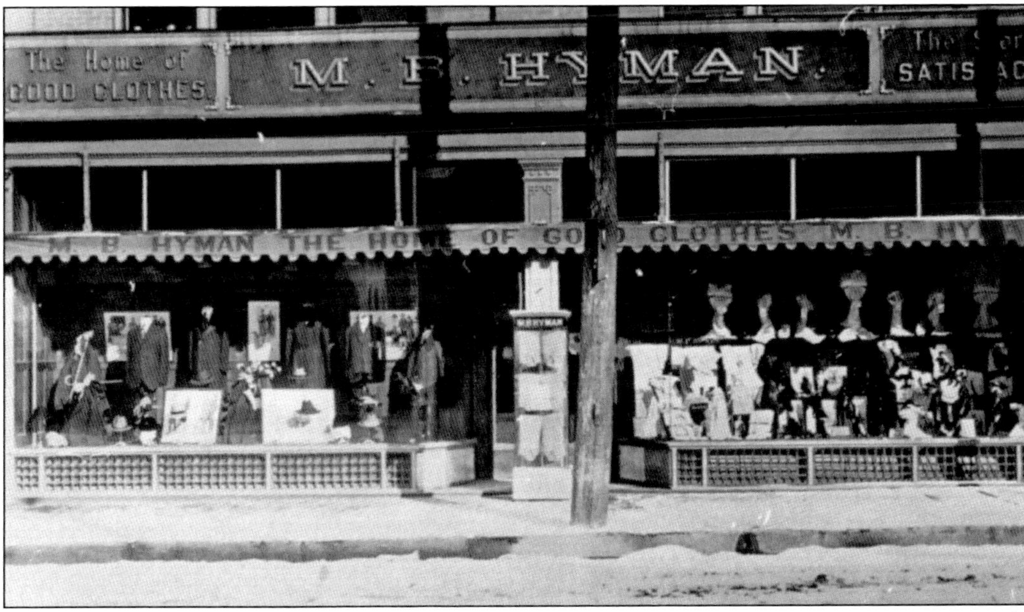

M. B. Hyman's men's clothing store was located on the northeast side of Mulberry Street in the area now occupied by Lebanon Citizen's National Bank. The store, staffed by Sam Hyman and later Isadore "Hy" Hyman, offered Hart Schaffner and Marx suits, an expensive line of clothing for such a small town. After Hyman's closed, another men's store, Keever's, occupied part of the space. (Courtesy of WCHS Museum.)

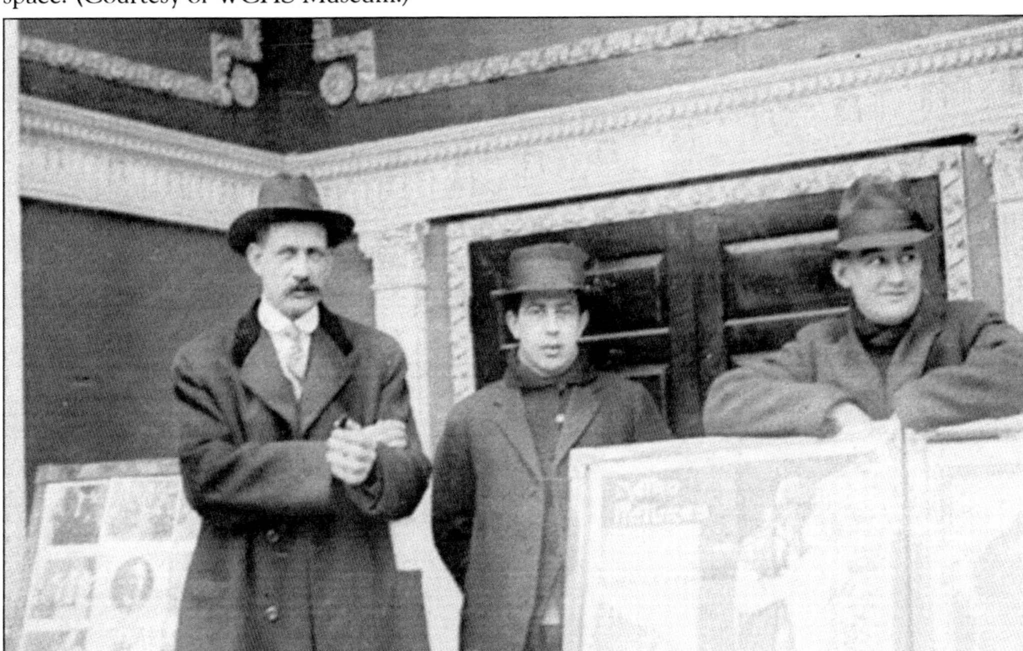

This c. 1910 image, taken from a glass negative, shows three men posing outside the site of the Grand Theater on West Mulberry Street. It highlights the ornamental detail of the exterior of the theater. This area is now occupied by Knickerbocker Gallery. (Courtesy of the Scott and Traci Gallagher collection.)

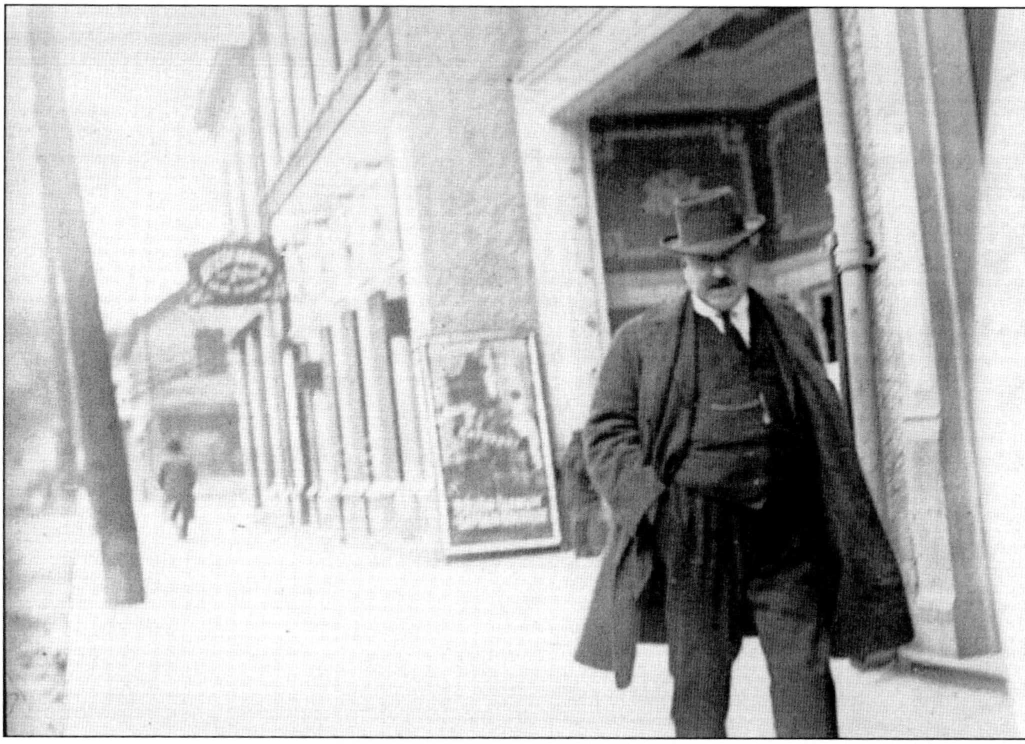

Another 1910 image of the theater on West Mulberry Street has been taken from a glass negative. This photograph also shows another remaining building on West Mulberry Street. The first two-story building in the background was home to a pool hall until the mid-1970s. The second building, on the corner, was then, and still is, a barbershop. (Courtesy of the Scott and Traci Gallagher collection.)

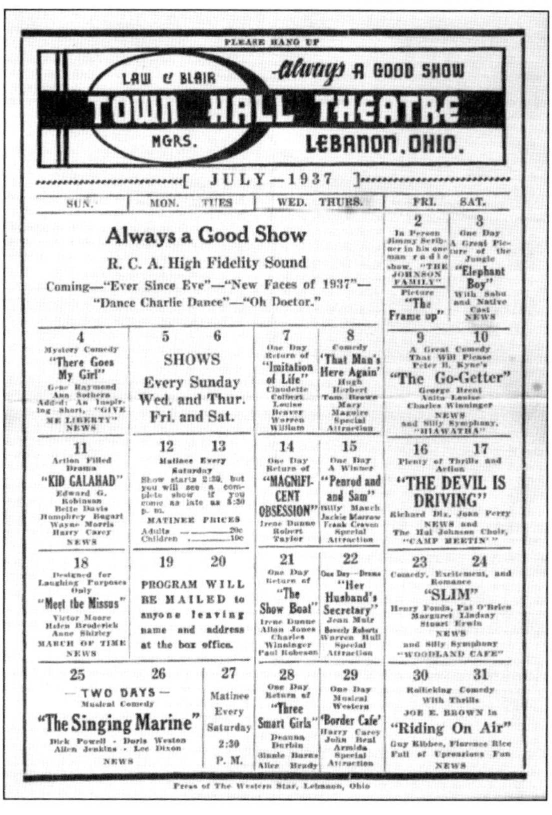

PLEASE HANG UP

LAW & BLAIR MGRS.

TOWN HALL THEATRE

Always A GOOD SHOW

LEBANON, OHIO.

[JULY—1937]

SUN.	MON.	TUES	WED.	THURS.	FRI.	SAT.
Always a Good Show R. C. A. High Fidelity Sound Coming—"Ever Since Eve"—"New Faces of 1937"—"Dance Charlie Dance"—"Oh Doctor."					2 In Person Jimmy Scribner in his one man radio show, "THE JOHNSON FAMILY" Picture "The Frame up"	3 One Day A Great Picture of the Jungle "Elephant Boy" With Sabu and Native Cast NEWS
4 Mystery Comedy "There Goes My Girl" Gene Raymond Ann Sothern Added: An Inspiring Short, "GIVE ME LIBERTY" NEWS	5 SHOWS Every Sunday Wed. and Thur. Fri. and Sat.	6	7 One Day Return of "Imitation of Life" Claudette Colbert Louise Beaver Warren William	8 Comedy 'That Man's Here Again' Hugh Herbert Tom Brown Mary Maguire Special Attraction	9 A Great Comedy That Will Please Peter B. Kyne's "The Go-Getter" George Brent Anita Louise Charles Winninger NEWS and Silly Symphony, "HIAWATHA"	10
11 Action Filled Drama "KID GALAHAD" Edward G. Robinson Bette Davis Humphrey Bogart Wayne Morris Harry Carey NEWS	12 Matinee Every Saturday Show starts 2:30, but you will see a complete show if you come as late as 3:30 p. m. MATINEE PRICES Adults 20c Children 10c	13	14 One Day Return of "MAGNIFICENT OBSESSION" Irene Dunne Robert Taylor	15 One Day A Winner "Penrod and and Sam" Billy Mauch Jackie Morrow Frank Craven Special Attraction	16 Plenty of Thrills and Action "THE DEVIL IS DRIVING" Richard Dix, Joan Perry NEWS and The Hal Johnson Choir, "CAMP MEETIN'"	17
18 Designed for Laughing Purposes Only "Meet the Missus" Victor Moore Helen Broderick Anne Shirley MARCH OF TIME NEWS	19 PROGRAM WILL BE MAILED to anyone leaving name and address at the box office.	20	21 One Day Return of "The Show Boat" Irene Dunne Allan Jones Charles Winninger Paul Robeson	22 One Day—Drama "Her Husband's Secretary" Jean Muir Beverly Roberts Warren Hull Special Attraction	23 Comedy, Excitement, and Romance "SLIM" Henry Fonda, Pat O'Brien Margaret Lindsay Stuart Erwin NEWS and Silly Symphony "WOODLAND CAFE"	24
25 — TWO DAYS — Musical Comedy "The Singing Marine" Dick Powell - Doris Weston Allen Jenkins - Lee Dixon NEWS	26	27 Matinee Every Saturday 2:30 P. M.	28 One Day Return of "Three Smart Girls" Deanna Durbin Binnie Barnes Alice Brady	29 One Day Musical Western 'Border Cafe' Harry Carey John Beal Armida Special Attraction	30 Rollicking Comedy With Thrills JOE E. BROWN in "Riding On Air" Guy Kibbee, Florence Rice Full of Uproarious Fun NEWS	31

Press of The Western Star, Lebanon, Ohio

This July 1937 movie listing is from the Law and Blair Town Hall Theater. After the disastrous opera house fire in 1932, another movie theater was included in the new town hall built on the same site. The Town Hall theater would last into the early 1960s when it was replaced with city offices. Of particular note is the admission price of 20¢. (Courtesy of the Sally Foster collection.)

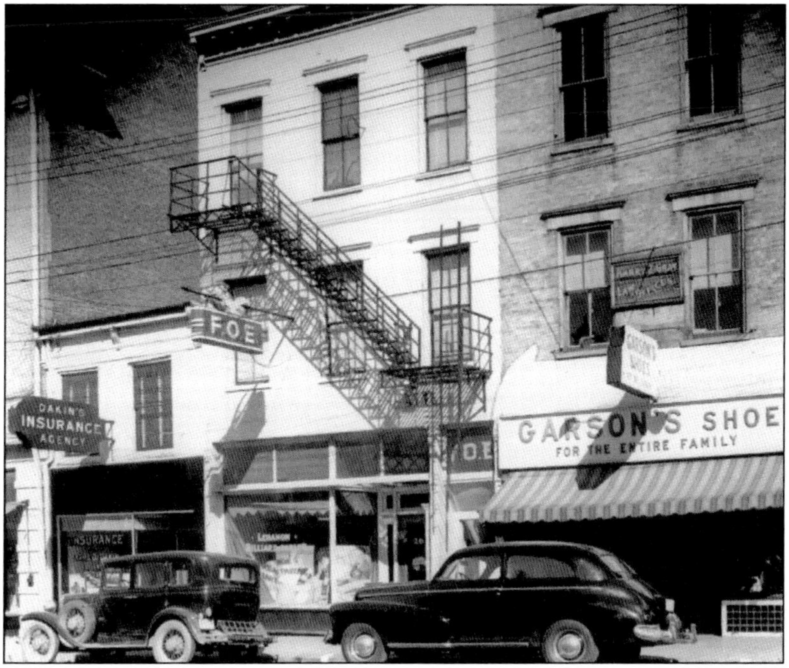

This 1930s view of West Mulberry Street shows two long-standing Lebanon businesses. Dakin Insurance (now part of LCNB National Bank) is still located on the same block, although in a different location. Garson's Shoes (owned and operated by Garson Saddleman) was a mainstay in Lebanon retail until the mid-1960s. (Courtesy of WCHS Museum.)

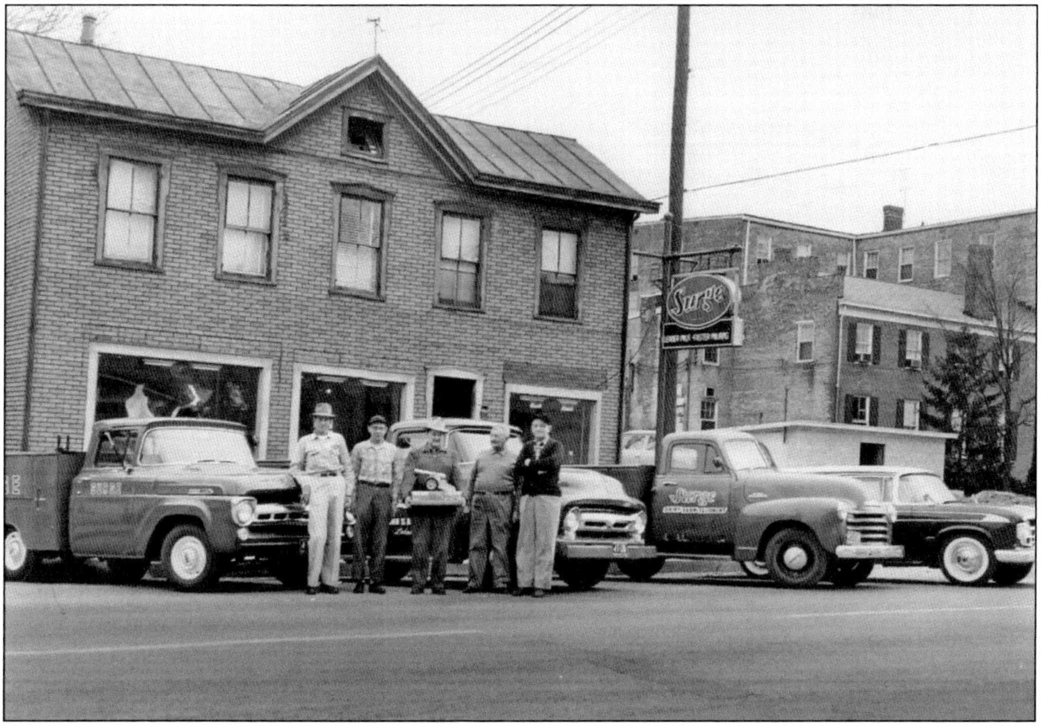

This 1950s photograph shows the original Buchanan's Equipment store on West Main Street in Lebanon. This building was located on what is now the parking lot of the Golden Lamb (visible in the rear). Standing in the center holding a replica cannon is owner John Buchanan. The business, still in operation, is now located in a larger facility on State Route 63 in Lebanon. (Courtesy of WCHS Museum.)

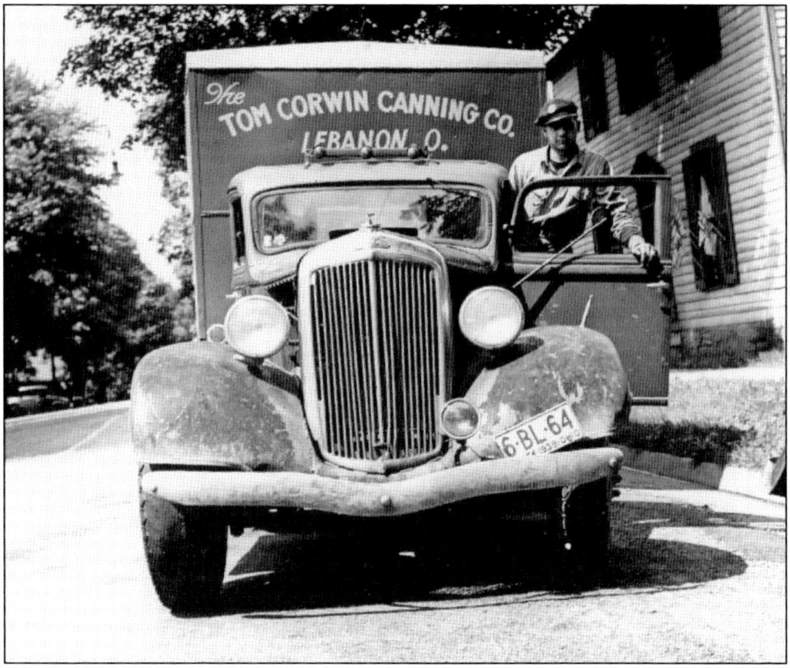

The Tom Corwin Canning Company was located on West Street in what was then a strictly industrial area of Lebanon. With the slogan "Our Products are as Good As Our Name," the company was named for Lebanon's most famous resident. The company canned and sold pumpkins, tomatoes, spinach, rhubarb, and baked beans. (Courtesy of WCHS Museum.)

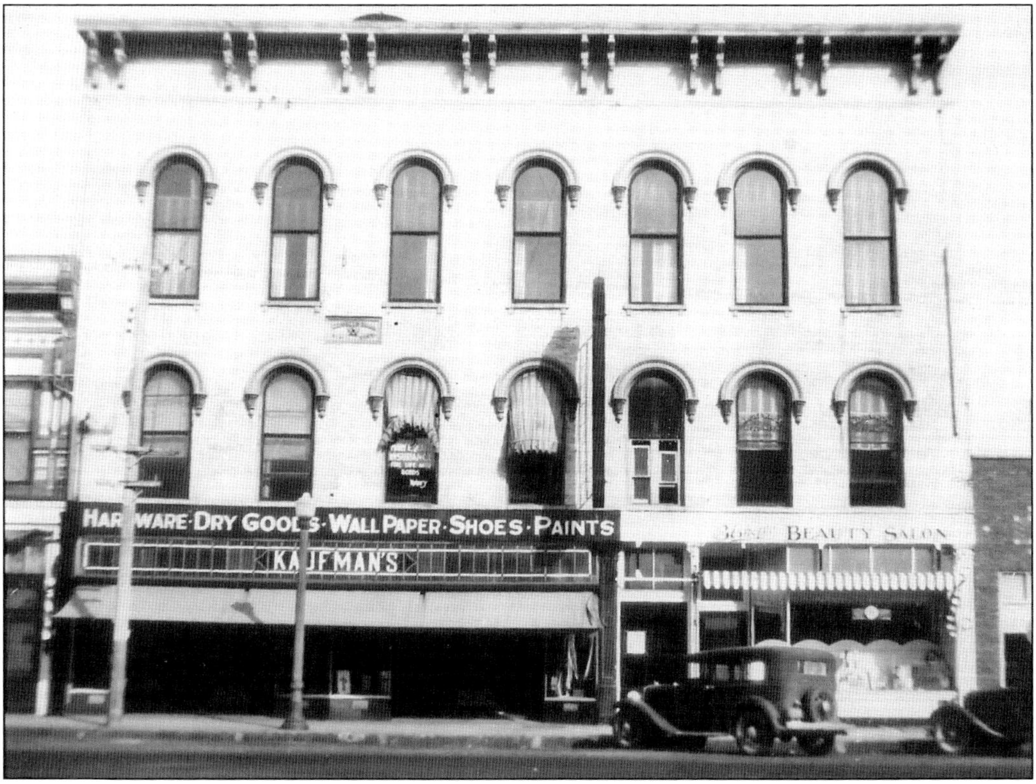

This 1930s image shows a Lebanon mainstay, Kaufman's, in its new location in Lebanon's Masonic Temple. Beginning as the New York Racket Store in 1897, Kaufman's would eventually expand into these larger quarters and remain in Lebanon until 1983. (Courtesy of WCHS Museum.)

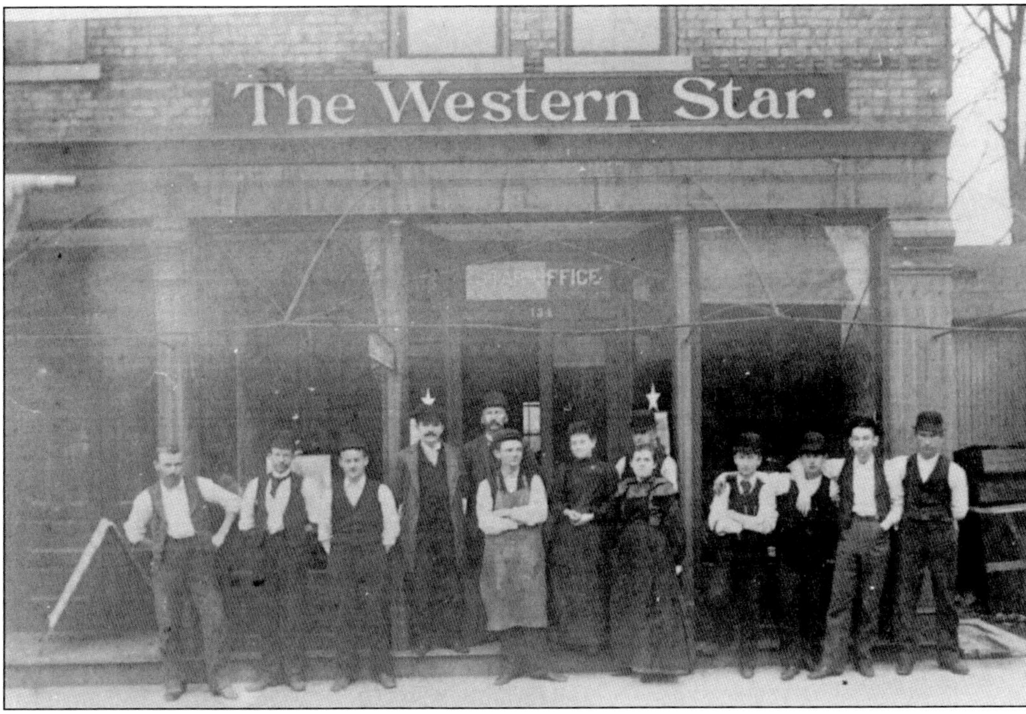

This 1900s photograph shows the offices and employees of *The Western Star*, the oldest weekly newspaper west of the Allegheny Mountains. Starting in Lebanon in 1807, this photograph shows the offices when they were on Silver Street in downtown Lebanon, now the site of a nursing home. (Courtesy of WCHS Museum.)

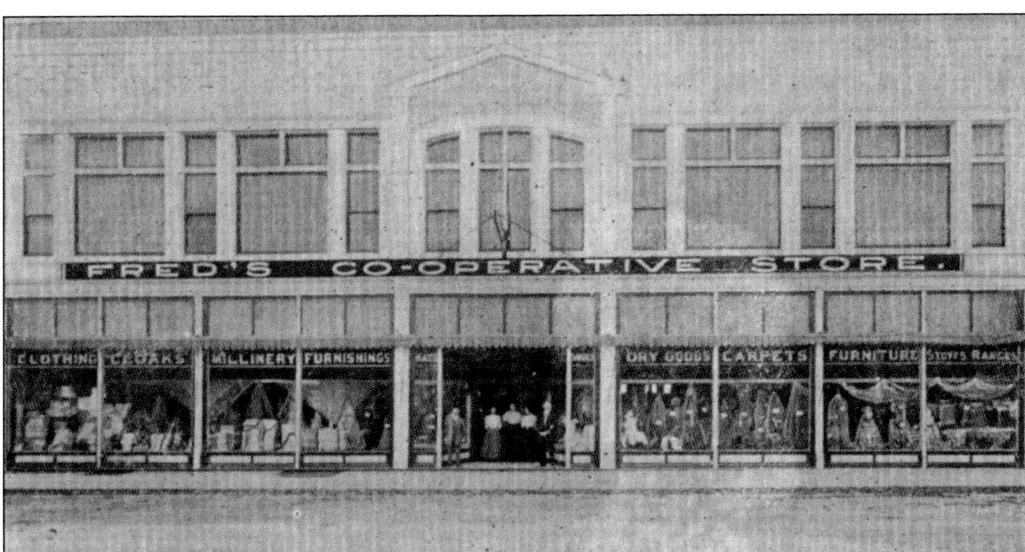

Another mainstay of Lebanon's downtown retail district was Fred's Department Store. Originally called Fred's Cooperative Store, it was on Mechanic Street in Lebanon until the late 1960s. (Courtesy of WCHS Museum.)

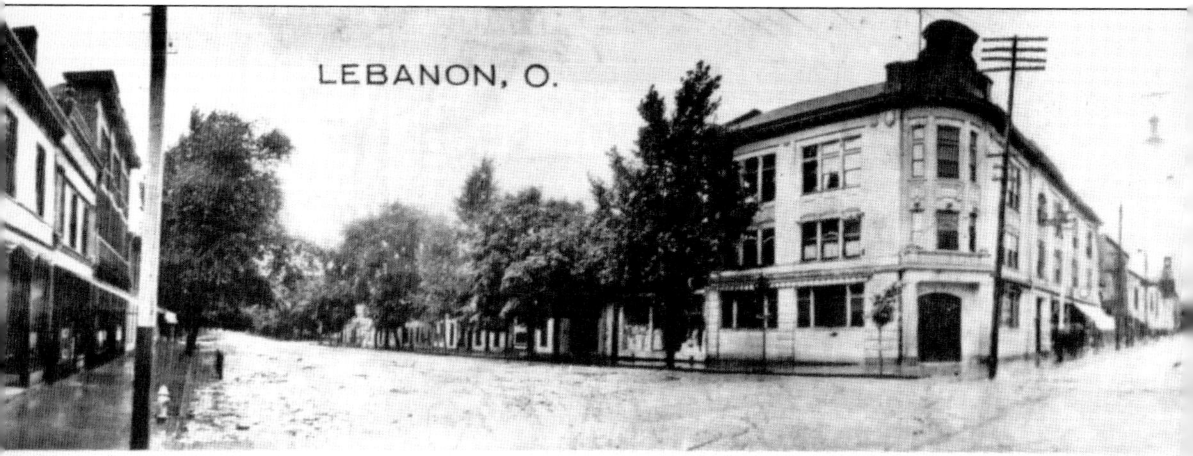

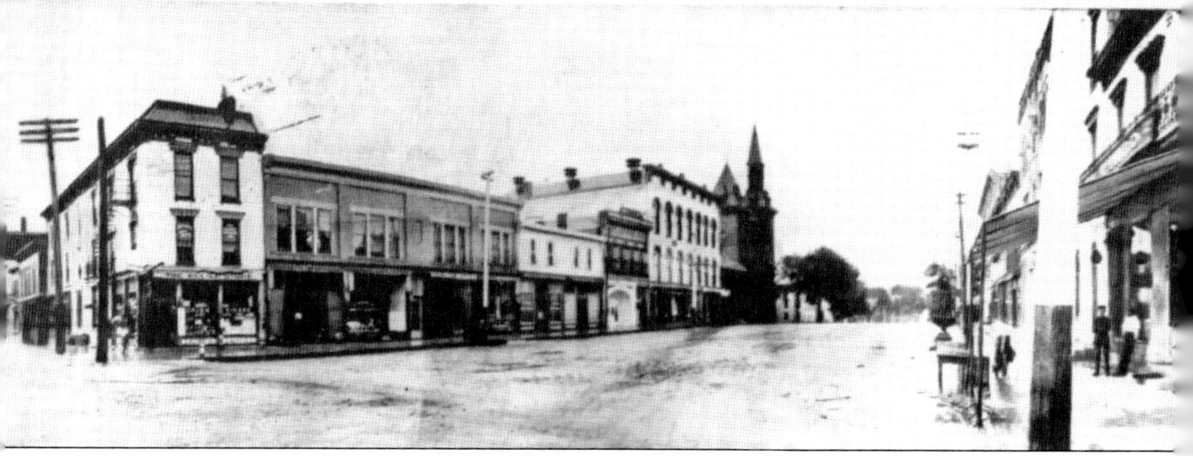

These two panoramic views of Lebanon's main street illustrates why it was named Broadway Street. The top view, looking west on Mulberry Street from the corner of Mulberry and Broadway, shows the wide expanse of the intersection as viewed in perspective of the Lebanon Citizens National Bank building. The bottom view easily illustrates Broadway's six-pole, or 100-foot, width from side to side. Most of the buildings in these two unique photographs are still standing today, with the exception of the Lebanon Opera House. (Courtesy of WCHS Museum.)

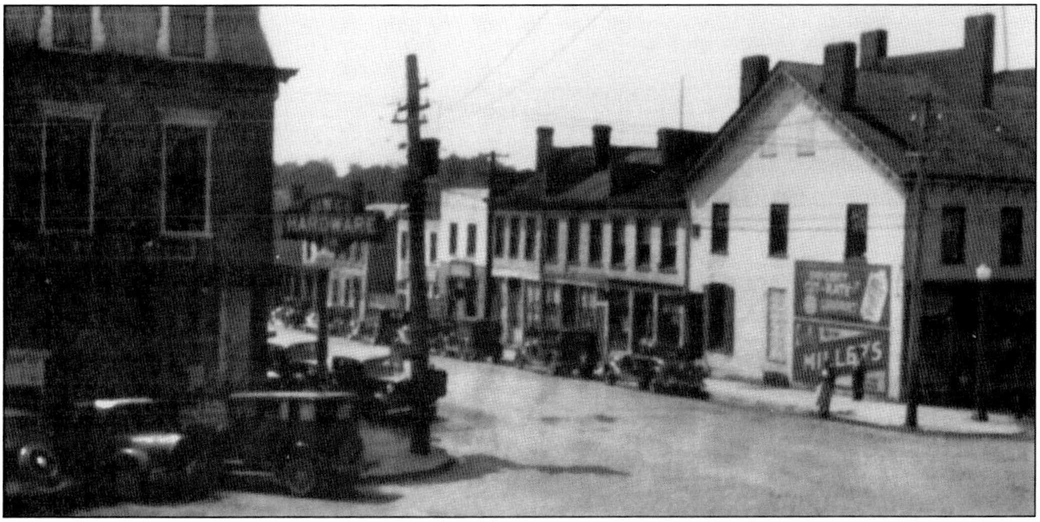

This 1935 image of the corner of Broadway and Mulberry Streets in Lebanon illustrates what was called Howery's Row. This particular section of Broadway Street, from J. W. Lingo's hardware store south, for years had been known as the Maplewood Block and so noted on plats and maps. The significance of the name Howery's Row has long been forgotten. Of particular note in this photograph is the freestanding Lingo Hardware sign on the corner. It was a rather short-lived attempt to further enhance the store known for its sales and promotions. (Courtesy of WCHS Museum.)

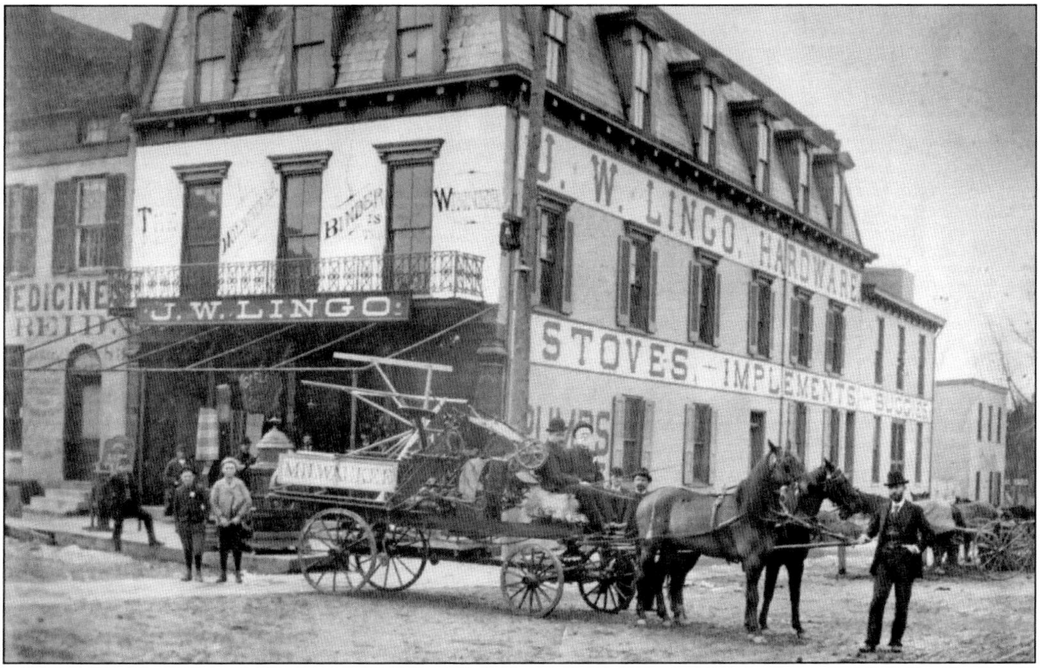

This early-1900s image is classic J. W. Lingo. Known as Lebanon's foremost entrepreneur, J. W. Lingo opened his store well before the turn of the early 20th century, and the store operated until the 1980s. Lingo was known for his constant sales and promotions, many of which extended out onto Broadway and Mulberry Streets. J. W. Lingo is pictured here sitting in the wagon with the white beard. The other men in the photograph are unidentified, but the two children to the rear are the sons of Henry Reid whose store was adjacent to Lingo's. (Courtesy of WCHS Museum.)

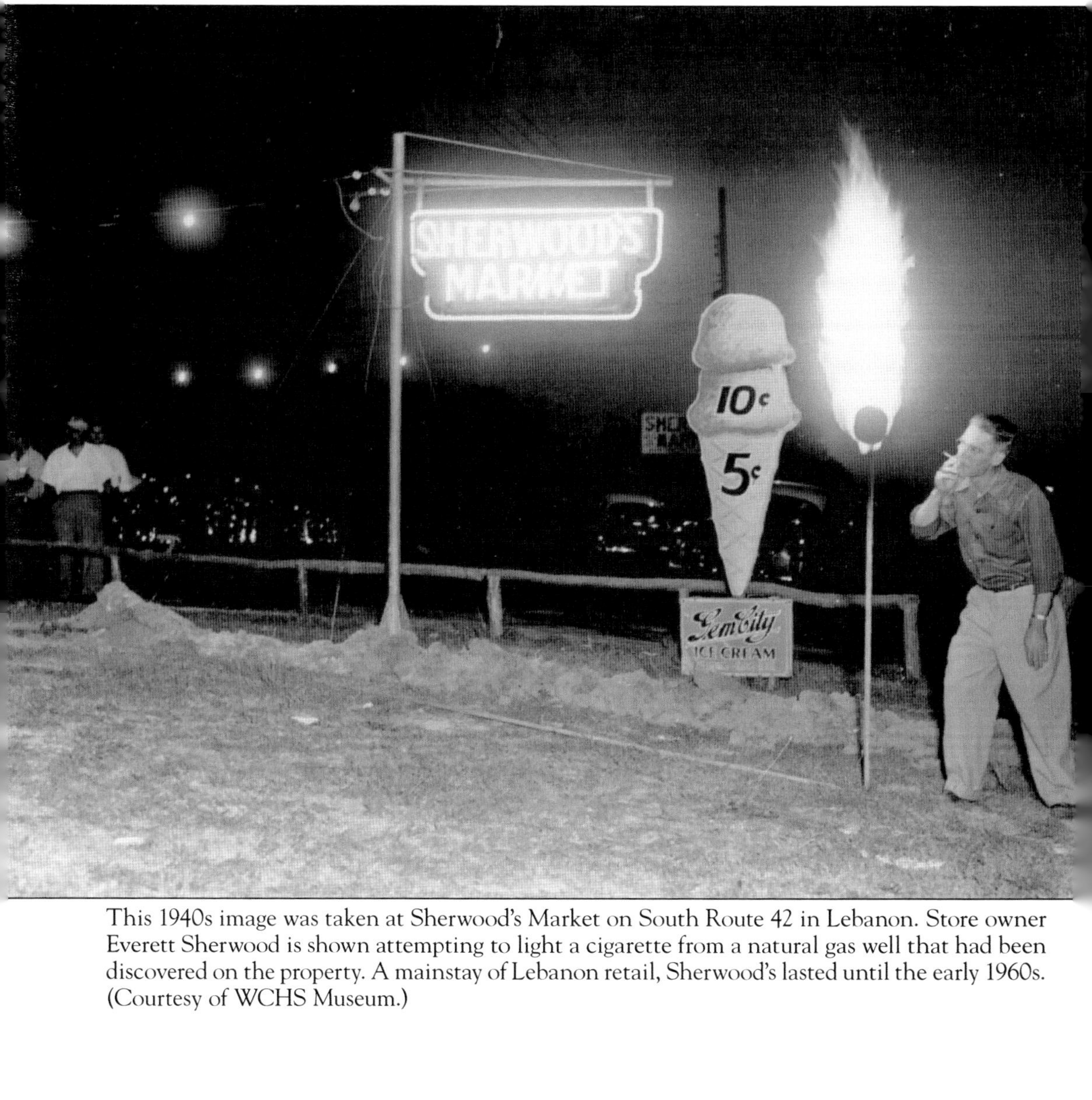

This 1940s image was taken at Sherwood's Market on South Route 42 in Lebanon. Store owner Everett Sherwood is shown attempting to light a cigarette from a natural gas well that had been discovered on the property. A mainstay of Lebanon retail, Sherwood's lasted until the early 1960s. (Courtesy of WCHS Museum.)

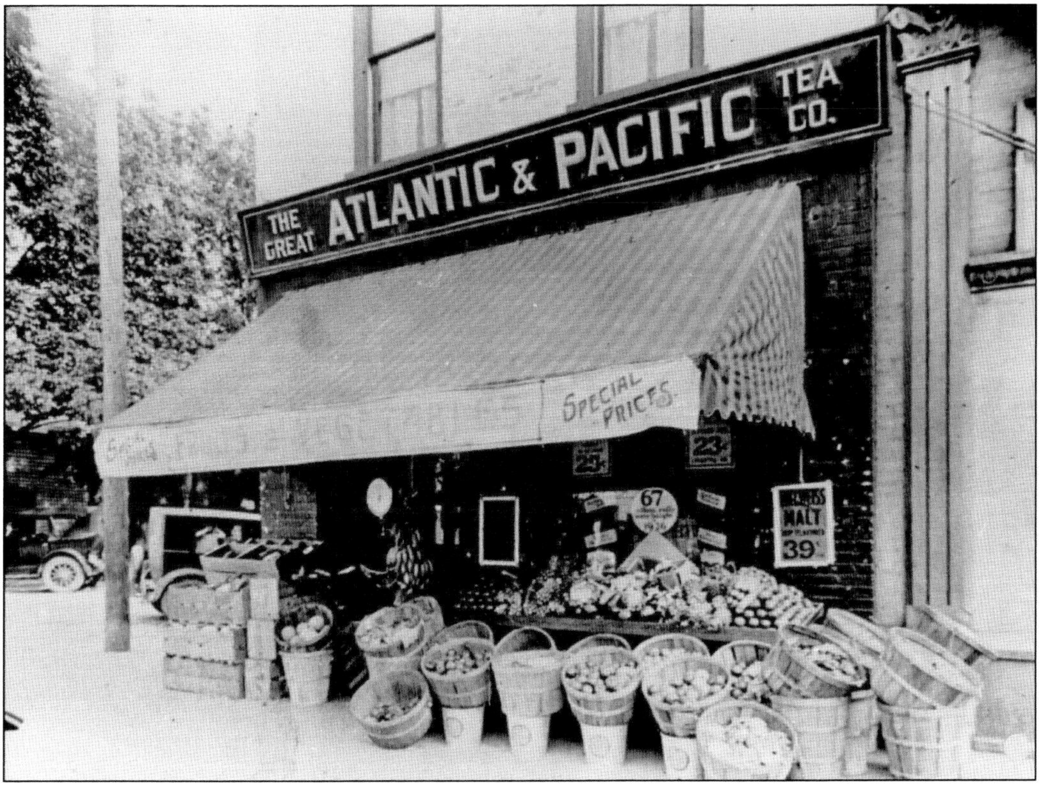

The Great Atlantic and Pacific Tea Company was one of the numerous markets located in downtown Lebanon. Then located at the corner of Mulberry and Mechanic Streets, the building is now a barbershop. (Courtesy of WCHS Museum.)

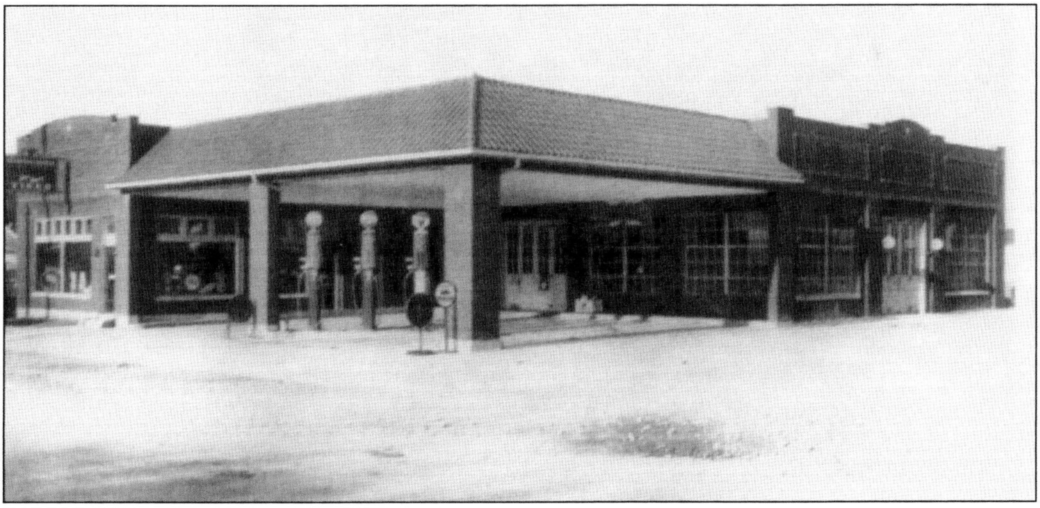

This 1930s view of an unidentified gas station at the base of Broadway Street shows an element of modern design creeping into Lebanon's historic downtown retail district. The building, still standing at the corner of Broadway and South Streets, has been extensively remodeled and at times housed two or three different Chevrolet dealerships. It is now the home to Millers Antique Mall. (Courtesy of WCHS Museum.)

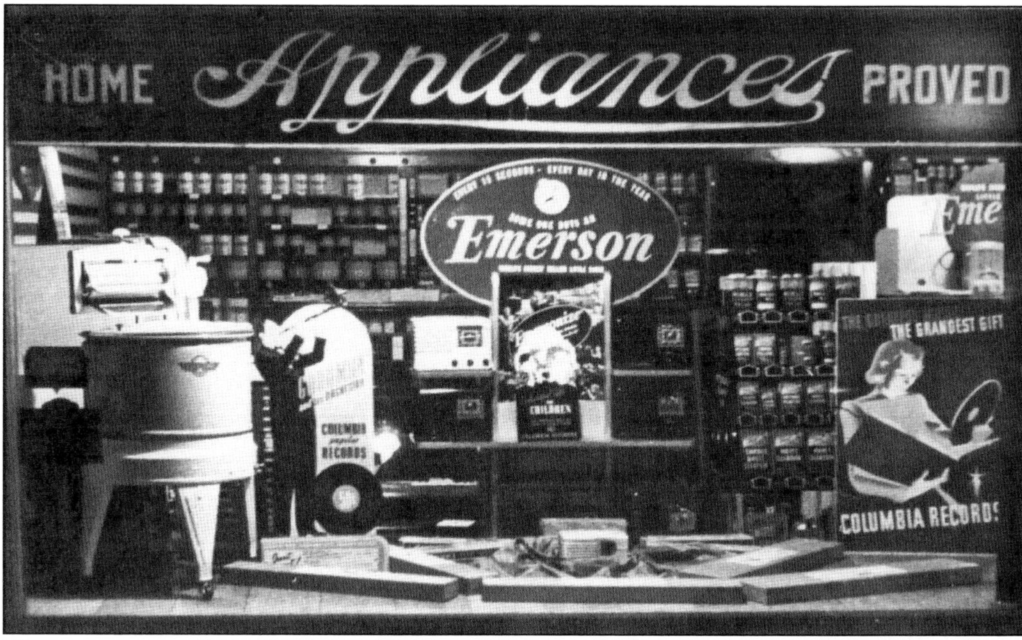

This 1940s image illustrates one of the most unusual retail stores in downtown Lebanon. Herrick's, which was located on the south side of Mulberry Street on the second block, was at one time a combination paint and music store. The store sold not only paint and records but also musical instruments. Lasting until the early 1970s, the location is now occupied by various retail stores. (Courtesy of WCHS Museum.)

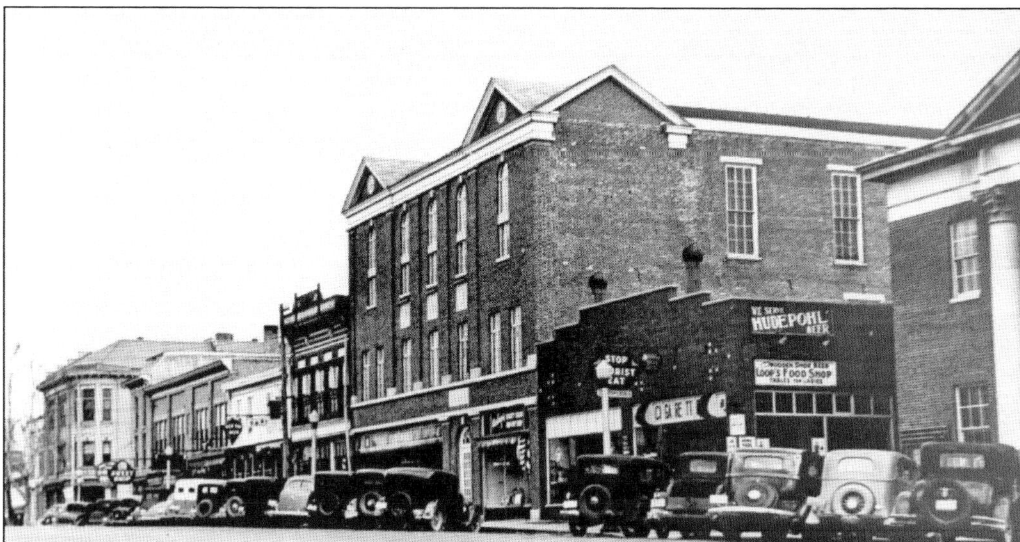

This mid-1930s image of Broadway Street is dominated by the Masonic Temple building with its new facade. The building next to it (now home to the Garden Gate and X-otic Antiques) always held a restaurant of some type, in this case Loop's. In later years, Phillips Restaurant would occupy the space. Another Lebanon landmark can be seen at the far end of the street with the sign for The Sweet Shop. This local soda fountain and restaurant lasted into the 1970s before closing. (Courtesy of WCHS Museum.)

This early book and music store in Lebanon is in an unidentified location. The concrete details on the building, including the dentil molding, heavily ornate columns, and windows, suggest a location on either Broadway or Mulberry Streets. (Courtesy of WCHS Museum.)

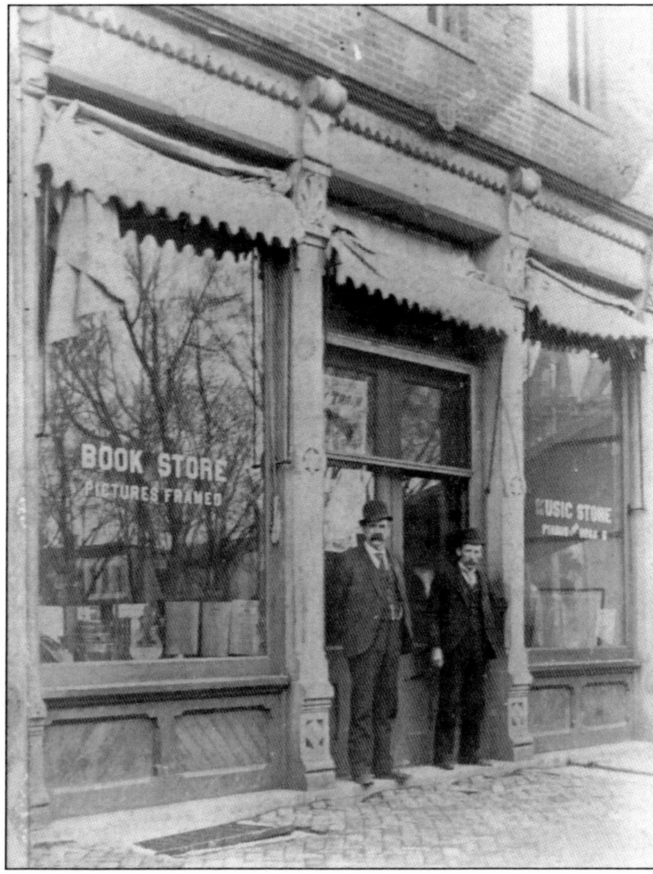

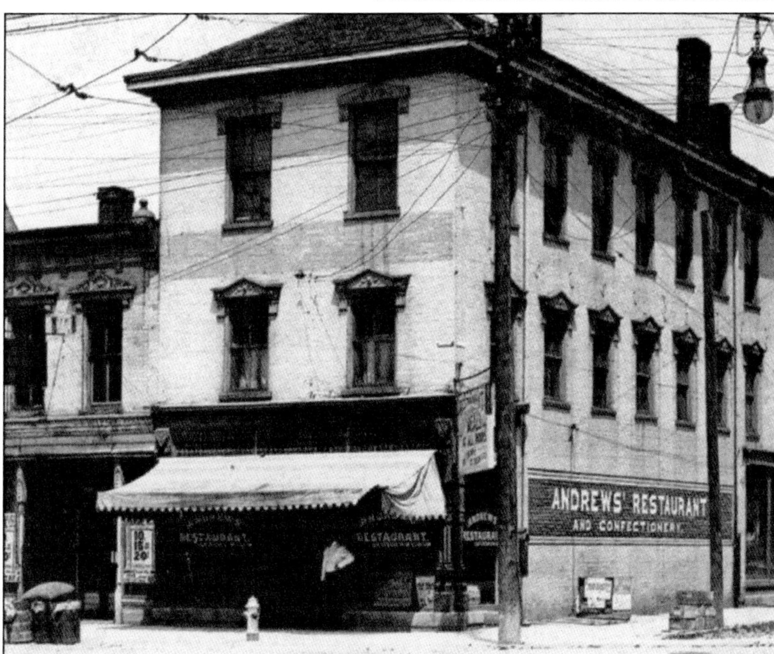

Andrews Restaurant was yet another food establishment in downtown Lebanon. This building, located at the corner of Mulberry and Mechanic Streets, has been restored, is still standing, and has been the location of various retail stores throughout the years. (Courtesy of WCHS Museum.)

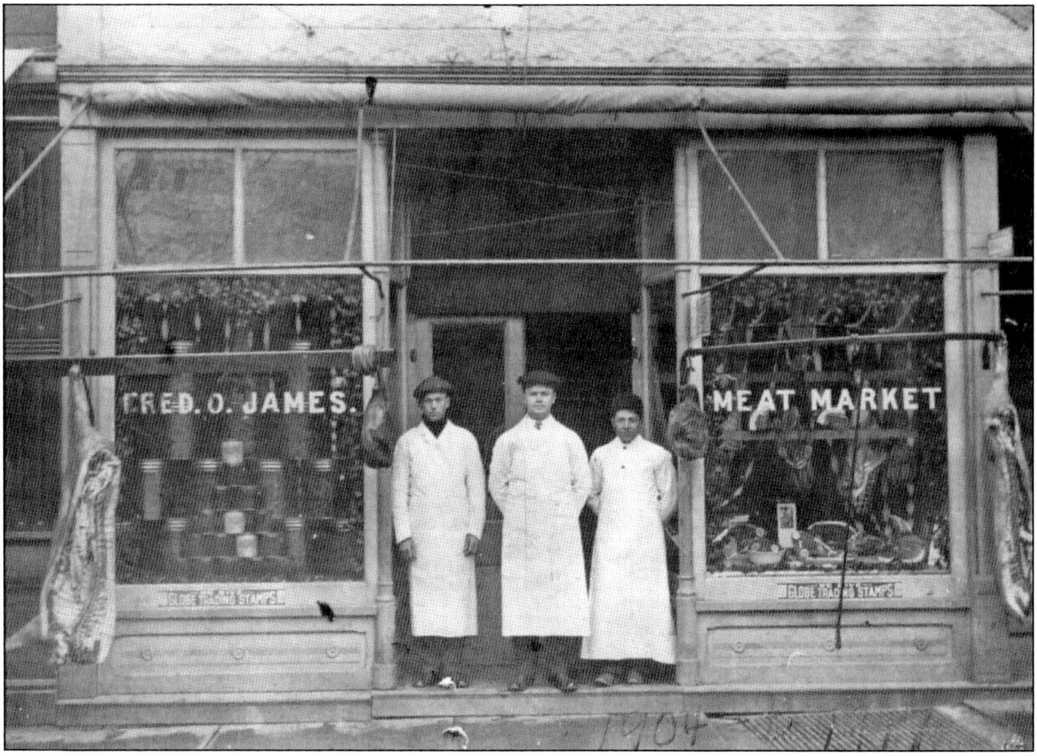

James Meat Market was located on the north side of Mulberry Street next to the Great Atlantic and Pacific Tea Company. This photograph shows owner Fred O. James in the center with two unidentified men. James Market is believed to have lasted until the mid- to late 1940s at this location. (Courtesy of WCHS Museum.)

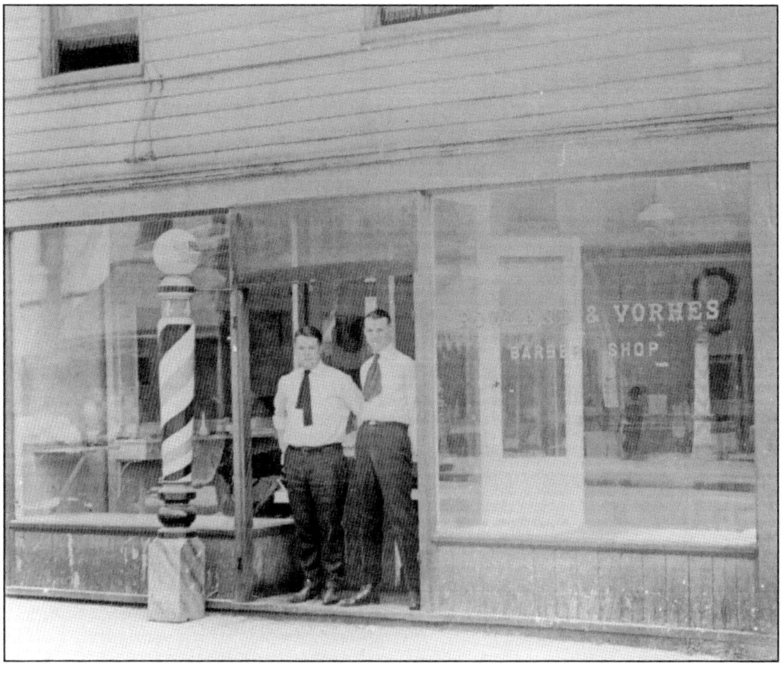

This image of the Rowland and Vorhes Barbershop shows owner "Puff" Vorhes on the left posing with an unidentified employee. The barbershop was located on Mulberry Street on the first block. (Courtesy of WCHS Museum.)

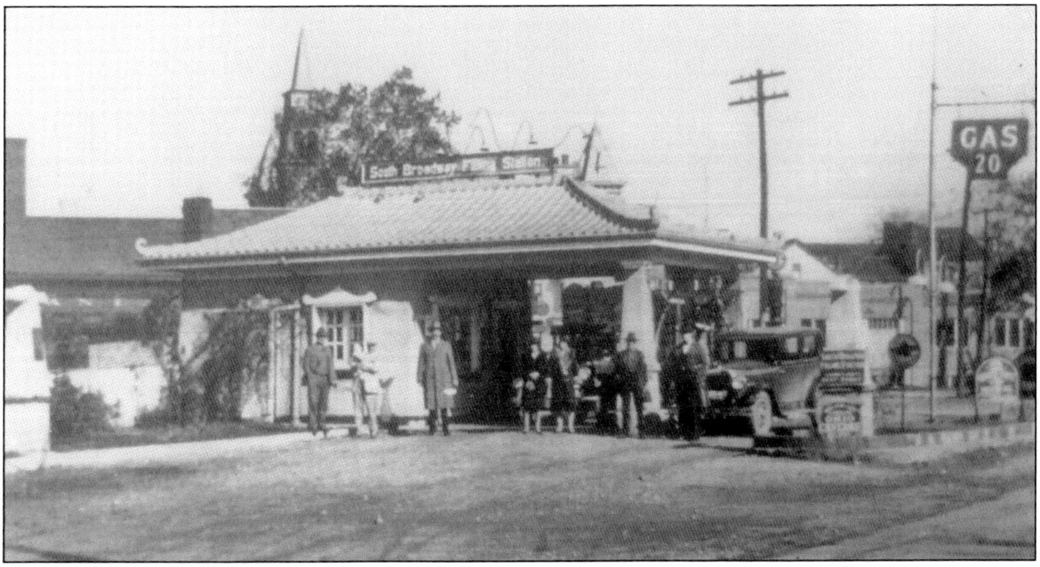

This 1920s image of the South Broadway Filling Station is one of many examples of Asian architecture that came to Lebanon in the early part of the 20th century. The buildings, all with distinctive tile roofs, can be seen in various locations throughout downtown, as witnessed by the next image. (Courtesy of WCHS Museum.)

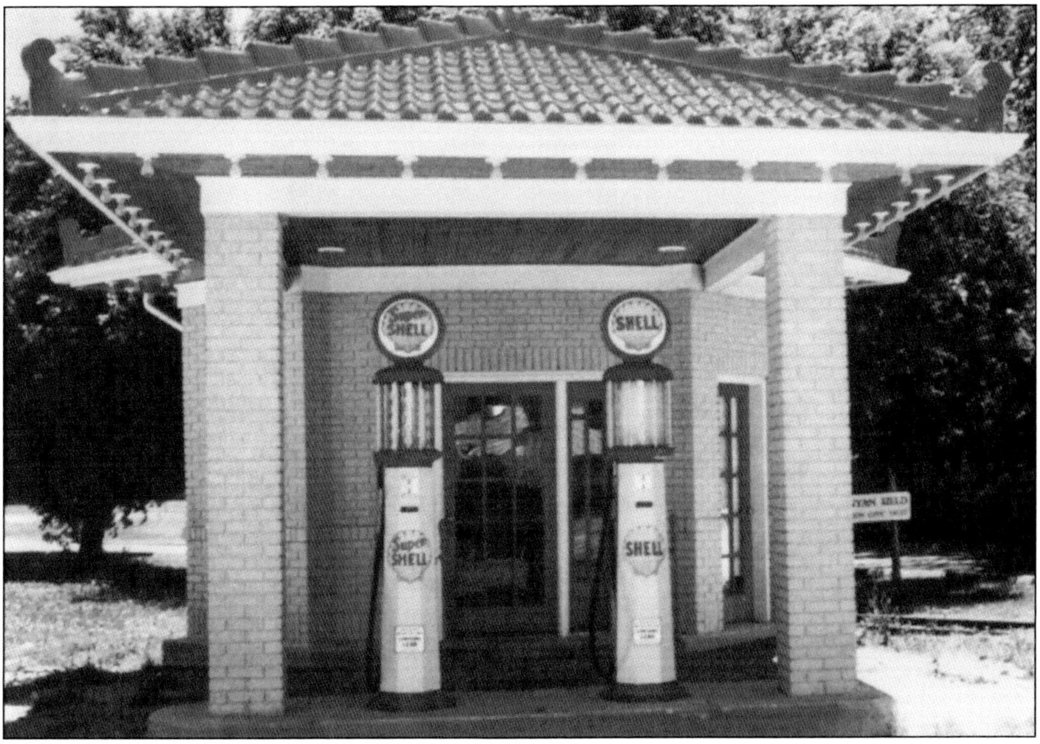

This small service station sat at the corner of Mulberry and Cherry Streets for decades before being completely moved in the 1990s to South Street near Harmon Park. Known for years by local residents as "The Taxi Stand," this restored station is now used by the Lebanon Police Department. (Courtesy of WCHS Museum.)

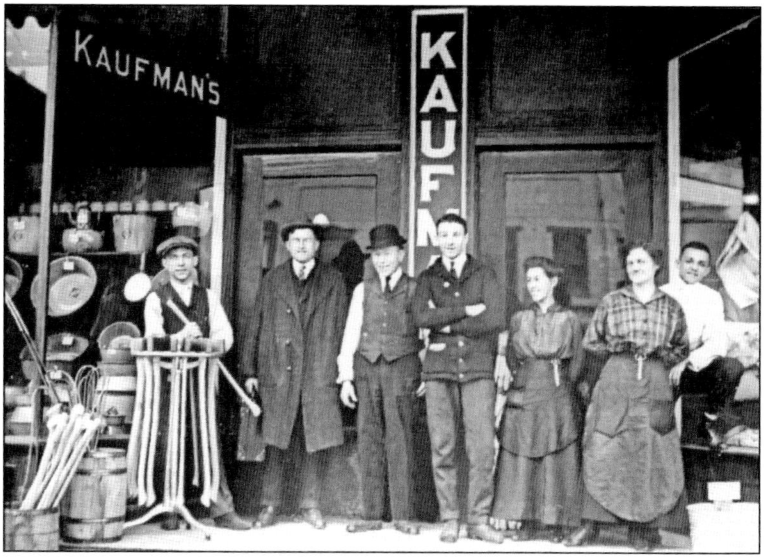

This early image of Kaufman's Department Store in Lebanon, taken from a glass negative, shows owner A. B. "Abe" Kaufman posing in the center with several unidentified employees. The large clothier was a staple in Lebanon's downtown retail district from 1897 until its closing in 1983. (Courtesy of the Scott and Traci Gallagher collection.)

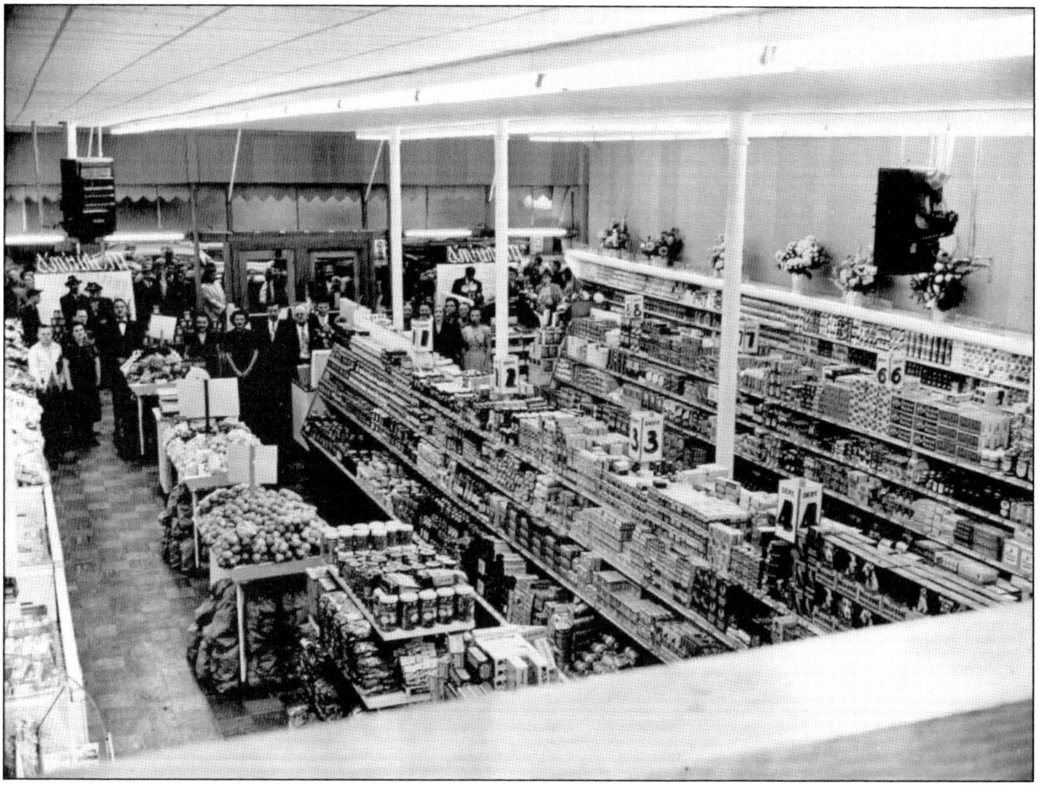

This 1950s image is an interior shot of Marvin's Super Value Grocery Store, which was located on the north side of Mulberry Street on the first block. By the 1950s, the smaller markets such as James and the A&P had been replaced with larger and more modern stores such as Marvin's and Kroger. This particular store served downtown until the mid-1970s. (Courtesy of WCHS Museum.)

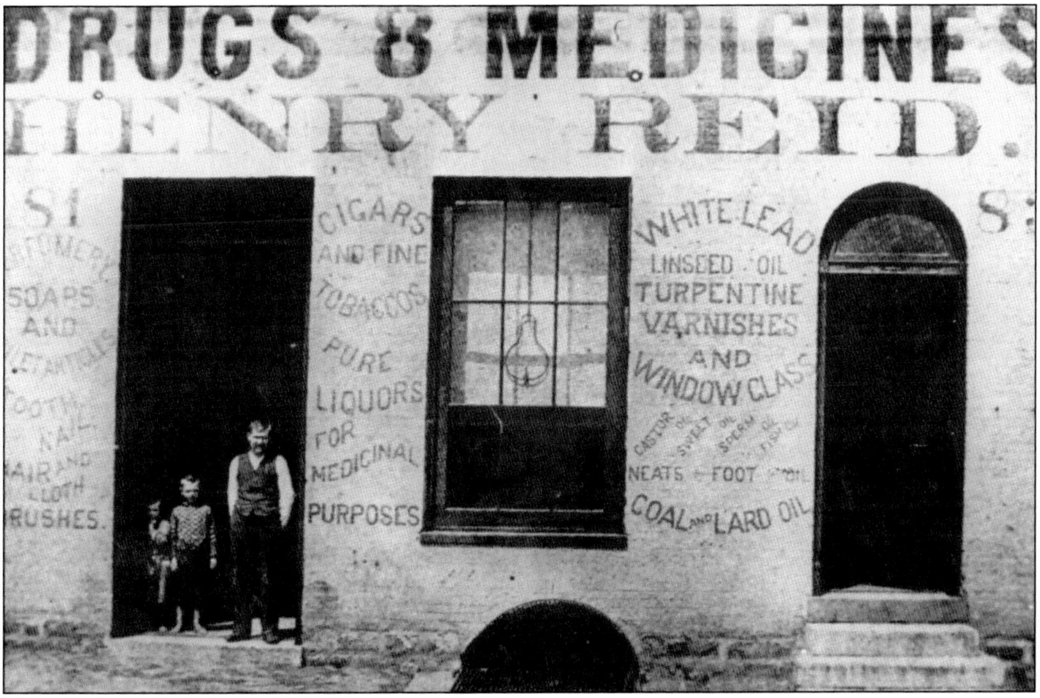

Reid's Drugstore was located on the Maplewood Block of Broadway Street between J. W. Lingo's and the Golden Lamb. It was adjacent to the old Lebanon National Bank building, now First Financial Bank. Much like the drugstores of today, Reid's offered a variety of merchandise besides drugs and patient medicines. According to local residents, there was always a drugstore of some type in this location. The last pharmacy was Hawke's, which occupied this storefront until after the turn of the 21st century. Posing in the doorway of the building, which is still standing, is owner Henry Reid and his two sons. (Courtesy of WCHS Museum.)

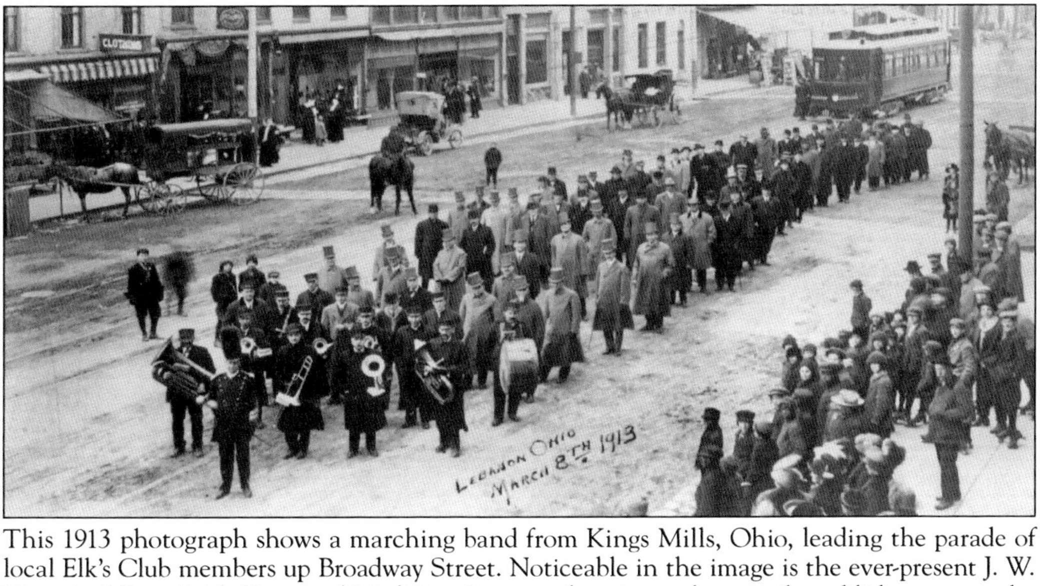

This 1913 photograph shows a marching band from Kings Mills, Ohio, leading the parade of local Elk's Club members up Broadway Street. Noticeable in the image is the ever-present J. W. Lingo building, Reids Drug and Medicine Store, and various other retail establishments on the west side of Lebanon's main street. (Courtesy of WCHS Museum.)

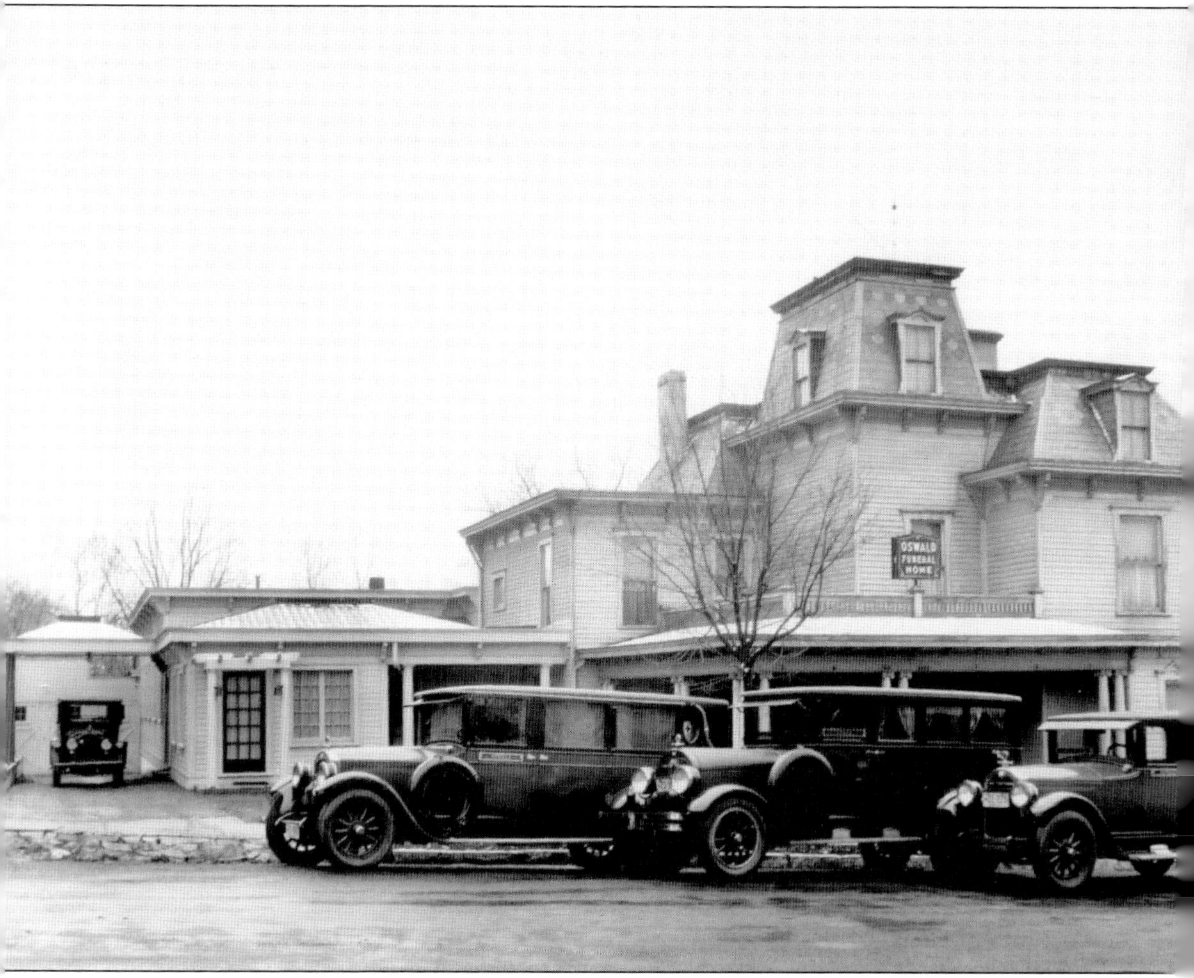

In this 1930s image, Oswald's Funeral Home is shown at 110 South Broadway Street. Beginning with casket and furniture maker John Oswald in 1866, the business soon began offering funeral services. The funeral home moved to its present Mulberry Street location in the early 1960s. The building pictured here was razed after a series of fires, with the property now being occupied by Henkle Schueler Realtors. (Courtesy of WCHS Museum.)

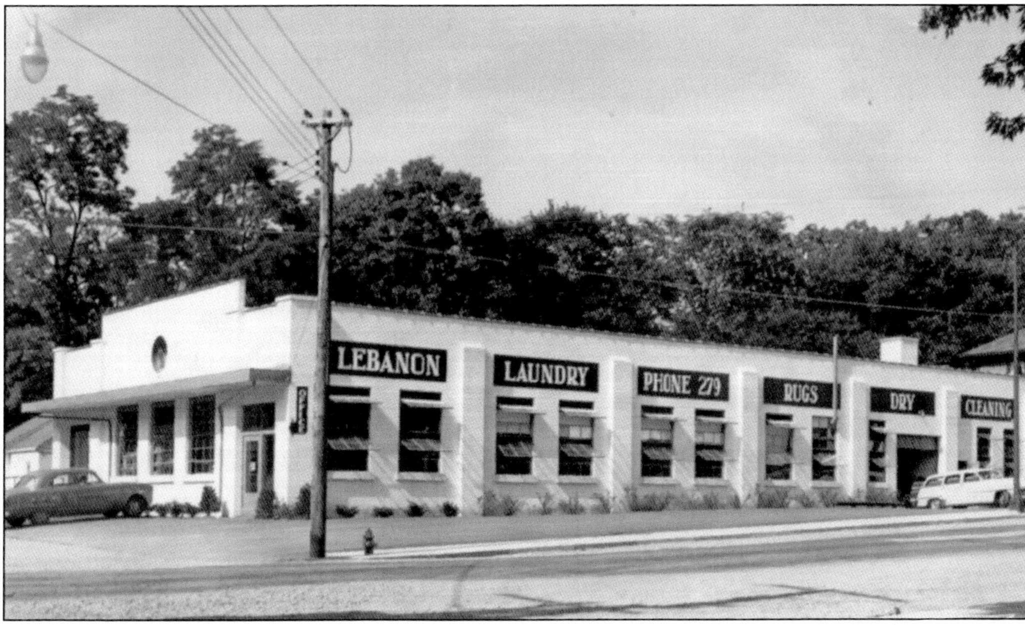

This 1950s image is of the long-standing Brown's Lebanon Laundry on West Silver Street in Lebanon. The modern cinder block building served as a laundry for Lebanon until the late 1960s or early 1970s. It was eventually purchased and now houses a portion of the Lebanon Fire Division. (Courtesy of WCHS Museum.)

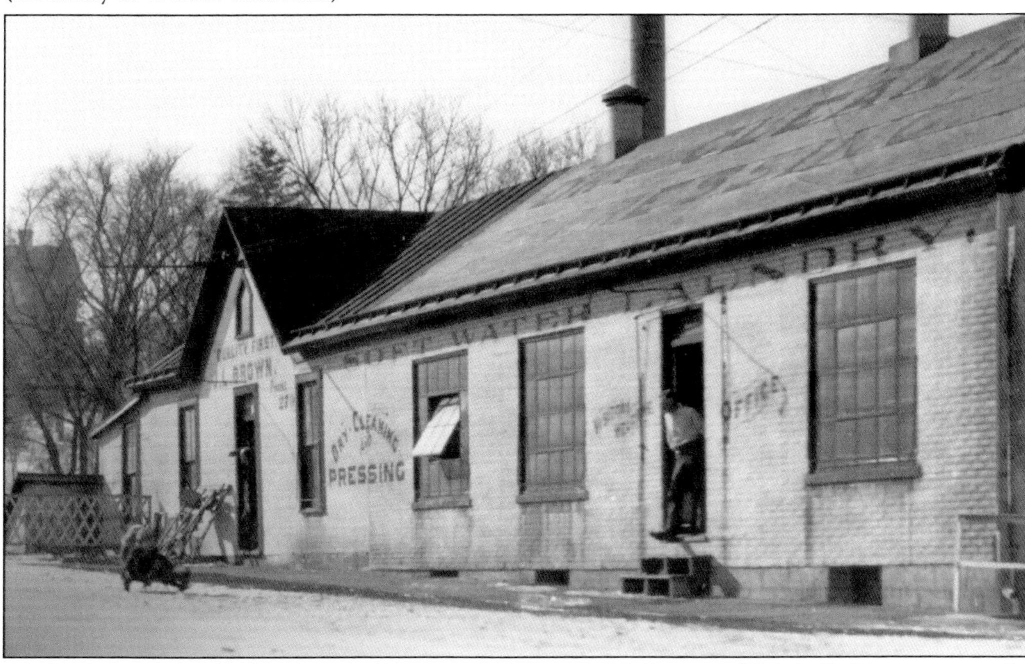

At the opposite end of town, on Cincinnati Avenue in Lebanon's Floraville District, was the original Brown's laundry of much more modest proportions. This 1920s image shows a business offering dry cleaning, a rarity in small towns at this time. This building located on the southeast side of Cincinnati Avenue is now the site of a small strip-mall shopping center. (Courtesy of WCHS Museum.)

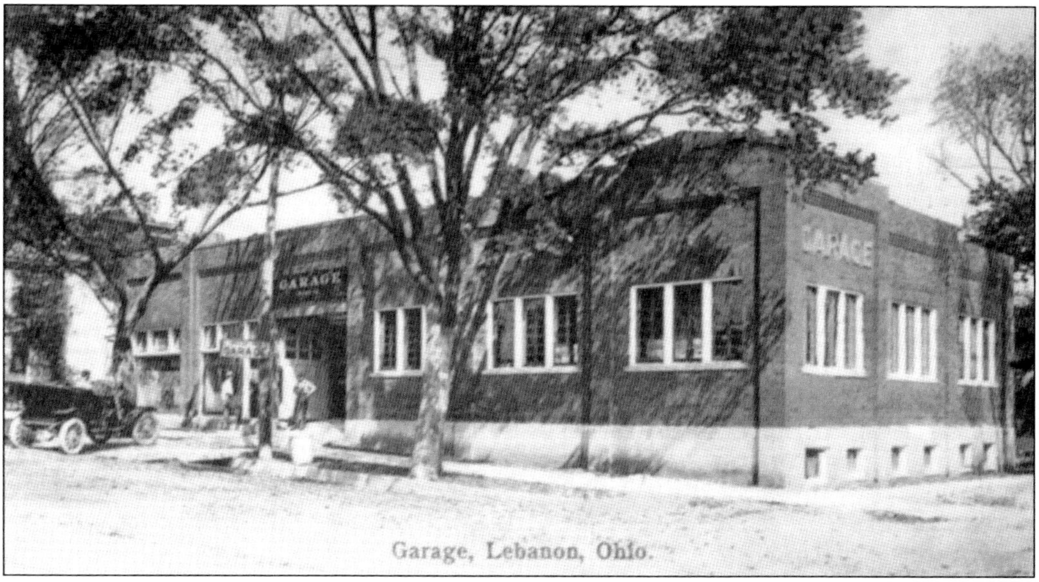

This building at the base of Broadway Street on the west side is known today by residents as the Roll Building, nicknamed for its longtime owner Robert Roll. In this early image, it was occupied by a garage, which later became the Kilpatrick-French Motor Inn and also a Chevrolet dealership. The building has remained virtually intact and is now home to Lebanon's famous Golden Turtle Chocolate Factory and several other businesses. (Courtesy of the Sally Foster collection.)

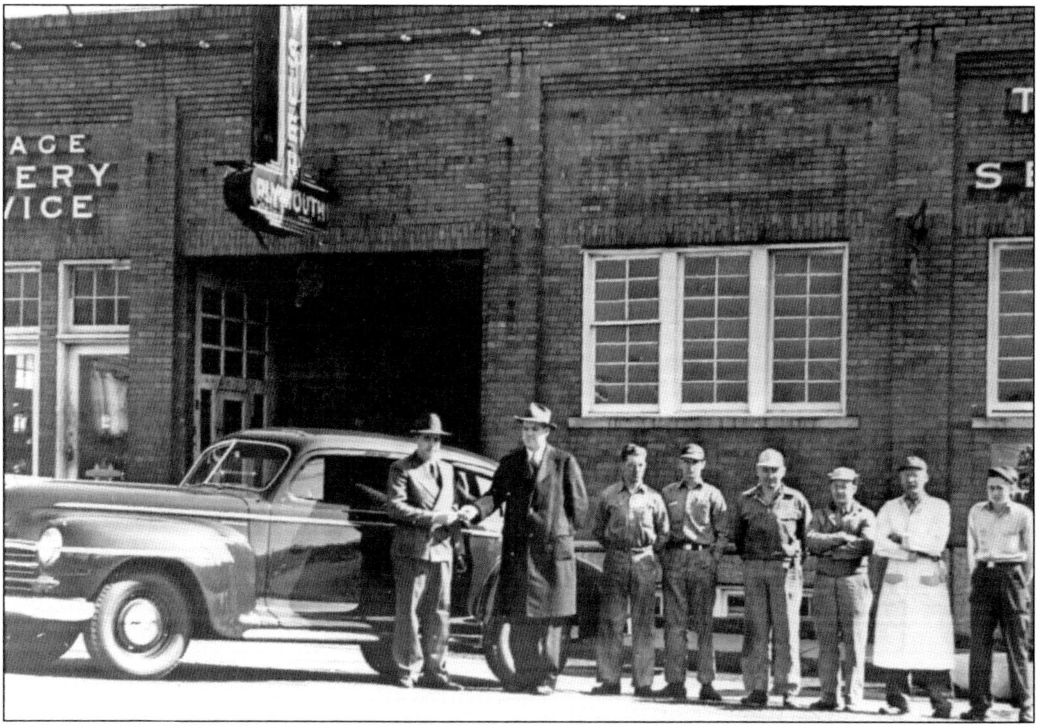

This 1940s image shows building owner Robert Roll (far left) accepting the delivery of the first new car in Lebanon after World War II. The building at this time was a Chrysler Plymouth dealership, having formerly been a Chevrolet dealership 20 years earlier. (Courtesy of WCHS Museum.)

Three

Shingles, Sticks, and Queens

Lebanon's Residential Architecture

The first home in Lebanon was constructed on Lot No. 1, which sits just beside Christmas Tree Park on East Main Street. Capt. John Thorpe built a simple two-story structure set back from the Main Street, probably with room behind for a small utility building or a garden. Thorpe's house and many soon to follow were simple structures that were designed for comfort and utility and not as testaments to wealth or accomplishment. As neighborhoods grew along Main Street, Mechanic Street, Orchard and Wright Avenues, and Silver and Mulberry Streets, words like Italianate, Gothic, Greek Revival, Federal, and Queen Anne started creeping into the city's language. Residences became larger and carriage houses started replacing the simple utility buildings of 30 years before.

Mathias Corwin, father of Gov. Thomas Corwin, is said to have built the first house designed by an architect. The residence still majestically stands guard today to the entrance of what was once known as Lebanon's Floraville District, the roughly 5-acre tract bounded by Cincinnati and Orchard Avenues. Also still surviving in Floraville are the Classic Revival home of Judge Willard Wright, father of famous designer Russel Wright, and the spectacular Greek Revival Pillars on Cincinnati Avenue built by Robert Boake. Just at the end of the Floraville District on Cincinnati Avenue is the very unique Hexagon House, built in 1858. This eight-sided home was constructed by Goldsmith Coffeen, who made his living selling Coffeen's Chinese Liniment, which was advertised as being "good for man or beast."

The grand homes in Lebanon are typically identified by local residents not by their architectural style but by the families who owned them. Lebanon residents do not speak in terms of Italianate, neoclassical, Greek Revival, or Queen Anne but rather refer to the Cropper House, the Herrick House, or the Corwin House. This casual familial identification serves as a constant reminder of the generations of families and their resiliency. They may be small homes like John Thorpe's or mansions like Mathias Corwin's, but they all exist as they have for almost two centuries, still making history for the families who live there with the continuation of everyday events, which brings one generation to a close and carries another forward.

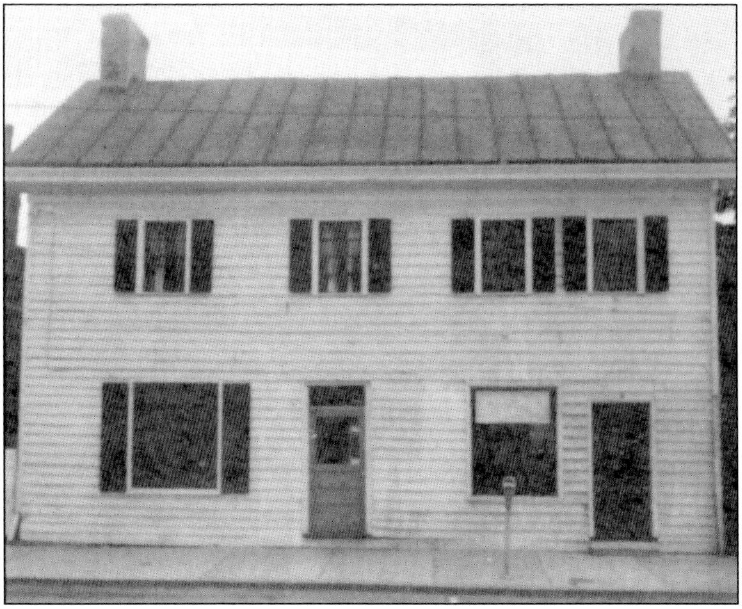

Identified as the oldest residence in Lebanon, the John Thorpe House stands on West Main Street in Lebanon. Built on Lot No. 1, on the southwest corner of Main and Broadway Streets, the house may have originally been a log cabin that has been covered over the years. The simple two-story home was built, as was the custom of the time, close to the street. The home is now part of Lebanon's downtown retail section. (Courtesy of WCHS Museum.)

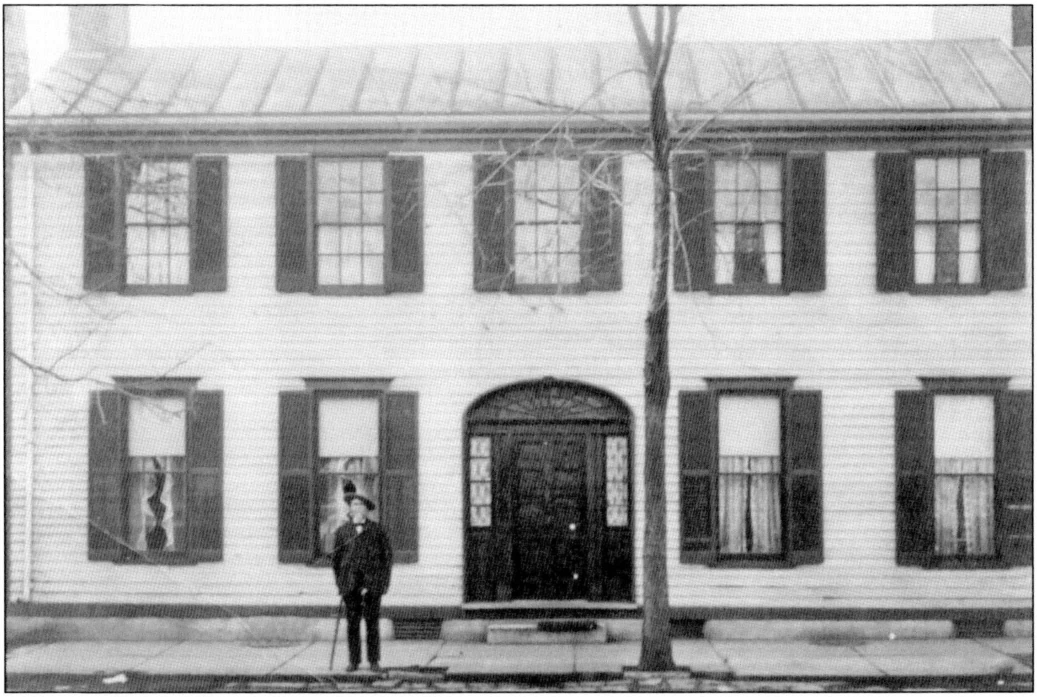

The Nixon-Brant House on north Mechanic Street is thought to be one of the oldest residences still standing in Lebanon. This Federal-style house was built by Samuel Nixon around 1807–1808. The home features an elliptical-fan window over the front door, a side gable roof, and an exterior that has been basically unaltered since its initial construction in 1807. In 1893, Warren County sheriff Al Brant purchased the property that remained in the Brant family until the 1920s. A devastating fire in 1999 almost destroyed the historic structure. Rescued and restored by the Lebanon Conservancy Foundation, the Nixon-Brant House now serves as the offices for the Lebanon Conservancy Foundation and is available for private functions. (Courtesy of WCHS Museum.)

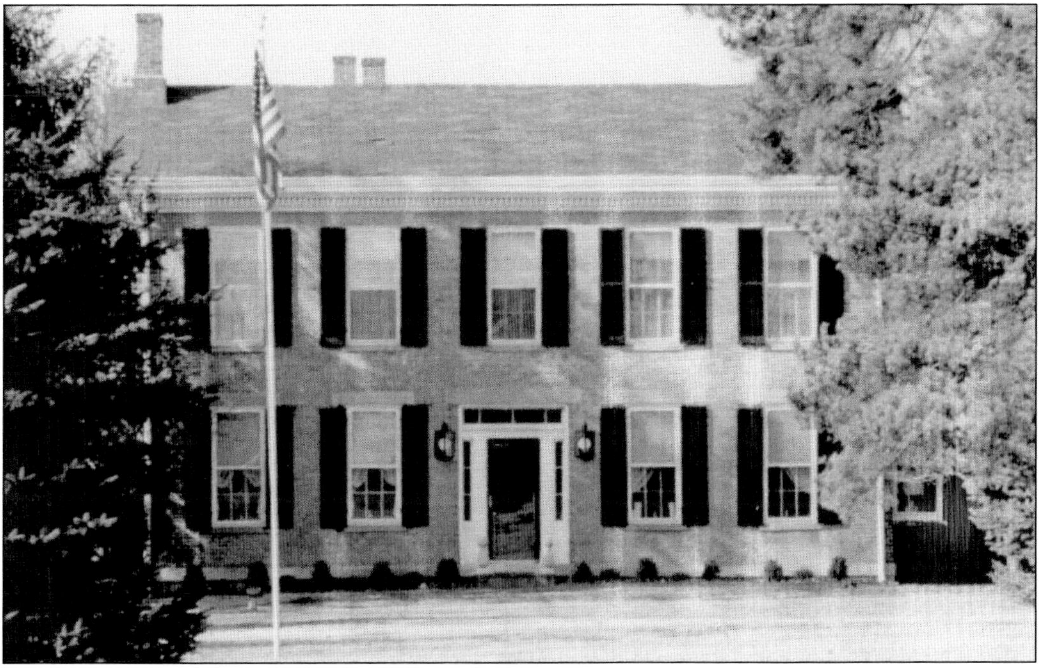

The Corwin-Bolin House at 1443 North Broadway Street was built by the youngest son of Lebanon's first settler, Ichabod Corwin. This Greek Revival–style residence features a center entrance and thick stone lintels on the windows. The Bolin name is attached to the family who owned the home for almost 60 years in the 20th century. Listed on the National Register of Historic Places, the home is now a private residence. (Courtesy of WCHS Museum.)

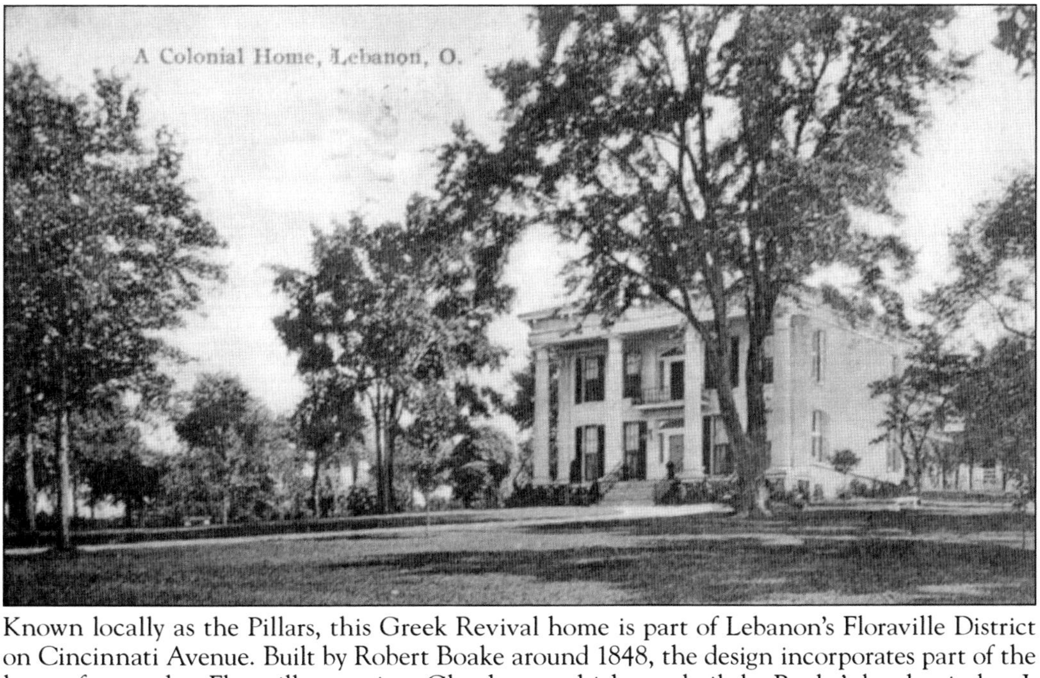

Known locally as the Pillars, this Greek Revival home is part of Lebanon's Floraville District on Cincinnati Avenue. Built by Robert Boake around 1848, the design incorporates part of the layout for another Floraville mansion, Glendower, which was built by Boake's brother-in-law J. Milton Williams. (Courtesy of the Sally Foster collection.)

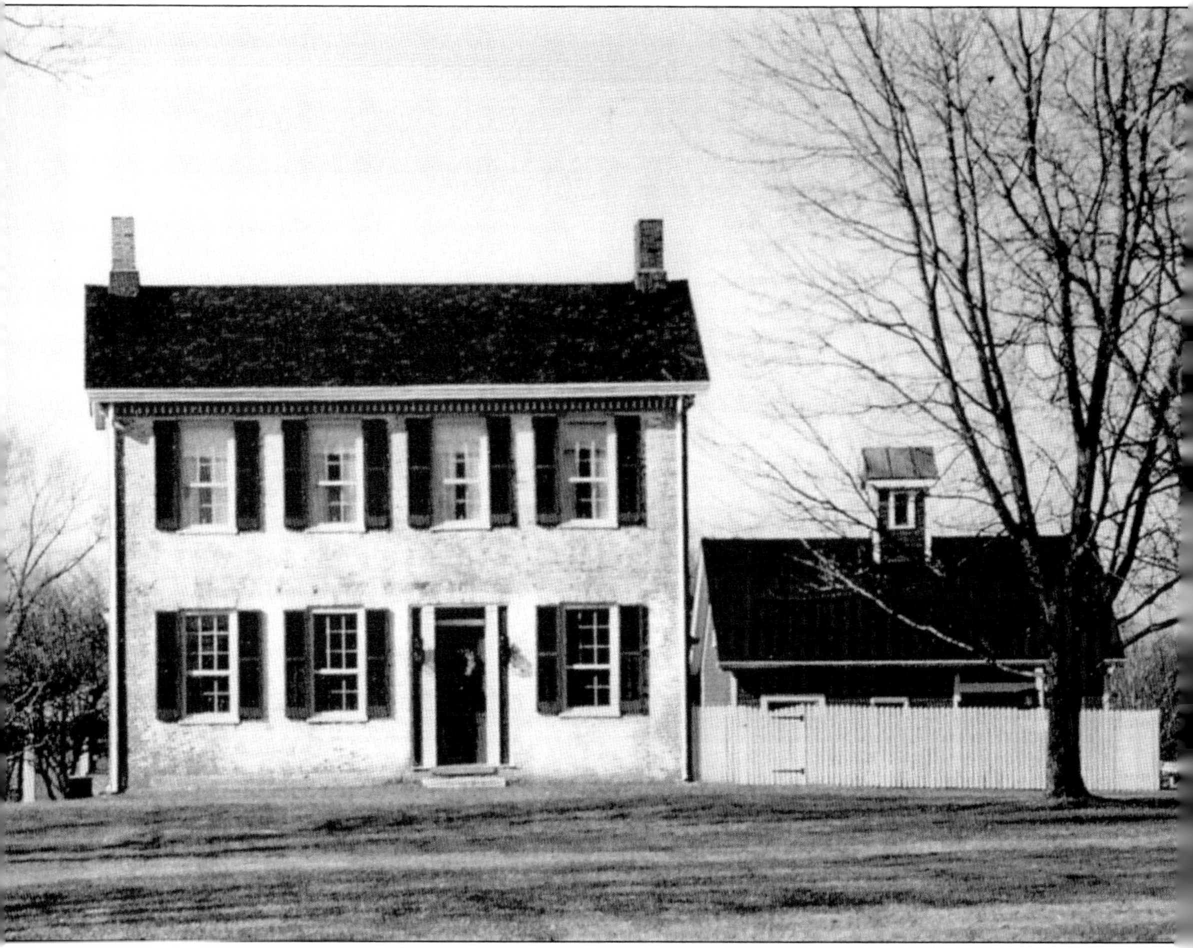

The Corwin House, located at 1255 North Broadway Street, remained in the Corwin family from the time of its construction around 1830 until 1978. This Federal-style home features an offset front entrance and windowless walls on either end. The unique front windows feature a nine-over-six pattern of panes. This home is listed on the National Register of Historic Places and is now a private residence. (Courtesy of WCHS Museum.)

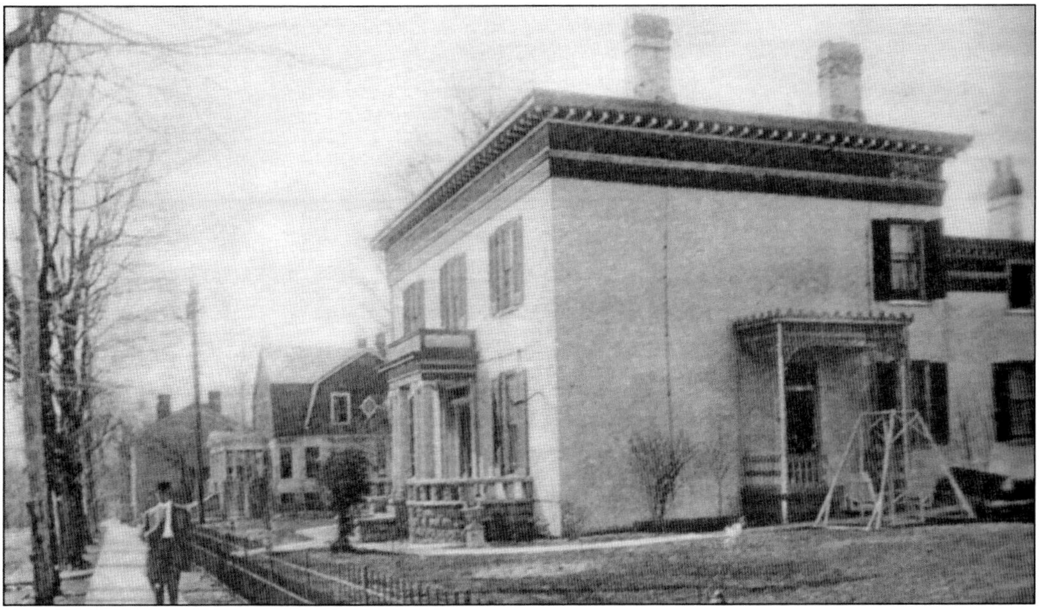

This early mansion on east Mulberry Street is another example of Greek Revival architecture in Lebanon. The classic architectural details include the heavy dentil molding at the roofline and the massive semicircular planting beds, which are still part of the structure today. (Courtesy of WCHS Museum.)

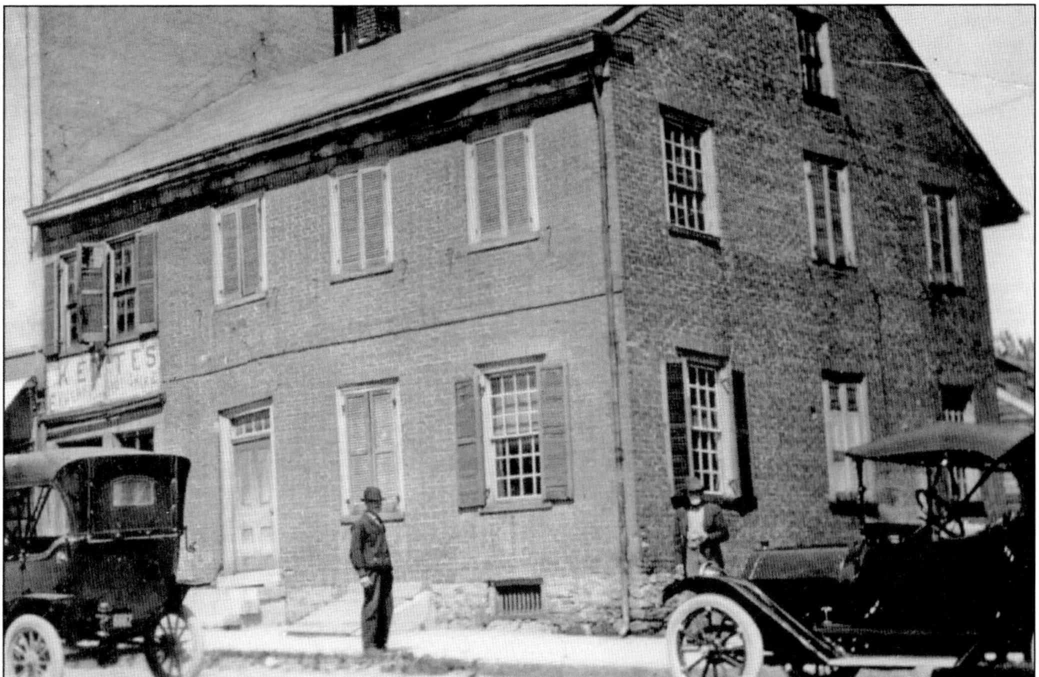

Samuel McCray, builder of Warren County's first courthouse at the corner of Main and Broadway Streets, constructed this home for himself on South Broadway using some of the courthouse designs. The home, damaged by an earthquake in 1811, stood until 1932 when it was destroyed by the opera house fire. (Courtesy of WCHS Museum.)

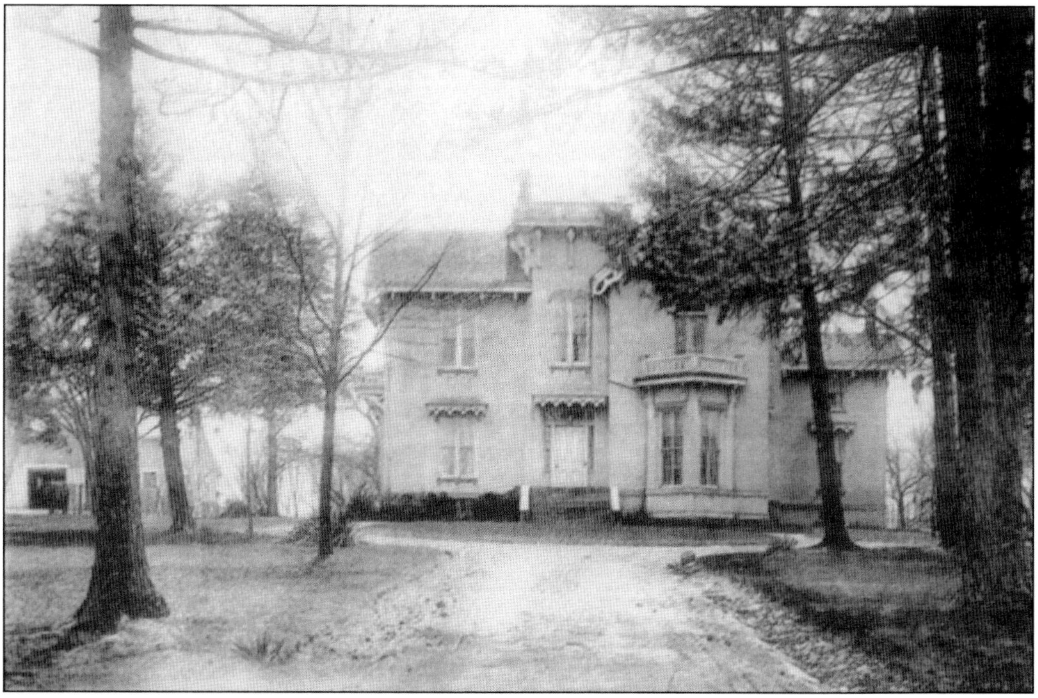

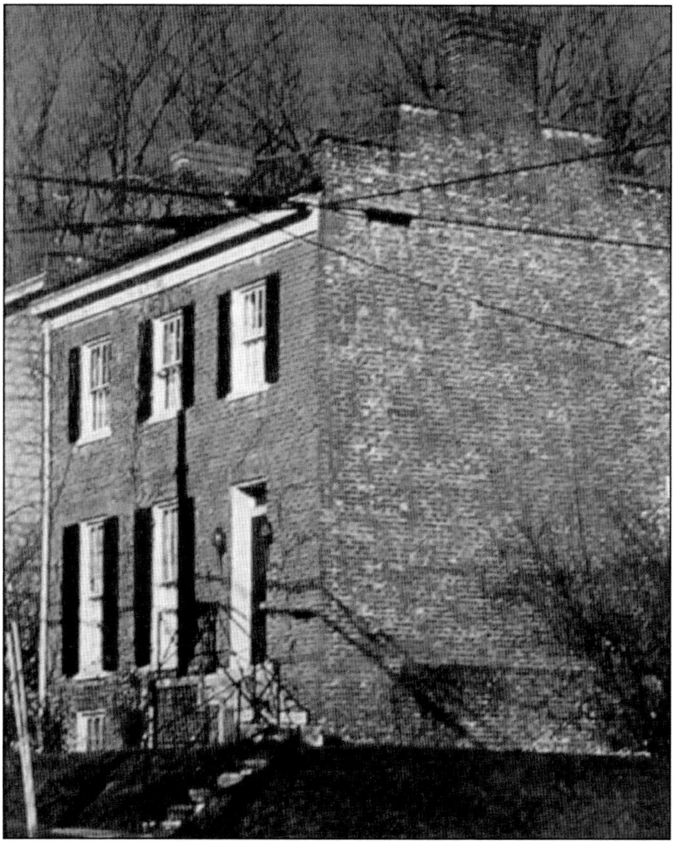

This Gothic-style mansion is another resident of Lebanon's Floraville District. Gothic style, evident in all parts of Lebanon, is typified by pointed arches, hood moldings over the windows, and gingerbread trim. This home, still standing on Cincinnati Avenue, is also noteworthy for its pink facade. (Courtesy of the Sally Foster collection.)

The Smith-Davis House on Silver Street in Lebanon is another Federal-style structure built with windowless walls at either end. The unique stepped-end gables indicate early European influences in the Federal style. The home, listed on the National Register of Historic Places, has had numerous additions throughout the years and was restored in the early 1980s. (Courtesy of WCHS Museum.)

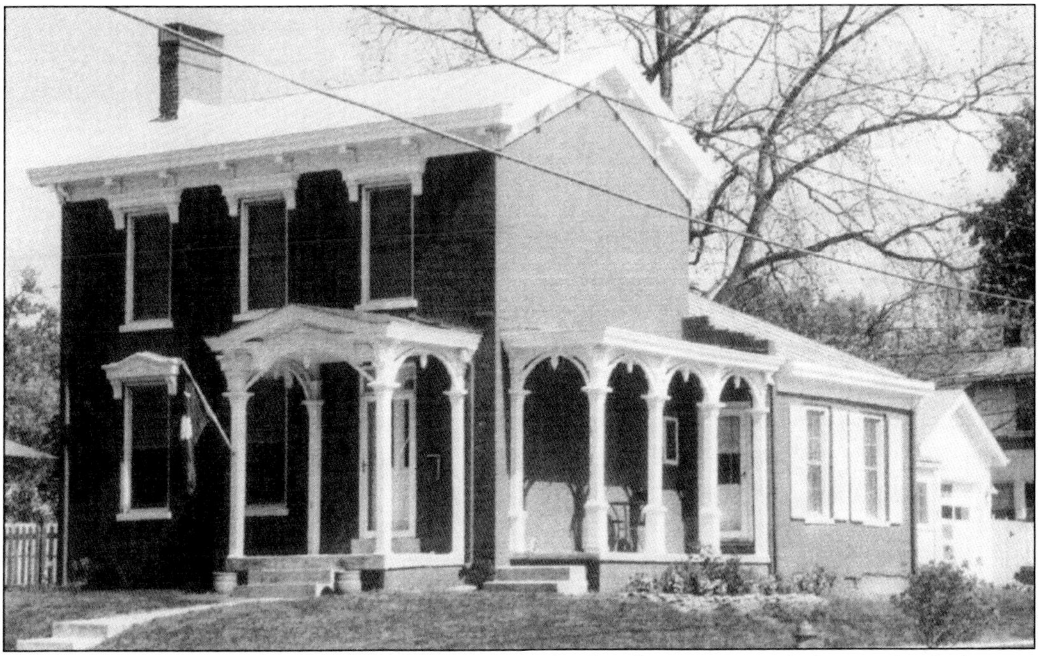

This home on Jackson Street shows numerous Federal influences in style but is also Italianate in design with its second-story trim above the windows and the columns on the front and side porches. (Courtesy of WCHS Museum.)

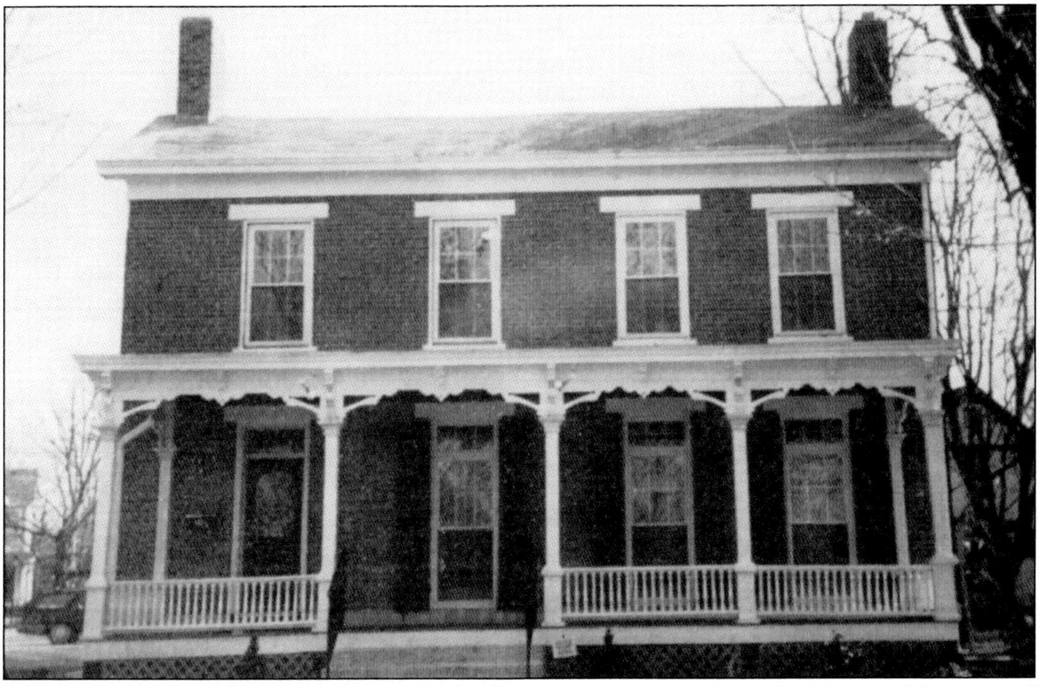

The Mohrman-Jack-Evans House on Columbus Avenue is listed on the National Register of Historic Places and is a modified example of Federal-style buildings around 1780–1820. A Victorian porch, which covers the extreme offset door to the left and the three windows to the right, was added sometime during the home's history. (Courtesy of WCHS Museum.)

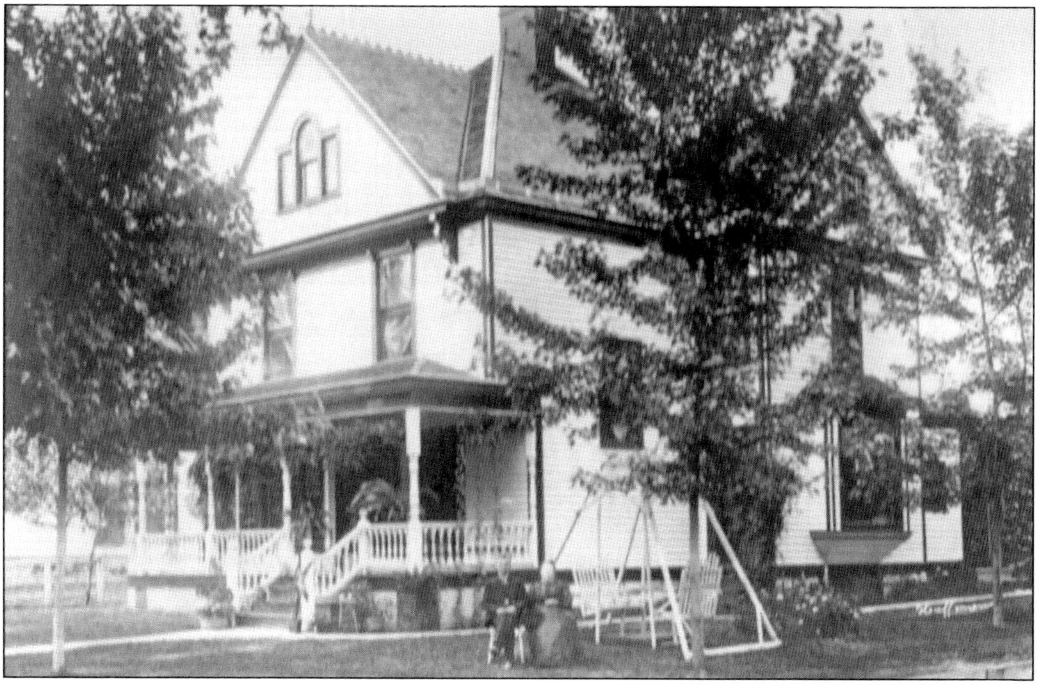

The Peter Hatfield home on Mound Street is an interesting mix of architectural styles. The Italianate porch fronts the main residence, which displays Gothic characteristics with the sharp angular peak to the front roofline, strong central chimney, and decorative moldings on both the second floor and the roofline. Pictured here in the 1890s are Peter Hatfield and his wife. (Courtesy of WCHS Museum.)

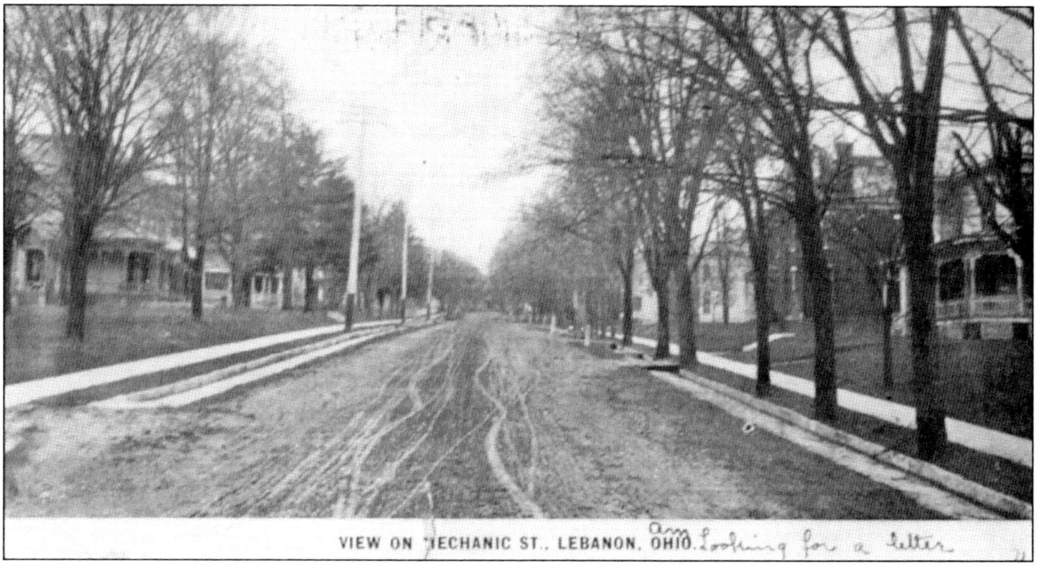

This early-1900s view, looking south on Mechanic Street, illustrates one of the most iconic streets in Lebanon for 19th-century architecture. The sheer number of shade trees gives evidence to a neighborhood of larger and more ornate homes. The City of Lebanon still maintains a shade tree commission, which meets monthly to preserve and protect the city's trees. (Courtesy of the Sally Foster collection.)

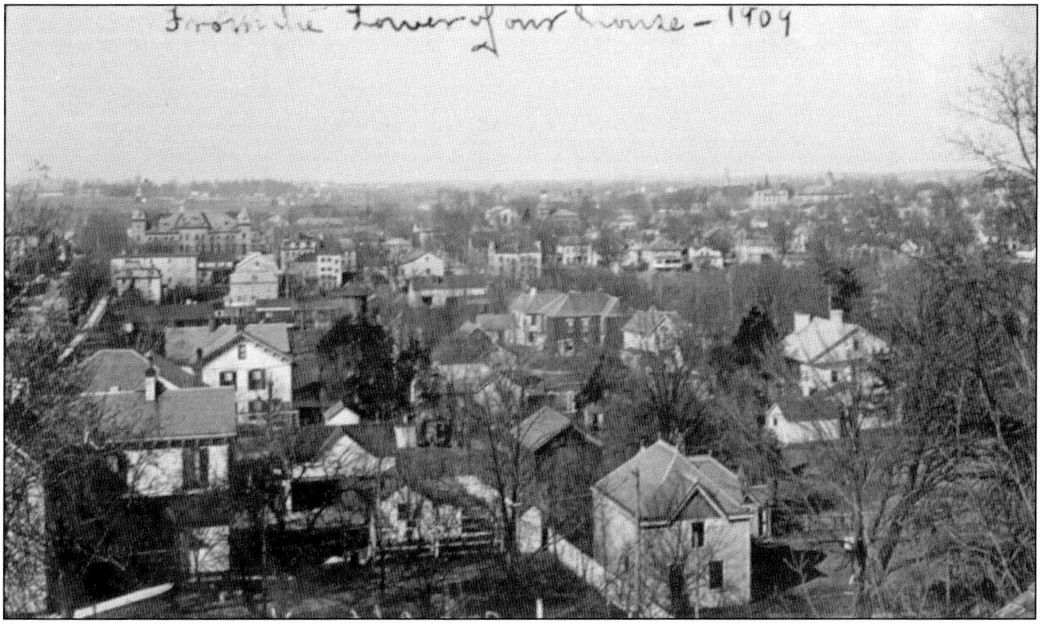

This rare bird's-eye view of Lebanon is aptly titled "From the Tower of My House." It is believed this photograph (which was produced on a postcard) was taken from the tower of a home that once stood on the southwest corner of Broadway Street and Orchard Avenue. Numerous local landmarks can be seen, including the Lebanon Opera House and the Golden Lamb. (Courtesy of the Sally Foster collection.)

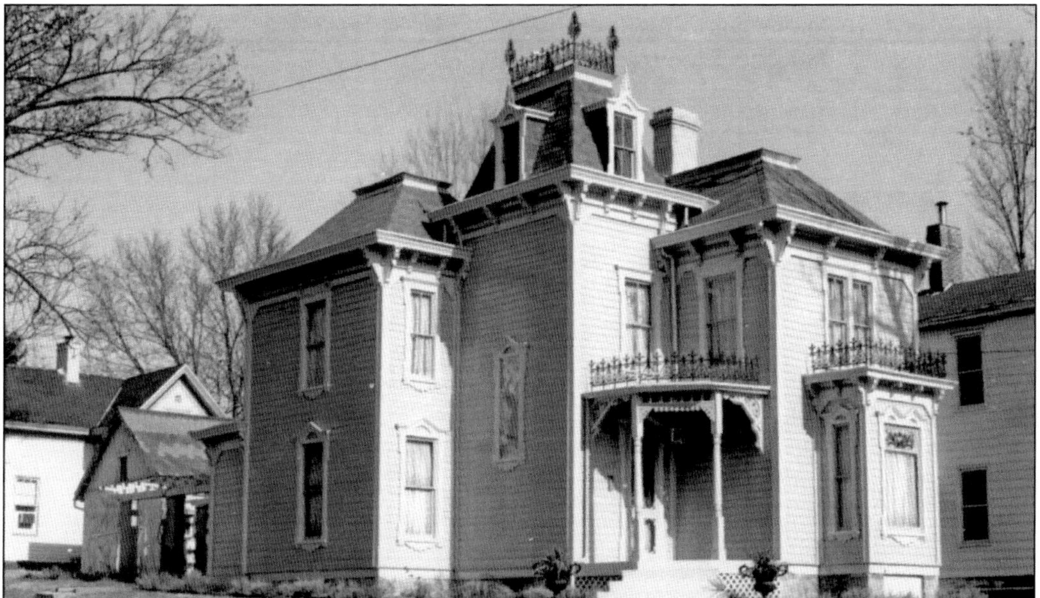

This classic Victorian home on High Street was a private residence for decades before becoming a bed-and-breakfast (Silver High Manor) and then a private residence again. The home displays some Italianate influence in the porch and the mansard-roofed tower with ornate detailing at the top. (Courtesy of WCHS Museum.)

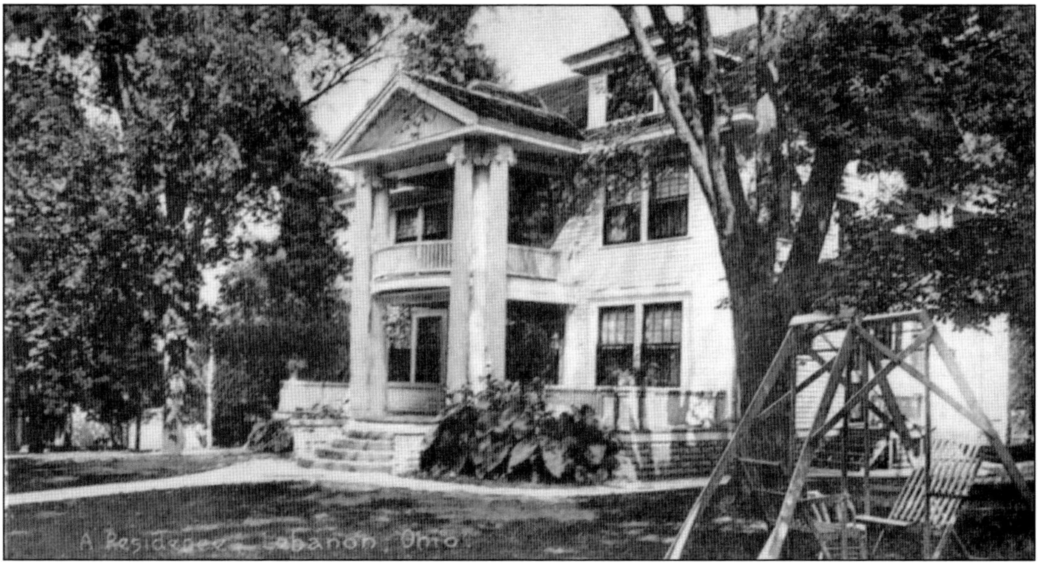

This classic revival home on South Broadway Street was built in 1910 for Judge Willard Wright, the father of Russel Wright who was an internationally known industrial designer. This three-story home features two-story Ionic columns supporting a classic cornice and pediment. The front door is flanked by oversized sidelights and topped by an elliptical fanlight. (Courtesy of the Sally Foster collection.)

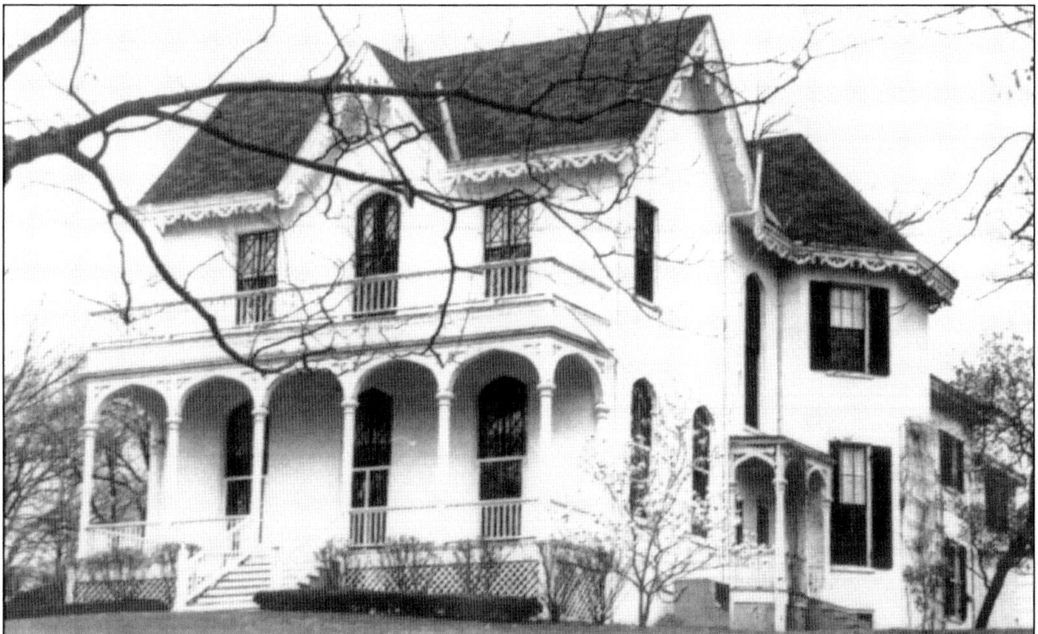

Known to generations of Lebanon residents as the Cropper House, this residence on south Broadway Street is more formally known as The Gables. Built around 1848, the Gothic Revival–style mansion was the first home in Lebanon designed and built by an architect. Mathias Corwin, father of Gov. Thomas Corwin, built the home with brick and cut stone. The mullioned windows contain 108 separate panes of glass. This front view of the home is one rarely seen by residents since the side and rear of the home face Broadway. (Courtesy of WCHS Museum.)

Four

The Finest Building in the County
Lebanon's Public Buildings

In February 1805, when the Ohio Legislature officially established Lebanon as the county seat of Warren County, a formal courthouse and administration building had yet to be built. Lebanon's first courthouse was constructed on the northeast corner of Main and Broadway Streets, the site of the current city administration building. This simple two-story building served as the county courthouse for over 30 years and then another 40 years as Lebanon's town hall. The building, along with much of the city block, was destroyed by a devastating fire in September 1874.

Warren County's next courthouse was located on donated land on Silver Street. At a cost of $25,000, the two-story Greek Revival–style structure housed county administration offices on the first floor. By 1895, this original courthouse had been transformed into a Renaissance Revival behemoth, which still stands today.

After the disastrous fire of 1874, a new and even bigger structure was erected on the site of the former modest Lebanon Town Hall. In September 1878, the Lebanon Opera House was dedicated and quickly declared "the finest public building in Warren County."

The new Opera House was a rambling Gothic structure with towers on all four corners and a dominating spire in the front. Housed within the Lebanon Opera House was a 1,200-seat auditorium with a proscenium arch decorated with a portrait of Thomas Corwin. County residents eagerly flocked to everything from traveling theatrical productions, local stage plays, and high school graduations.

The finest building in Warren County began suffering a slow death around 1900. Fewer theatrical productions came to Lebanon, and the opera house began exhibiting the newest craze, moving pictures. The final death knell for the grand old building came in the early hours of Christmas morning in 1932 when a disastrous fire swept through. Ironically the film that had been playing the night before was a little-known and long-forgotten movie with Cary Grant entitled *Hot Saturday*.

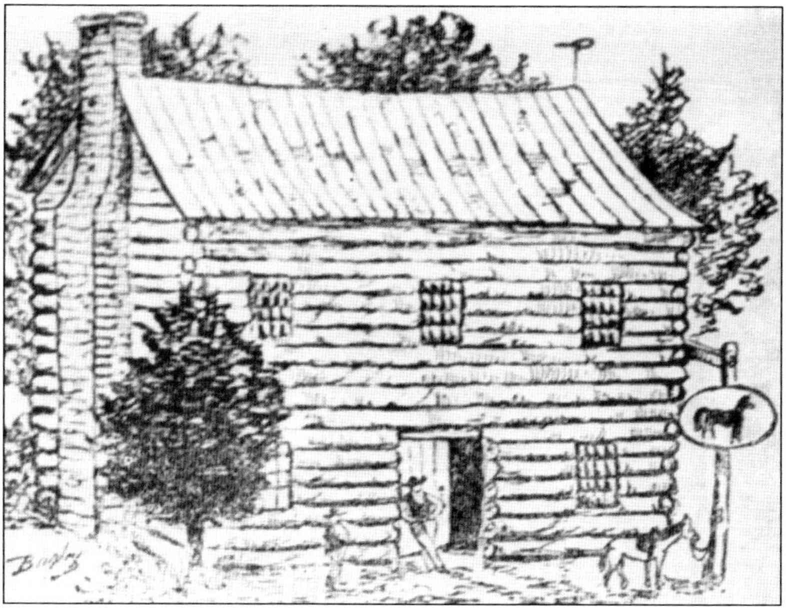

This early illustration is perhaps Lebanon's first public building. Ephraim Hathaway's Black Horse Tavern was located on North Broadway Street between Mulberry and Silver Streets. Taverns were usually the first buildings in a town and served as courts, public meeting halls, and sometimes even as a jail. (Courtesy of WCHS Museum.)

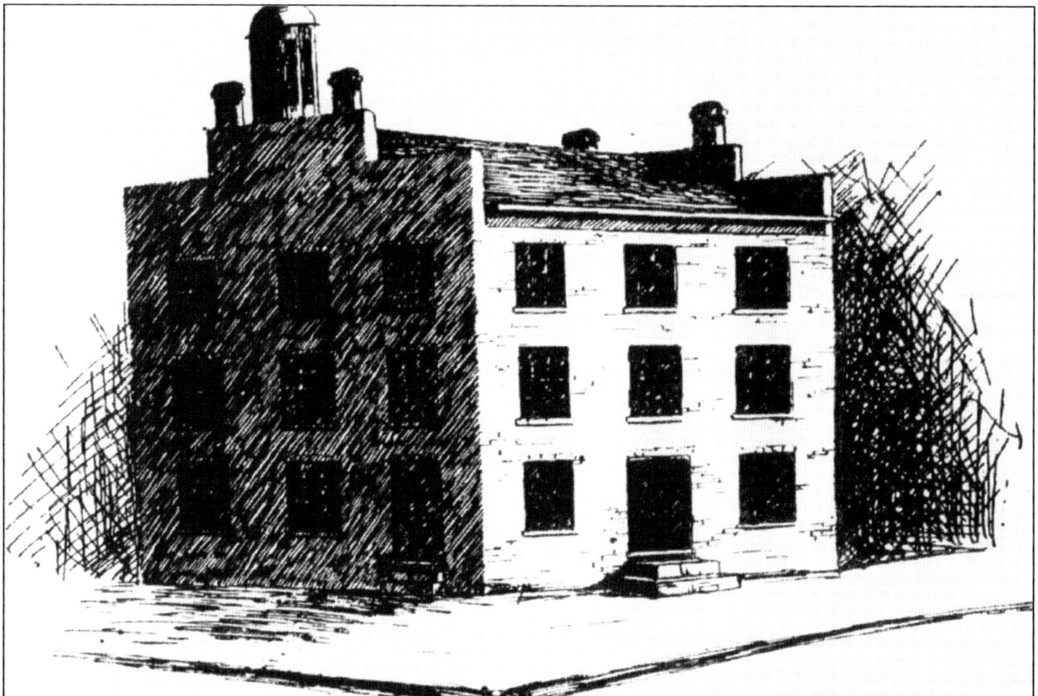

This drawing is of Warren County's first courthouse, which stood on the site of the present Lebanon City Building. Erected in 1805, it served as the county courthouse for 30 years until 1835, when it became Lebanon's town hall. The third story was added in 1844. The building, 36 feet square, was constructed at a cost of $1,450. It stood until September 1874, when it was destroyed by fire. (Courtesy of WCHS Museum.)

This 1950s image shows the current Lebanon City Building as it appeared for many years after it was dedicated in 1934. Of particular note are the movie poster signboards at either end of the building. In addition to city offices and the fire station, the building housed a popular movie theater until the mid-1960s. (Courtesy of the Sally Foster collection.)

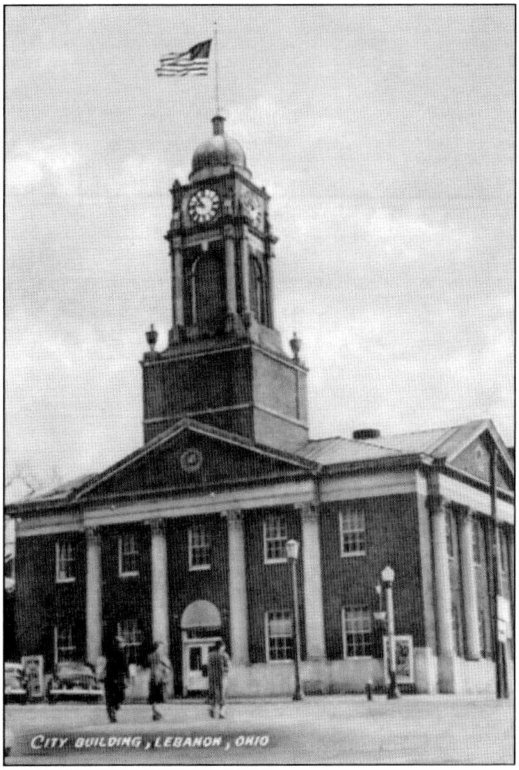

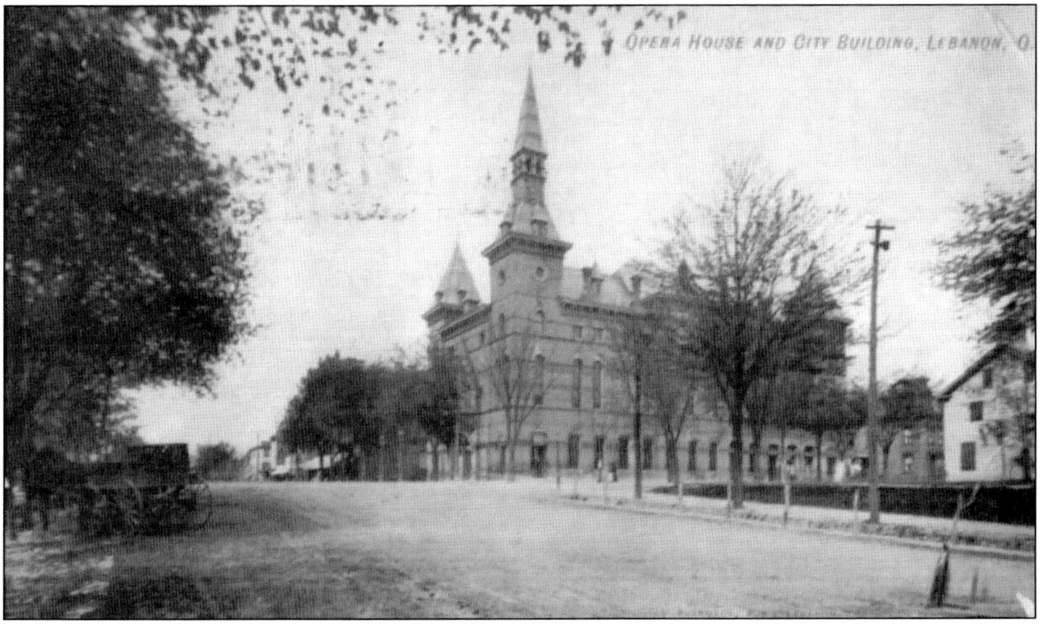

This early-1900s photograph shows the Lebanon Opera House, dubbed "the finest building in the county" when it was dedicated in September 1878. Built at a cost of $36,000, the opera house construction began in 1877 with the building being dedicated just over a year later. The rambling three-story Gothic structure dominated downtown with towers on all four corners and a grand spire in the front. (Courtesy of the Sally Foster collection.)

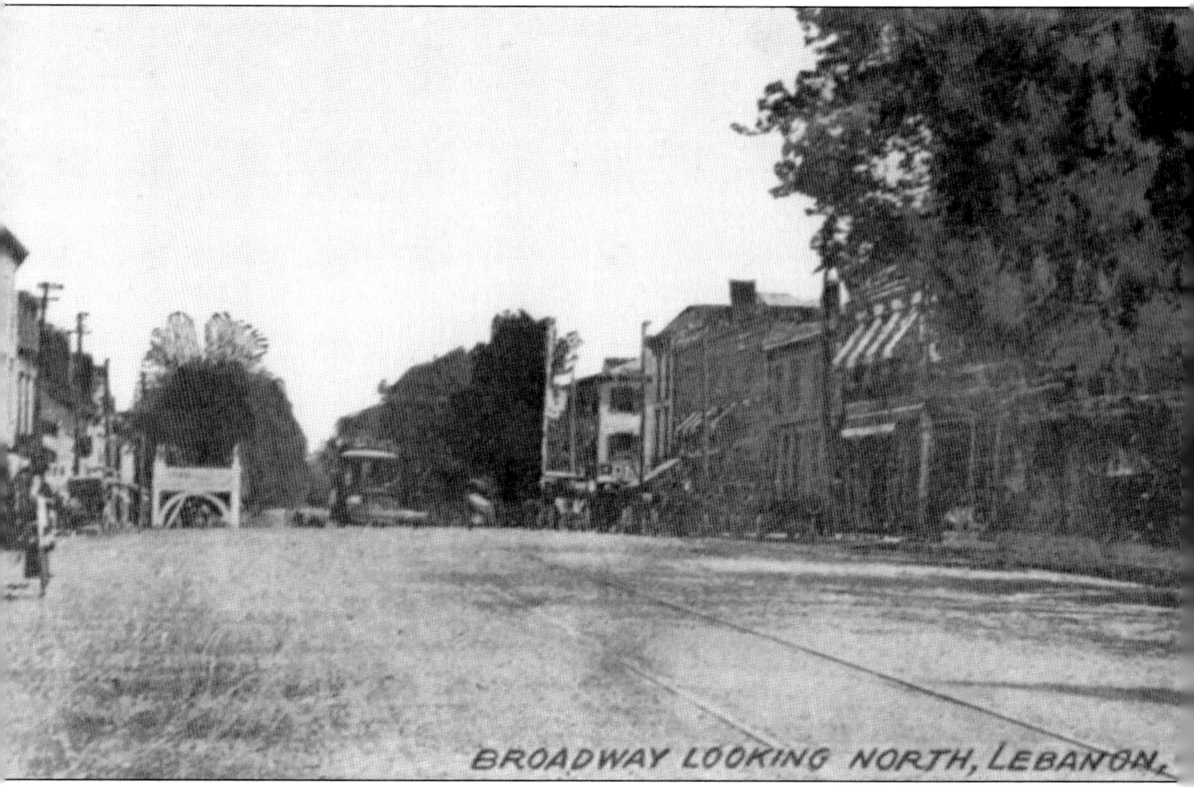

This 19th-century view of North Broadway Street features no public buildings but does offer a rare view of the town bandstand on the left-hand side of the image. Constructed at the northwest corner of Broadway and Mulberry Streets, concerts and entertainments were held there every Saturday night weather permitting. (Courtesy of the Sally Foster collection.)

This view of the Lebanon Opera House gives a much clearer view of the massive building that stood at the corner of Main and Broadway Streets for over 50 years. In addition to a 1,200-seat auditorium, the opera house also contained, at various times, the Lebanon Post Office, city offices, and a movie theater. (Courtesy of WCHS Museum.)

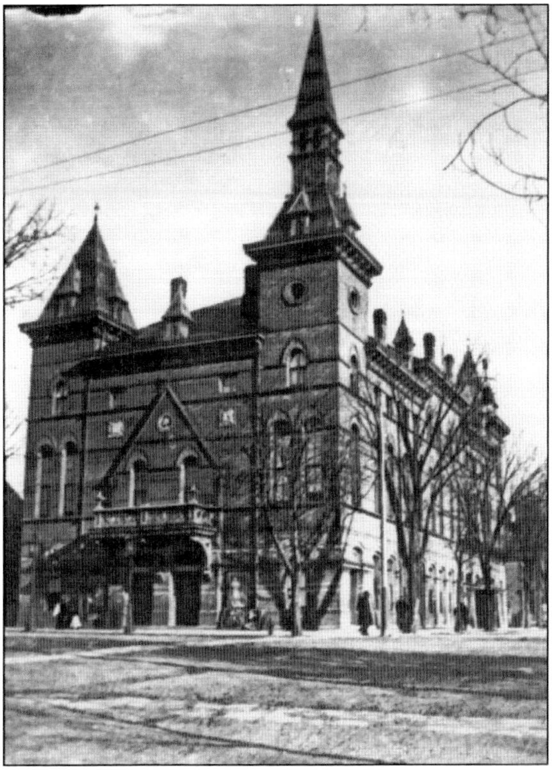

This photograph, taken in the Lebanon Opera House in 1902, is of a Tom Thumb wedding staged to celebrate the city's centennial. Though the children involved are unidentified, notes on the back of the photograph indicate the wedding was staged by a professional company who used local "actors" for various roles. (Courtesy of WCHS Museum.)

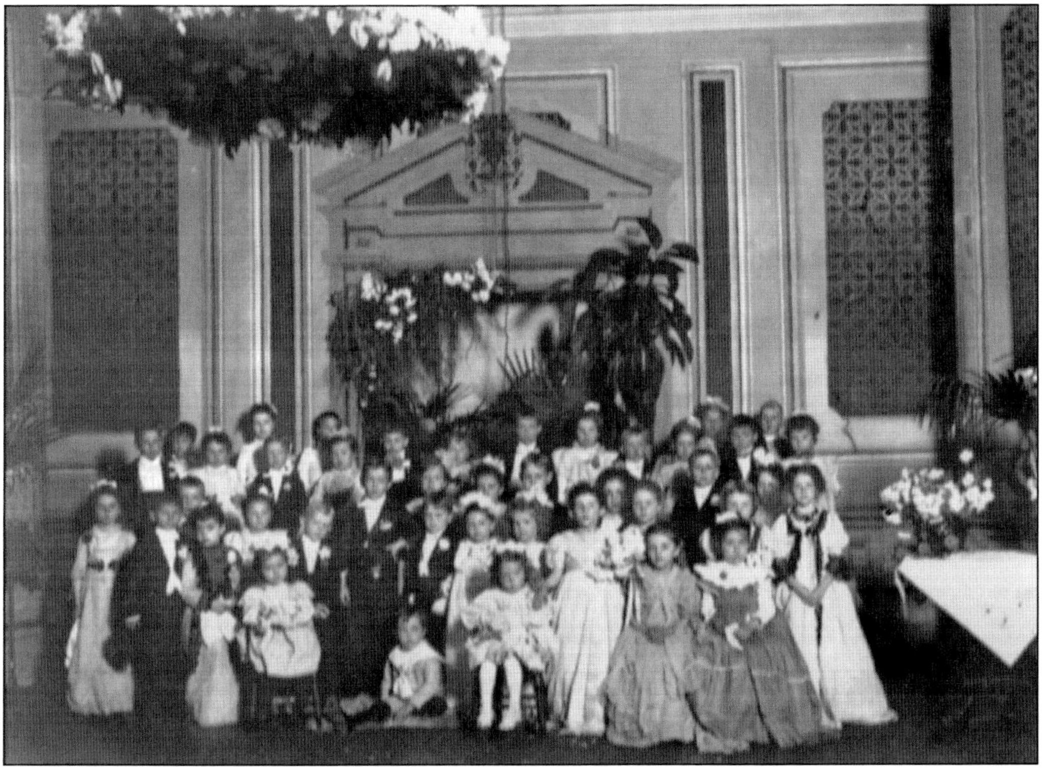

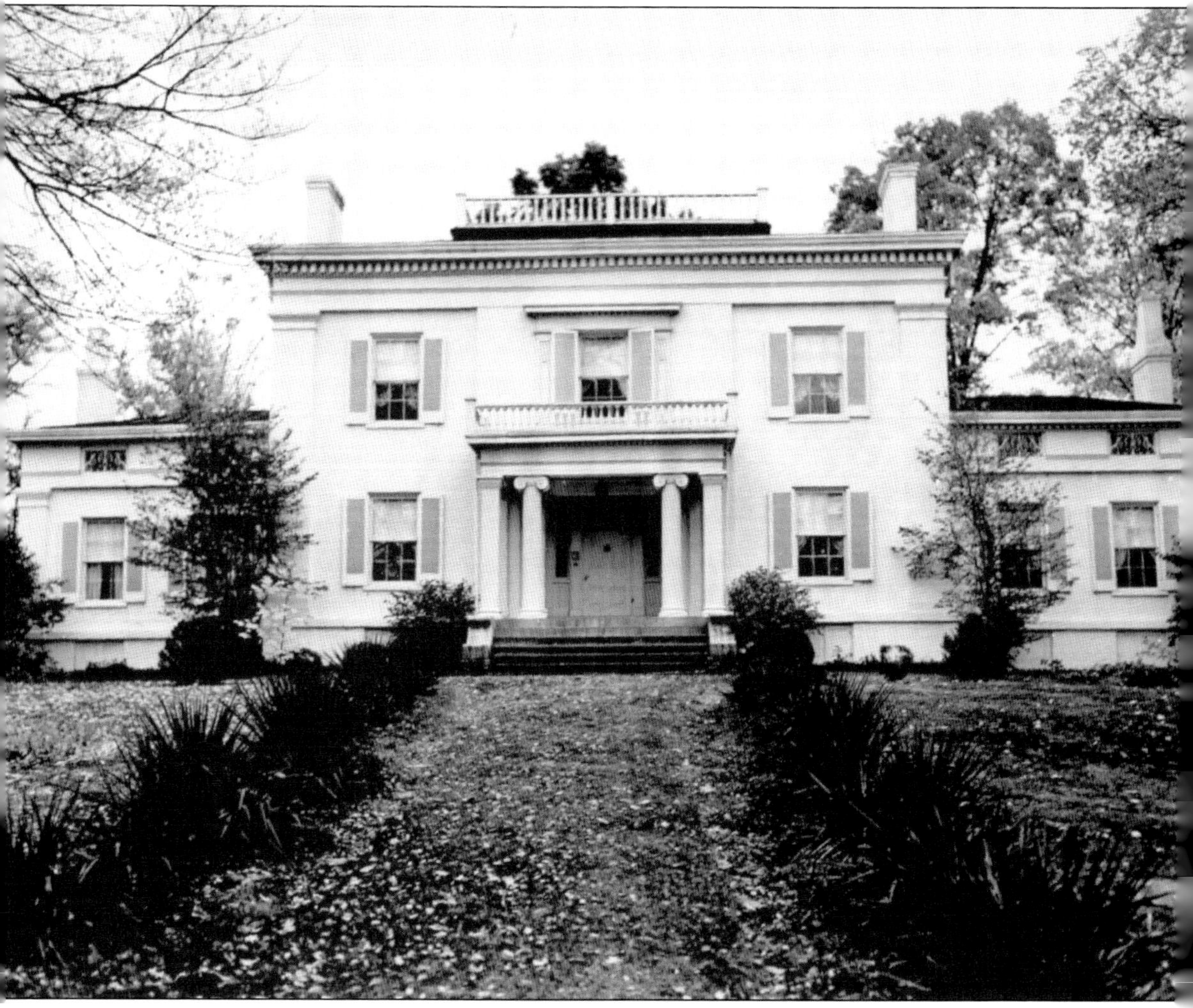

This 1930s image shows perhaps Lebanon's most famous public building, Glendower. Purchased by the Warren County Historical Society in 1944 (with $10,000 in private contributions for repairs), the mansion, named Glendower by its builder J. Milton Williams, and its collections were presented to the State of Ohio in a formal ceremony in the 1940s when it was renamed Glendower State Memorial. In 2007, the Warren County Historical Society regained ownership of the home and its collections from the State of Ohio. (Courtesy of WCHS Museum.)

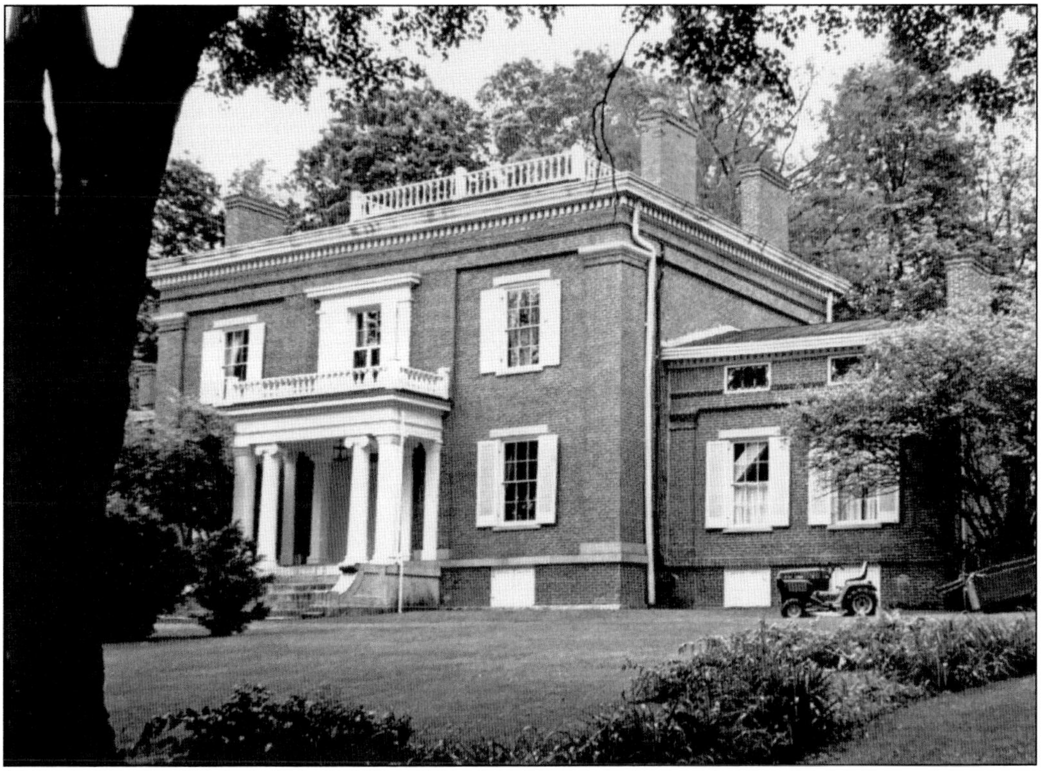

This 1960s image of Glendower shows the home after extensive renovations were performed by the State of Ohio. The building was sandblasted and restored to its original brick facade. Period trees and perennials were also planted to preserve the home's 19th-century history. (Courtesy of WCHS Museum.)

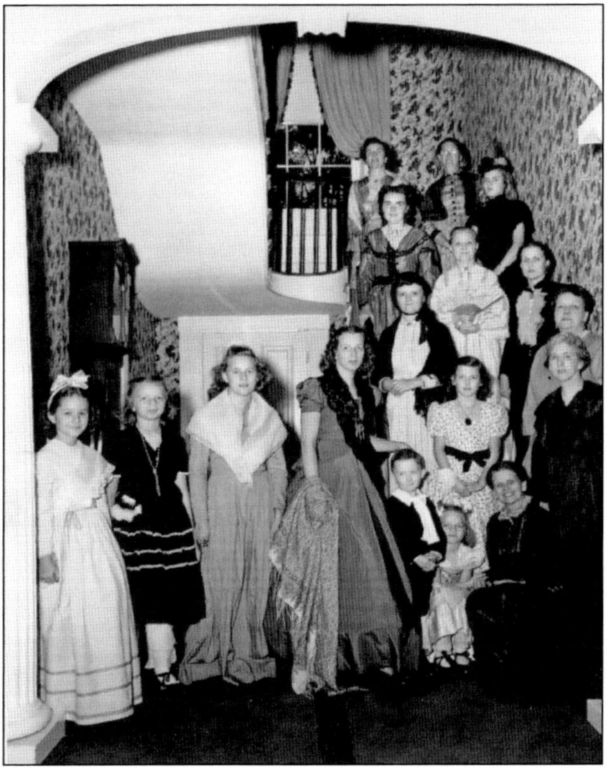

This photograph is of the opening-day ceremonies at Glendower Mansion. Local residents dressed in period costumes to welcome visitors to Lebanon's first museum. Though the people in the photograph are unidentified, sitting on the steps at the bottom right-hand corner of the image is Mrs. William Mason "Hazel" Phillips, one of the founders and longtime director of the Warren County Historical Society. (Courtesy of WCHS Museum.)

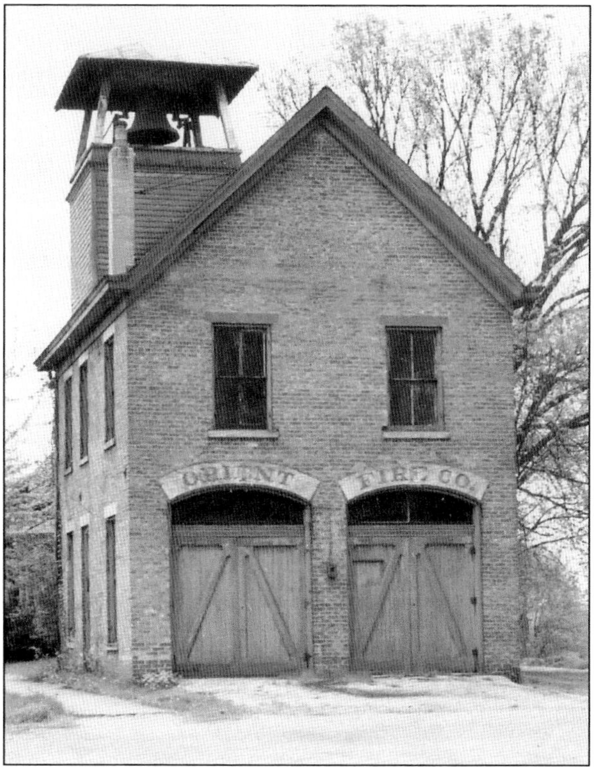

In 1878, with land donated by a local resident and at a cost of $2,000, the Orient Fire House began serving the east end of Lebanon. Located at the corner of Mulberry Street and Chillicothe Avenue, the building, which is still standing, has been restored by the City of Lebanon and services the Lebanon Fire Department. (Courtesy of WCHS Museum.)

Harmon Hall, erected with money donated by Lebanon philanthropist William Elmer Harmon, was dedicated in 1912 for use as a facility for "indoor amusements." Opened on November 6, 1913, Harmon Hall served for decades as first a YMCA and then an athletic facility for Lebanon school students. In 1961, the building was leased from the Harmon Civic Trust as a new and larger home for the Warren County Historical Society. (Courtesy of WCHS Museum.)

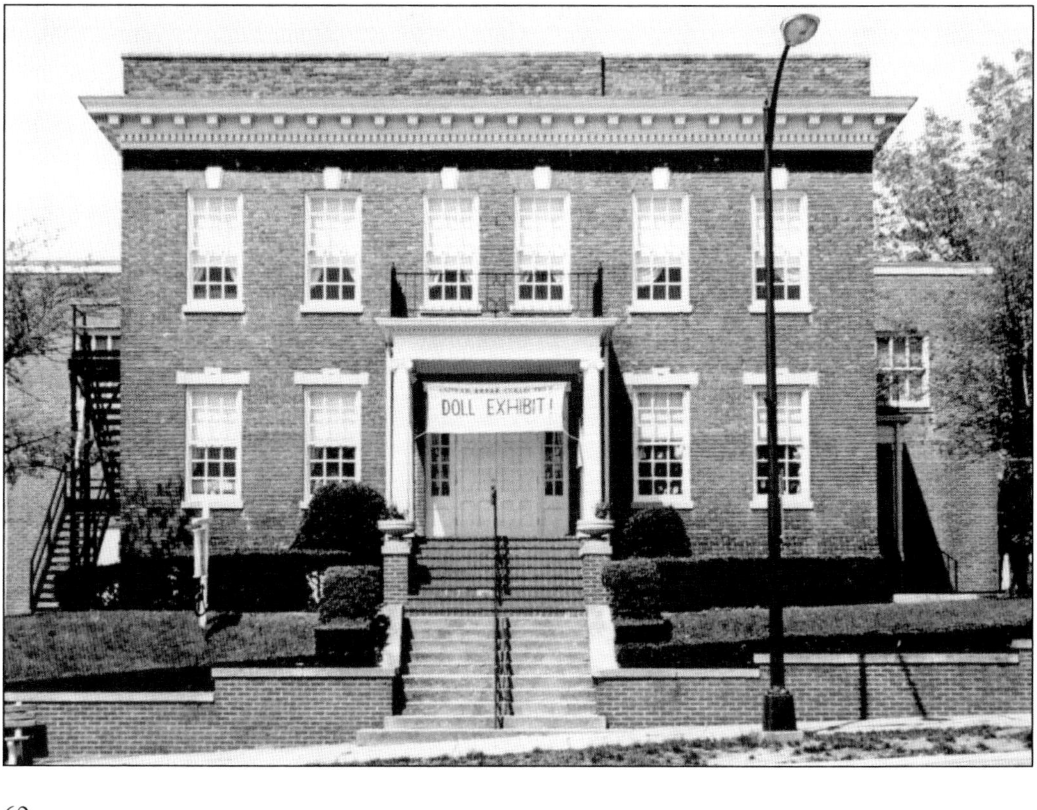

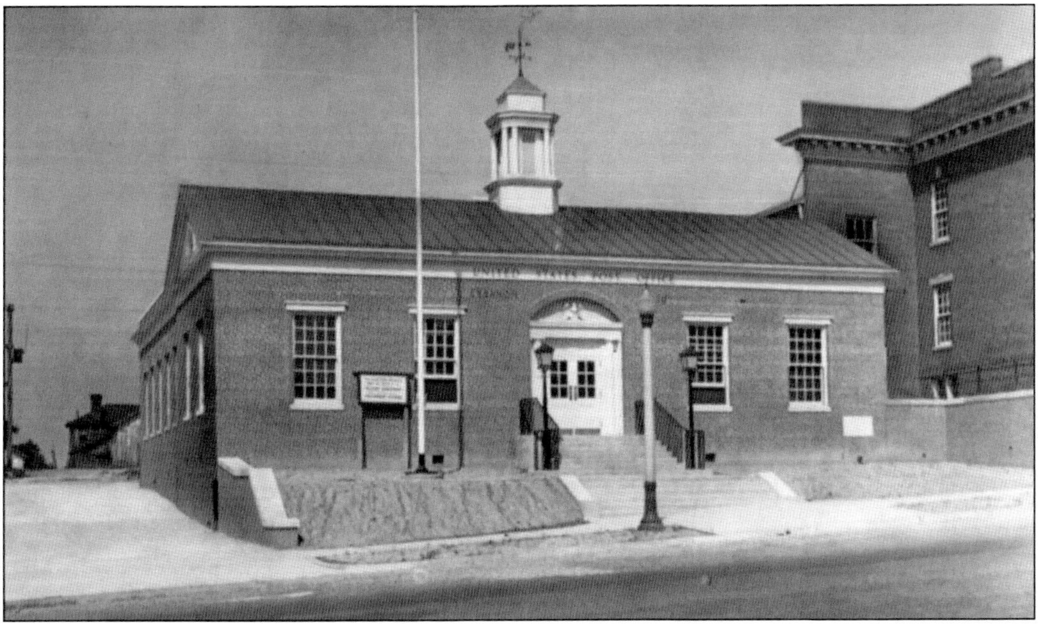

This late-1930s image shows Lebanon's post office, built as a Works Progress Administration (WPA) project in 1936. This historically significant structure replaced the previous post office, which had been housed in the Elks Building on Mulberry Street from 1912 until 1936. Prior to being located on Mulberry Street, Lebanon's post office had been housed in various locations, including a room at the Lebanon Opera House. (Courtesy of WCHS Museum.)

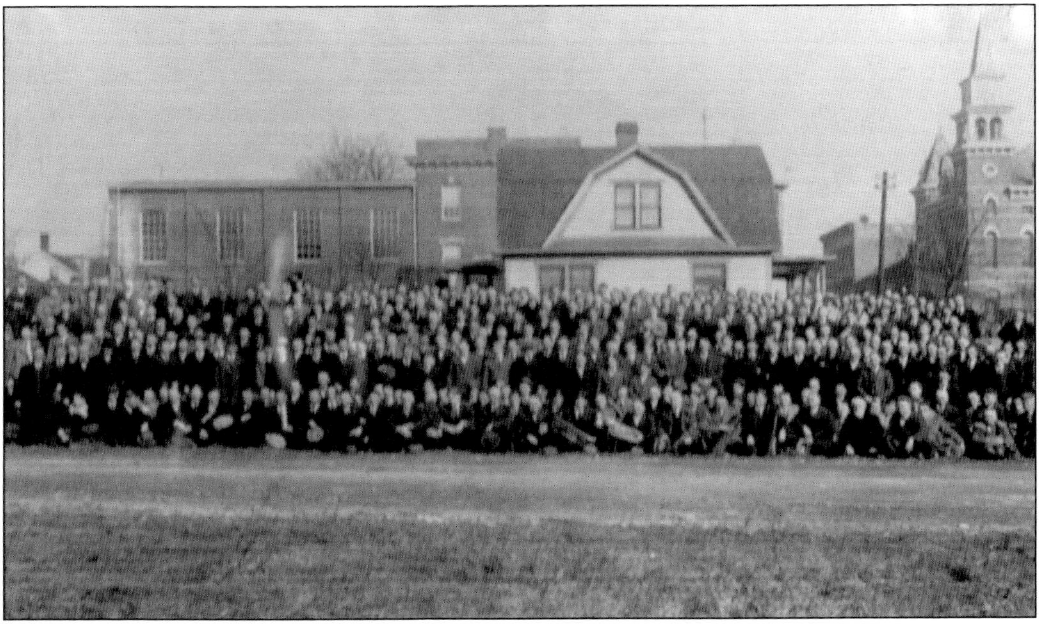

This 1920s image of an unidentified group of men is of interest only because of the small home in the background. Taken from the corner of Broadway and South Streets looking north, this photograph shows the future location of Lebanon's downtown post office. The home in the background was moved from South Broadway to a new location on Wright Avenue, where it still stands today. (Courtesy of WCHS Museum.)

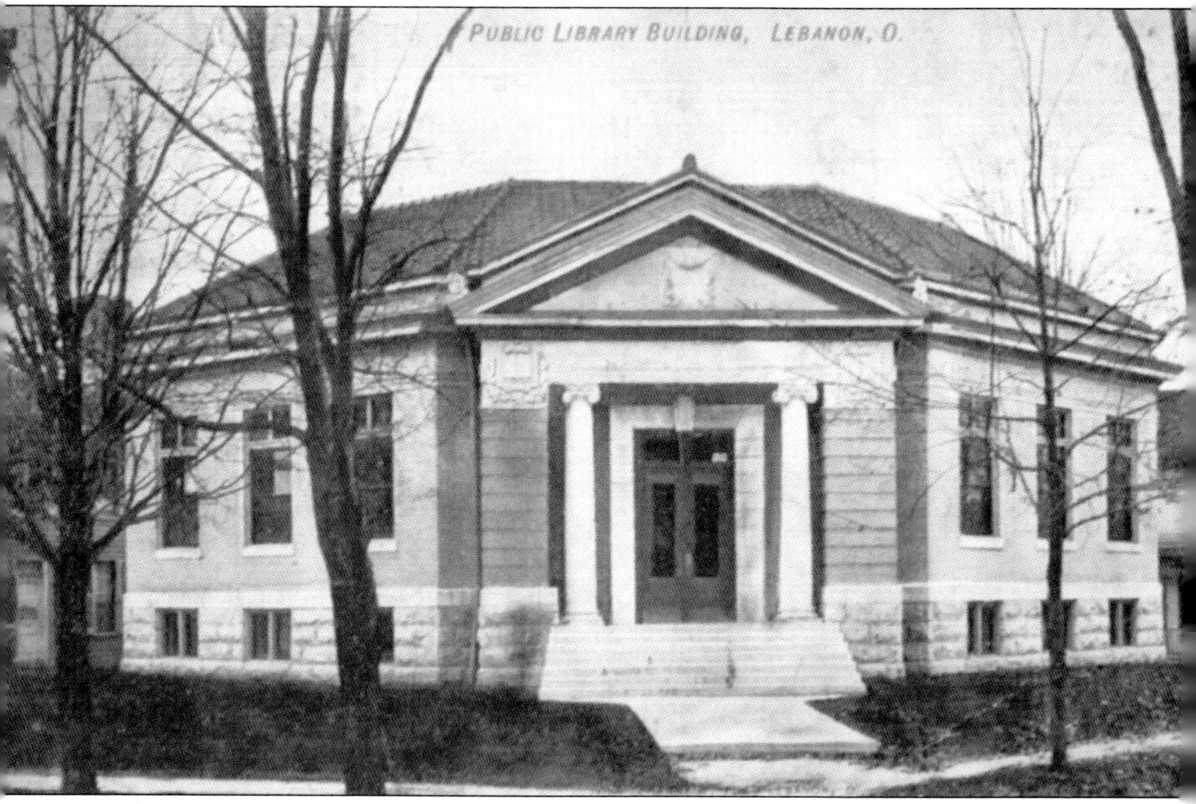

This undated postcard shows Lebanon's public library as it appeared shortly after it was built in 1908. One of the original Carnegie Libraries, the building was located on land donated to the city almost a century before and built at a cost of $13,500. In the late 1980s, the library was expanded to accommodate the needs of a growing county population. (Courtesy of the Sally Foster collection.)

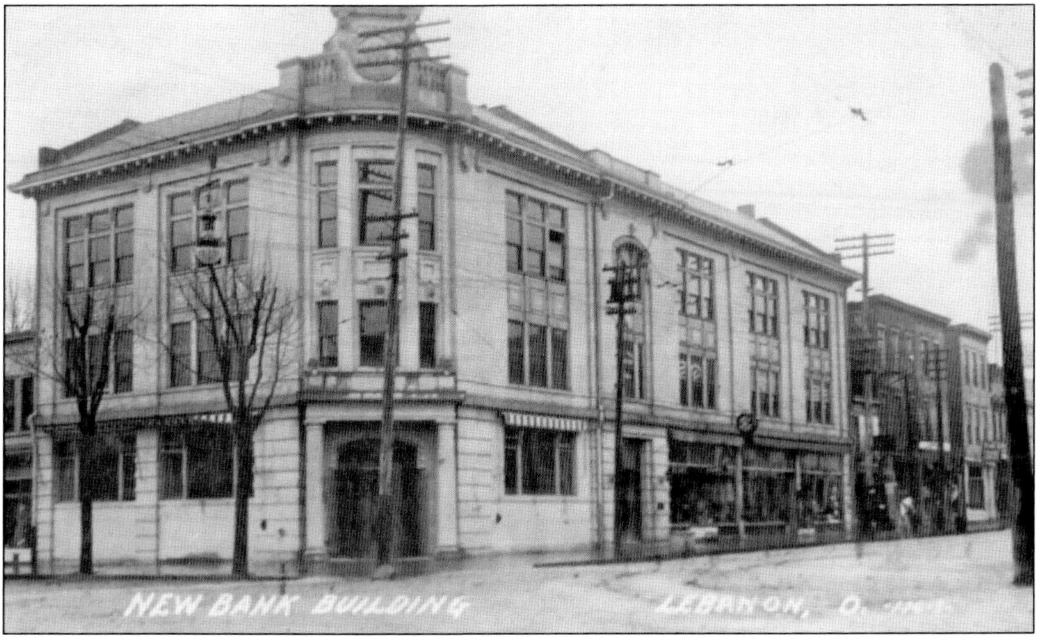

The Lebanon National Bank moved into this imposing and highly recognizable building on Broadway Street in 1908. In 1925, the bank merged with another local institution, The Lebanon Citizens Bank, to formally become Lebanon Citizens National Bank (LCNB). Beginning with a single location, LCNB National Bank now has over 20 locations throughout southwestern Ohio. (Courtesy of the Sally Foster collection.)

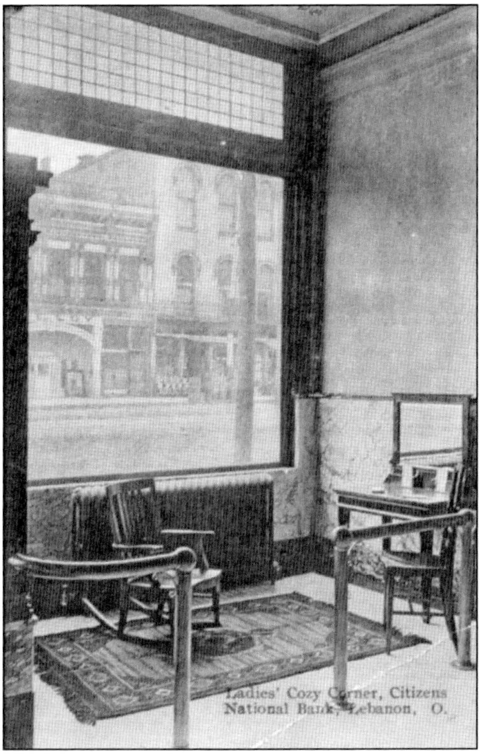

This early-20th-century postcard shows the "Woman's Cozy Corner" at the then Citizens National Bank prior to its merger with Lebanon National Bank in 1925. The view out the window shows Meloy's Theater, which was located in the first block of Mulberry Street. (Courtesy of the Sally Foster collection.)

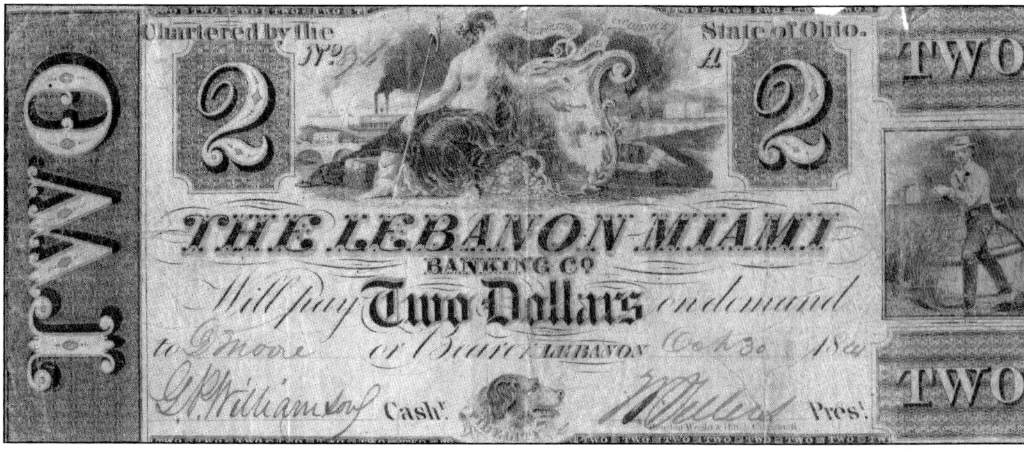

Many banks printed and signed their own currency prior to 1935. This rare early $2 note was issued by the Lebanon Miami Banking Company, which was chartered in 1814 as the county's first bank. The bank lasted for only 27 years, closing in 1841. The "two dollar bill" was signed by the head cashier of the bank and the bank president. (Courtesy of the Robert Kuhns collection.)

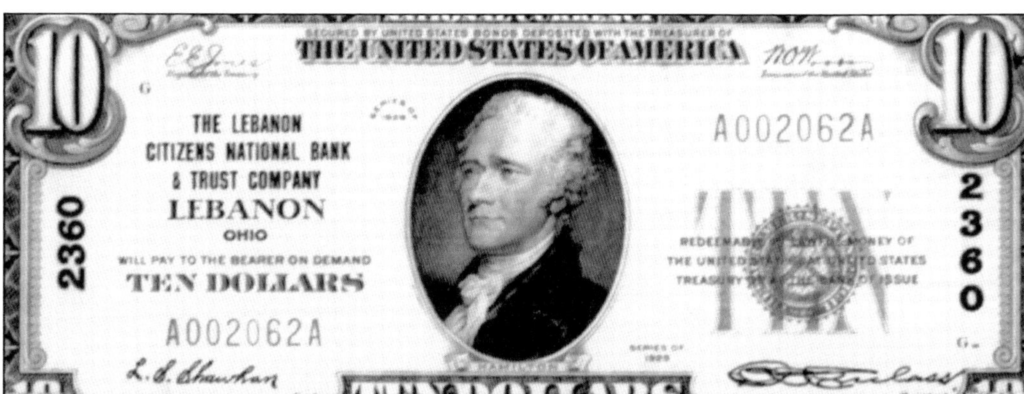

This much later note, issued over a century later, now bears the recognizable symbols of modern-day currency but was still issued by the Lebanon Citizens National Bank. This $10 bill, emblazoned with the bank's name on the front, was signed not by the secretary of the treasury or the treasurer of the United States but by the bank president and L. S. Shawhan, the bank cashier. (Courtesy of LCNB National Bank.)

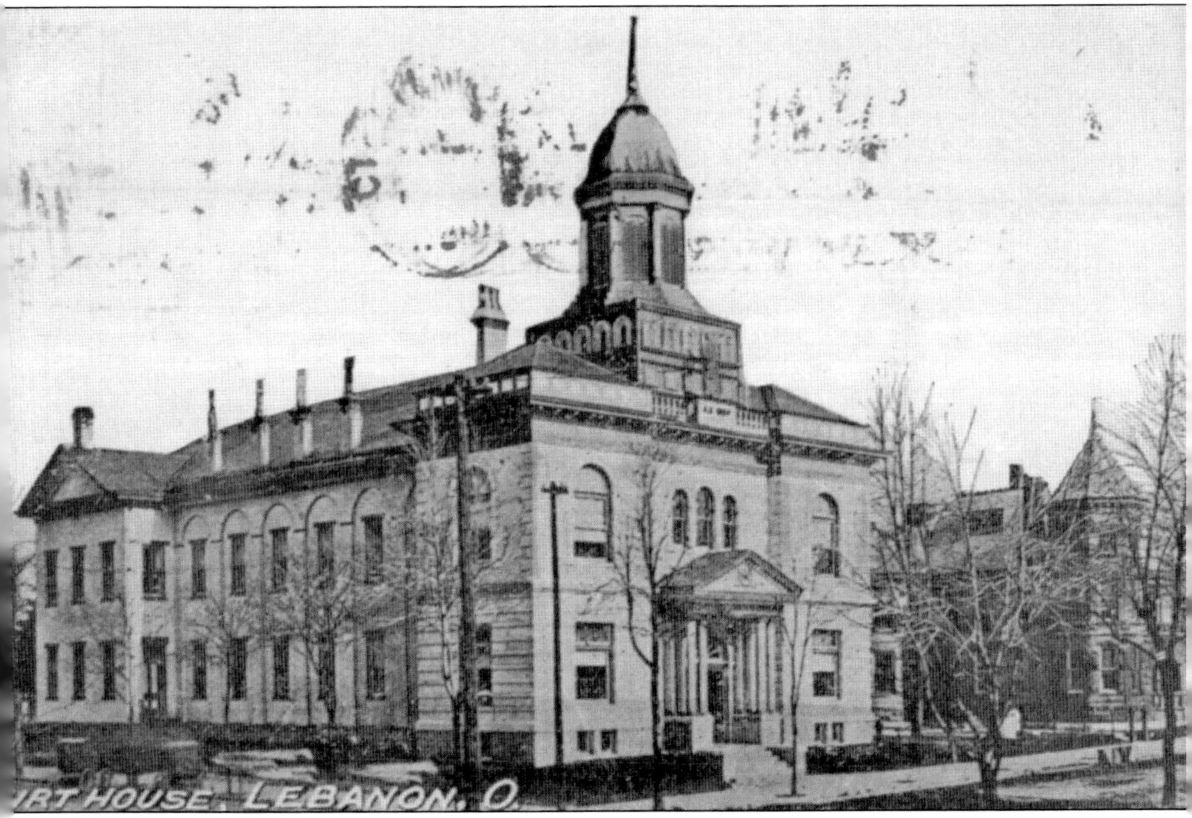

The Warren County Courthouse was erected on Silver Street on donated land with a construction cost of $25,000. The building was originally a simple Greek Revival–style structure, but subsequent additions in 1890 and 1895 left the building with various architectural influences and styles. The building, still standing, houses various county offices, with a larger courthouse having been built in the latter part of the 20th century. (Courtesy of the Sally Foster collection.)

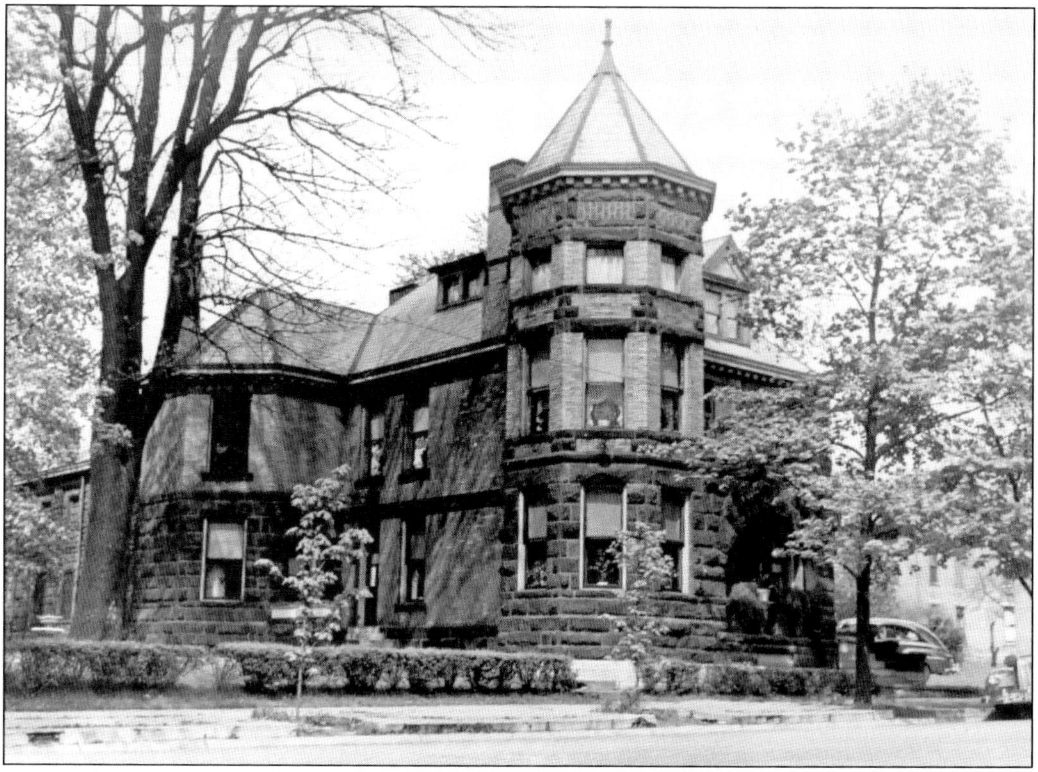

This early image is of the Warren County Courthouse, which was built in 1889. Four years later, in 1893, the jailer's residence was added to the front of the building. This structure replaced two previous jails on Silver Street: the first built in 1820 and the second built on the same spot in 1844. The jail was in use for over 100 years until the new corrections center on Justice Drive was built in the latter part of the 20th century. (Courtesy of WCHS Museum.)

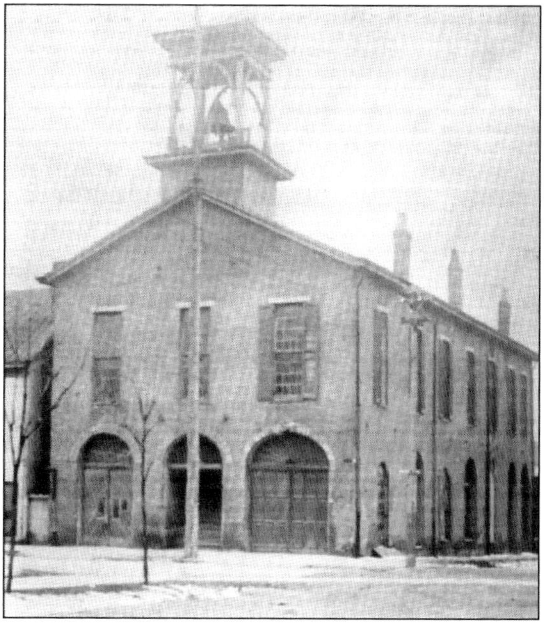

Washington Hall, Lebanon's market house, was built at the southwest corner of Mechanic and Silver Streets in 1856. This hall replaced the previous structure that had stood in the middle of Silver Street. Throughout its 100-year history, Washington Hall served numerous functions, including a public hall and eventually a chapel for National Normal University. (Courtesy of WCHS Museum.)

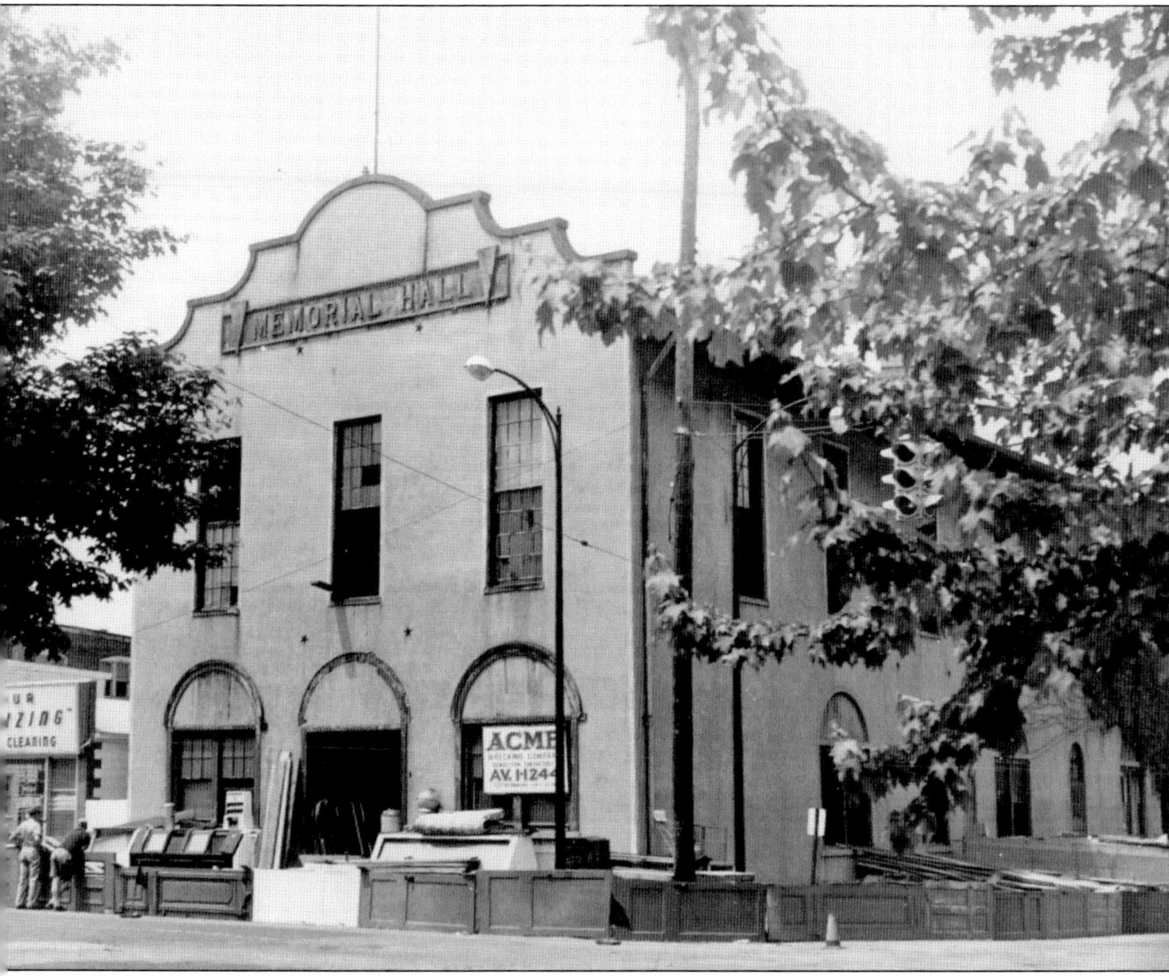

One hundred years after its dedication, Washington Hall, renamed Memorial Hall in the 20th century, had outlived its usefulness. This early-1960s image shows the hall in its latter days before its eventual demolition in 1963. (Courtesy of WCHS Museum.)

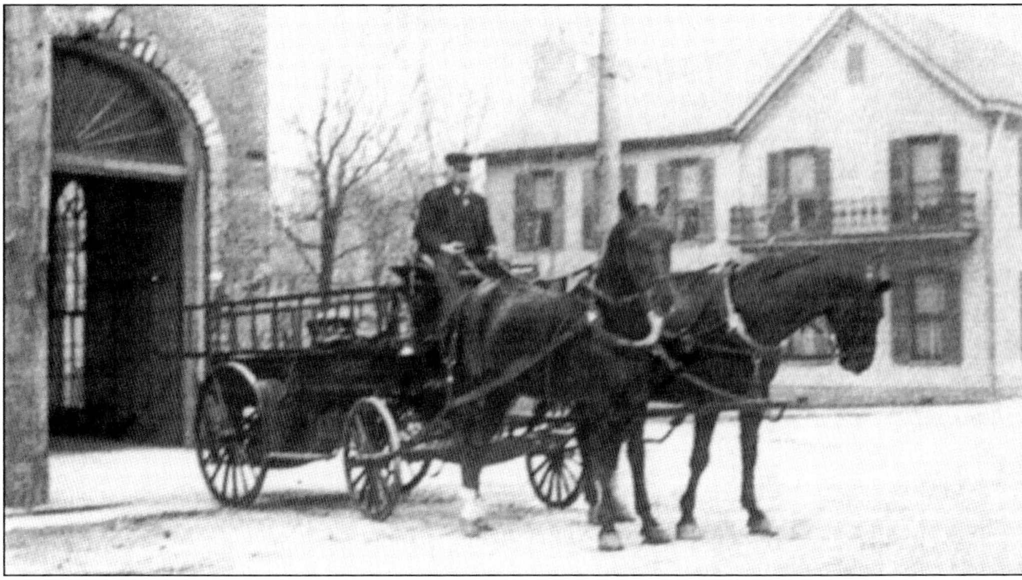

During its 100-year history, Washington Hall also served as a home for the Lebanon Fire Department. This rare glass-negative image shows one of Lebanon's earliest pieces of horse-drawn firefighting equipment exiting Washington Hall. (Courtesy of the Scott and Traci Gallagher collection.)

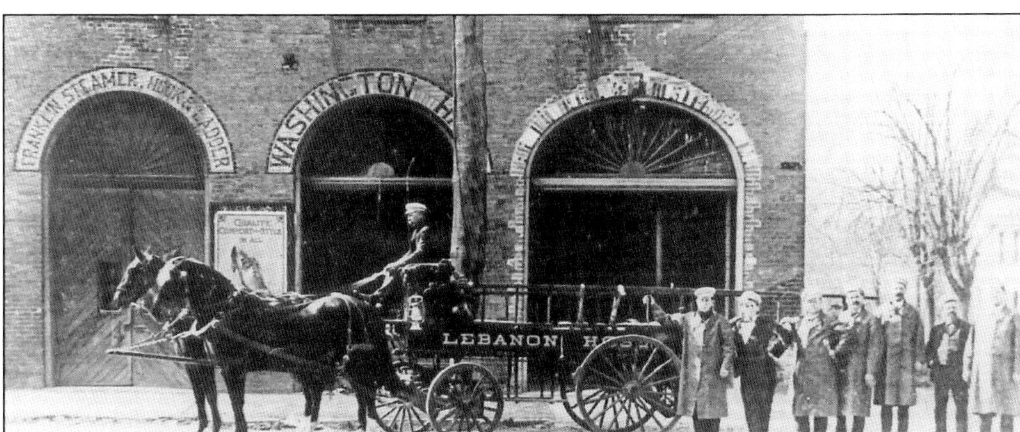

This late-19th-century image shows a complete fire company with horse-drawn equipment posing outside of Washington Hall. Of particular note is the advertising poster between the left and center openings. (Courtesy of WCHS Museum.)

Five

The Ownly Hotel
Lebanon's Golden Lamb Inn

Over 200 years after Jonas Seaman was issued a license to operate "a house of public entertainment" by the December term of the Warren County Court, Lebanon's Golden Lamb remains the most recognized landmark in this historic community. Though the building today bears no resemblance to Seaman's simple log tavern of 1803, the traditions of good food and gracious hospitality inspired by Seaman continue to this day.

The original Golden Lamb was a simple, one-story log tavern located probably 50 to 60 feet back from Broadway Street. In 1815, innkeeper Ichabod Corwin built a two-story brick structure in front of the original tavern, which is now the Golden Lamb's lobby and second floor.

In 1825, the original log tavern to the rear was replaced with a two-story brick building that completed the hotel's second floor. By 1845, the Golden Lamb had expanded to three floors and now trumpeted the name the Lebanon House in advertisements and over the hotel's door. The last pre-20th-century expansion came in 1874 with the addition of the hotel's fourth floor. The building would remain relatively unchanged until 1965, when the current tavern and gift shop were added.

In 1926, Robert Jones purchased the inn and began renovations to the then century-old landmark. Jones and his wife, Virginia, began furnishing the old hotel with antiques, researching the inn's history, and turning the old hotel into the recognizable Golden Lamb of today. In April 1940, the Golden Lamb was recognized by the Daughters of the American Revolution as Ohio's oldest hotel. Thirty-eight years later, in 1978, the Golden Lamb was certified by the Ohio Historical Society as the oldest continuous business in the state of Ohio.

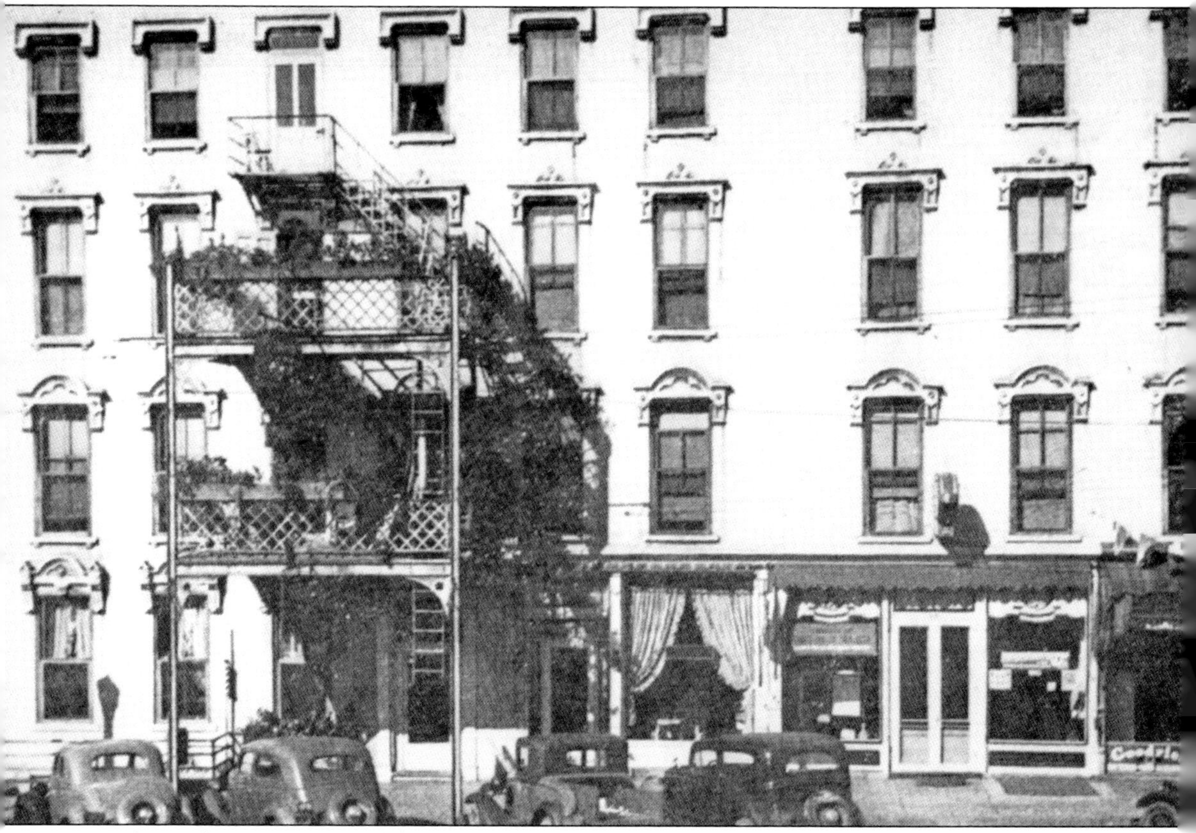

This early-1930s image of the Golden Lamb shows the building prior to the major renovation in 1935. Of particular note is the vintage ornate concrete work capping the windows on the front of the building. As was the fashion in the 19th century when the building was constructed, the concrete work gets less ornate as the floors get higher. Also noteworthy is the ornate ornamental iron balcony, which was probably added in the late 19th century. During this period of the inn's history, retail stores occupied the two northernmost dining rooms: one was a grocery store and the other an auto supply store and AAA office. (Author's collection.)

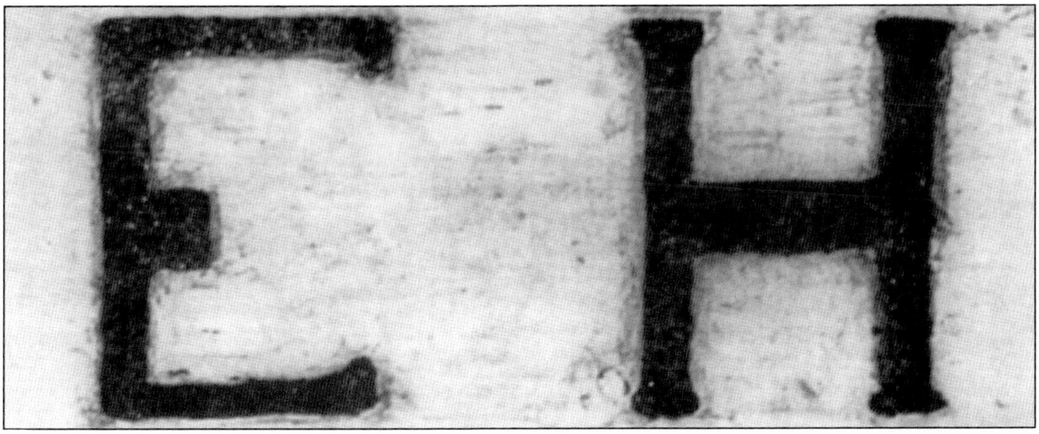

This tavern sign now hanging in the Golden Lamb is from Ephraim Hathaway's Black Horse Tavern. These handwrought initials, pounded out of iron, are purported to be the oldest antique in Warren County in private hands. (Courtesy of WCHS Museum.)

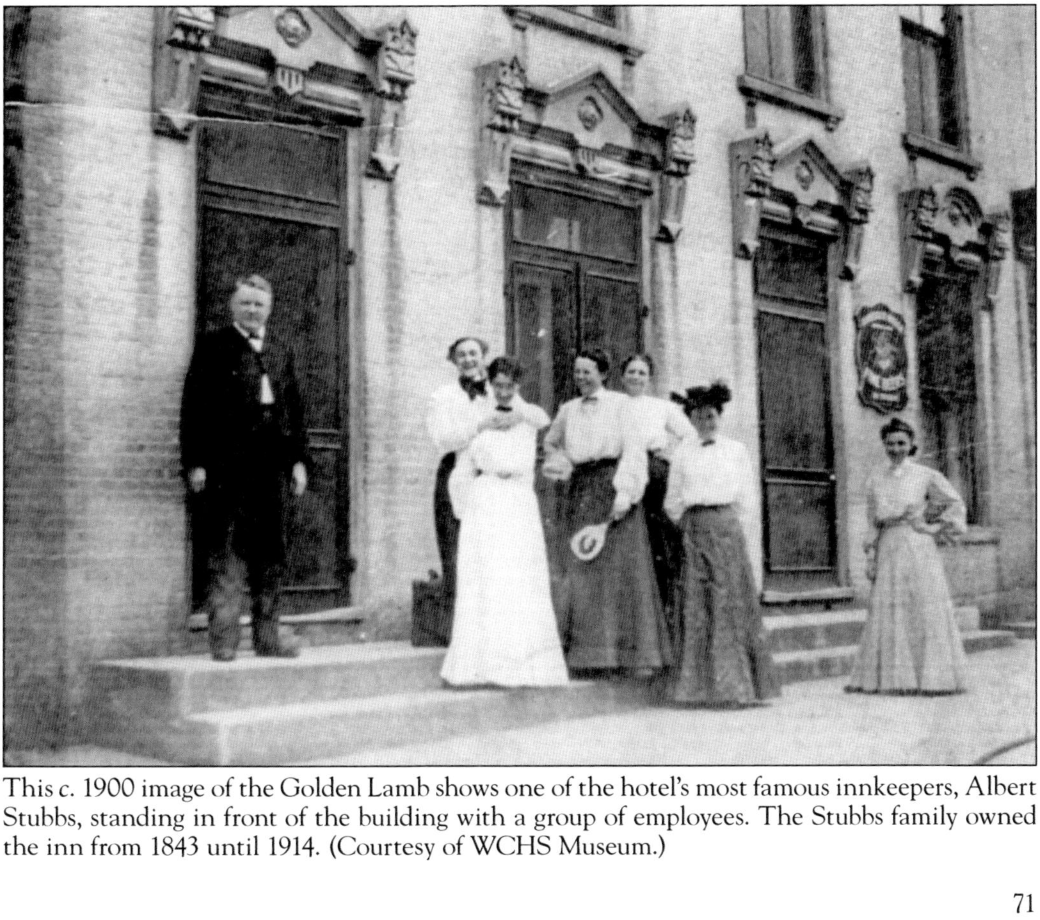

This c. 1900 image of the Golden Lamb shows one of the hotel's most famous innkeepers, Albert Stubbs, standing in front of the building with a group of employees. The Stubbs family owned the inn from 1843 until 1914. (Courtesy of WCHS Museum.)

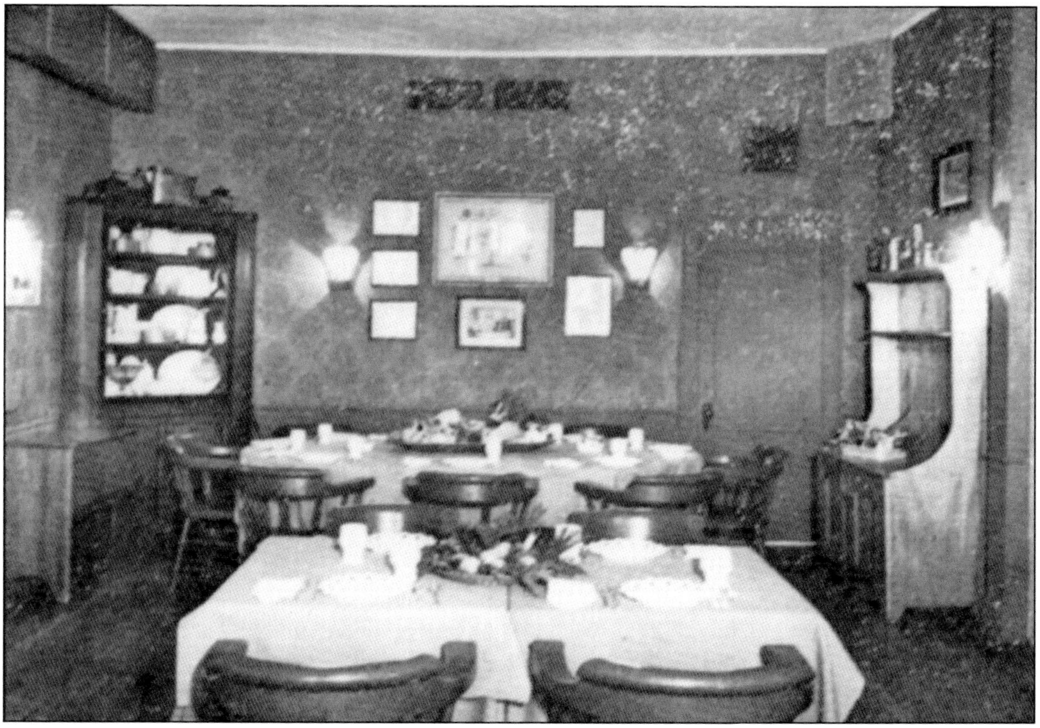

This 1940s image is of one of the Golden Lamb's dining rooms prior to renovation and redecorating. This room is now the inn's Shaker Dining Room and houses much of the hotel's Shaker antique collection. The door in the back right of the image led to the hotel's bar, which innkeeper and owner Robert Jones attempted to keep hidden from guests. (Courtesy of the Portman family collection.)

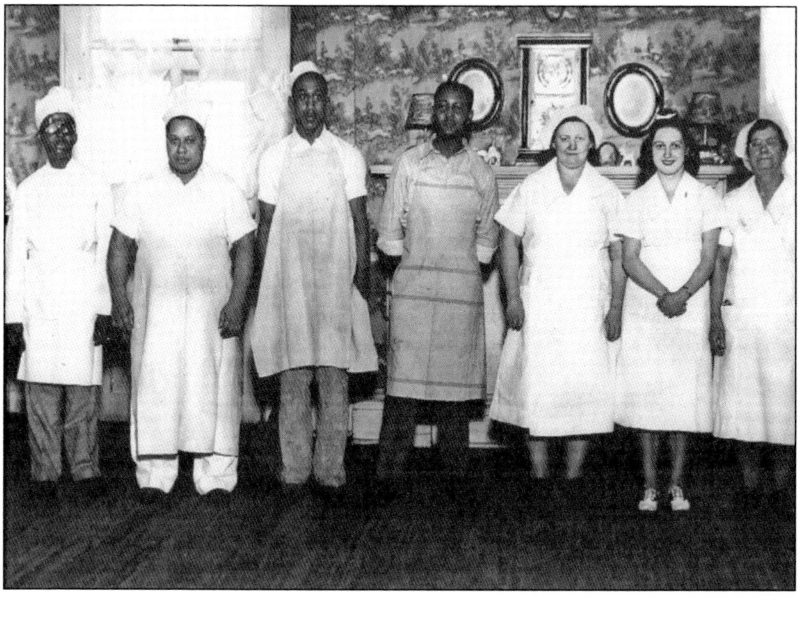

This early-1940s image is of the Golden Lamb's kitchen staff posing in the hotel lobby. Though most of the individuals are unidentified, second from the left is a very young Norman Sims, the Golden Lamb chef who came to the inn in the late 1920s and retired in 1969. (Courtesy of the Portman family collection.)

As early as the mid-1930s, the Golden Lamb was cited for historical significance in its architecture. This certificate, issued as part of a historic buildings survey by the WPA in 1935, was thought to have placed the Golden Lamb on the National Register of Historic Places. It was not until 1978 that the Golden Lamb discovered it had never been given national register recognition. In a rare move, the Department of the Interior nominated the Golden Lamb for inclusion to the register and approved the nomination, all in one meeting. (Courtesy of the Portman family collection.)

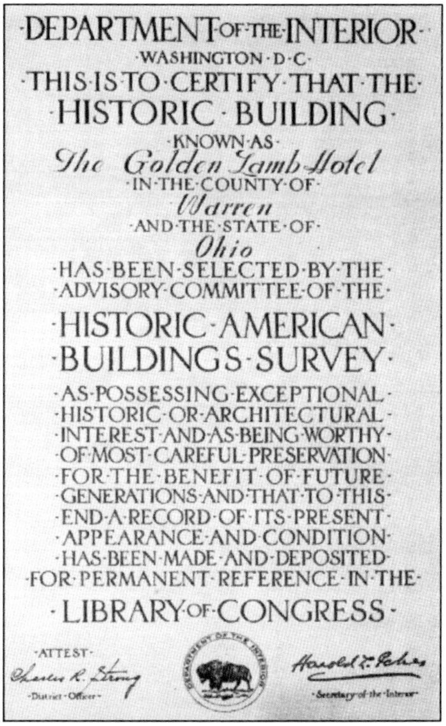

DEPARTMENT OF THE INTERIOR
WASHINGTON D C
THIS IS TO CERTIFY THAT THE
HISTORIC BUILDING
KNOWN AS
The Golden Lamb Hotel
IN THE COUNTY OF
Warren
AND THE STATE OF
Ohio
HAS BEEN SELECTED BY THE
ADVISORY COMMITTEE OF THE
HISTORIC AMERICAN
BUILDINGS SURVEY
AS POSSESSING EXCEPTIONAL
HISTORIC OR ARCHITECTURAL
INTEREST AND AS BEING WORTHY
OF MOST CAREFUL PRESERVATION
FOR THE BENEFIT OF FUTURE
GENERATIONS AND THAT TO THIS
END A RECORD OF ITS PRESENT
APPEARANCE AND CONDITION
HAS BEEN MADE AND DEPOSITED
FOR PERMANENT REFERENCE IN THE
LIBRARY OF CONGRESS

ATTEST
District Officer
Secretary of the Interior

This room on the Golden Lamb's second floor is now known as the Corwin Dining Room. When this photograph was taken, it was known as the conference room, a public space set aside by innkeeper Robert Jones for hotel guests. It is interesting to note that the cane seat armchairs around the large central table were still in use at the Golden Lamb through the 1970s. (Courtesy of the Portman family collection.)

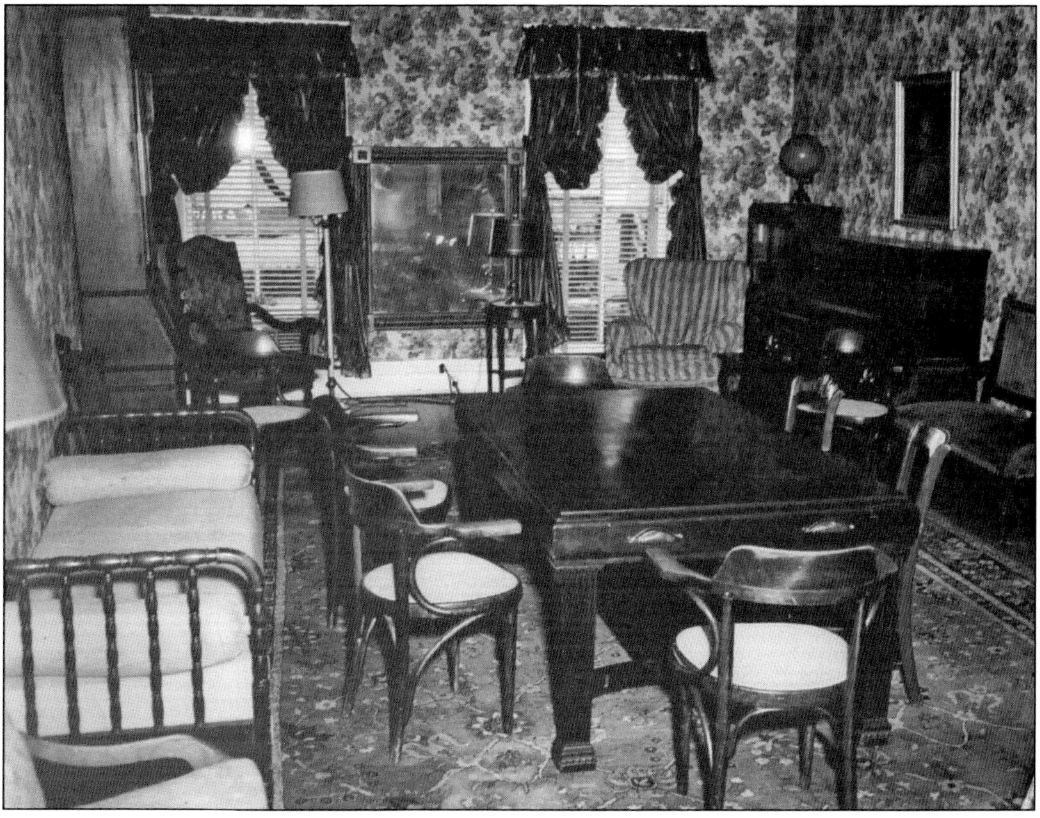

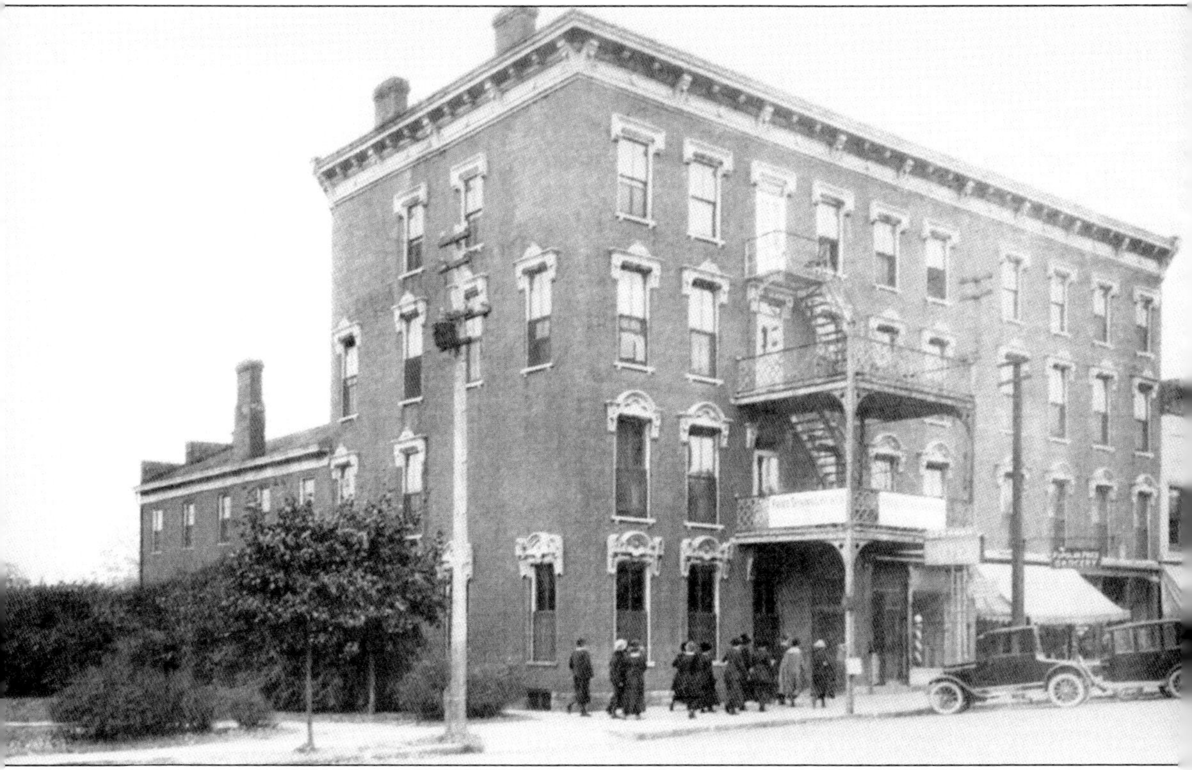

This c. 1920 image of the Golden Lamb shows it operating as the Lebanon Hotel. Noteworthy is the early advertisement for specially priced fried chicken dinners as an inducement to the public now traveling by car, as opposed to train or by horse and buggy. The Popular Price Grocery occupied what is now the Shaker Dining Room, and an unidentified retail store occupied the northernmost dining room, now the Buckeye Room. (Courtesy of the Portman family collection.)

This rare handbill advertises an appearance by the famed Siamese twins at the Golden Lamb sometime in the late 1820s or early 1830s. Inns and taverns were common locations for entertainments and exhibitions in the 19th century. This handbill advertises an appearance at "Mrs. Shares Hotel," which would indicate the period when it was owned my Mary Share, widow of Henry Share, who was one of the Golden Lamb's most well-known innkeepers. It is of particular note that admission price for viewing the twins in their room was 25¢. (Courtesy of WCHS Museum.)

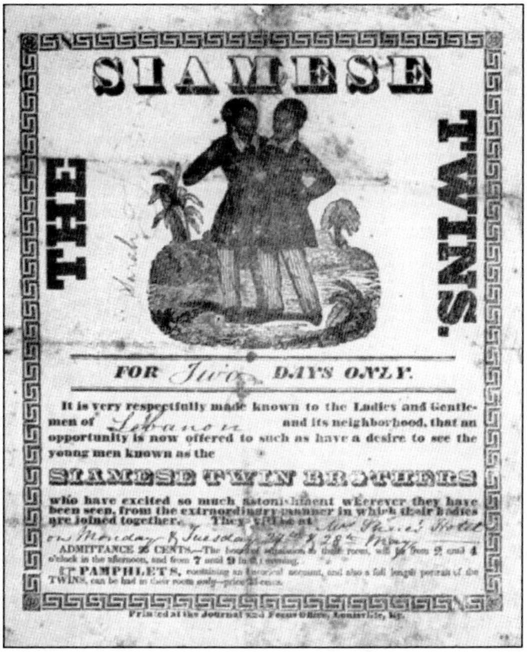

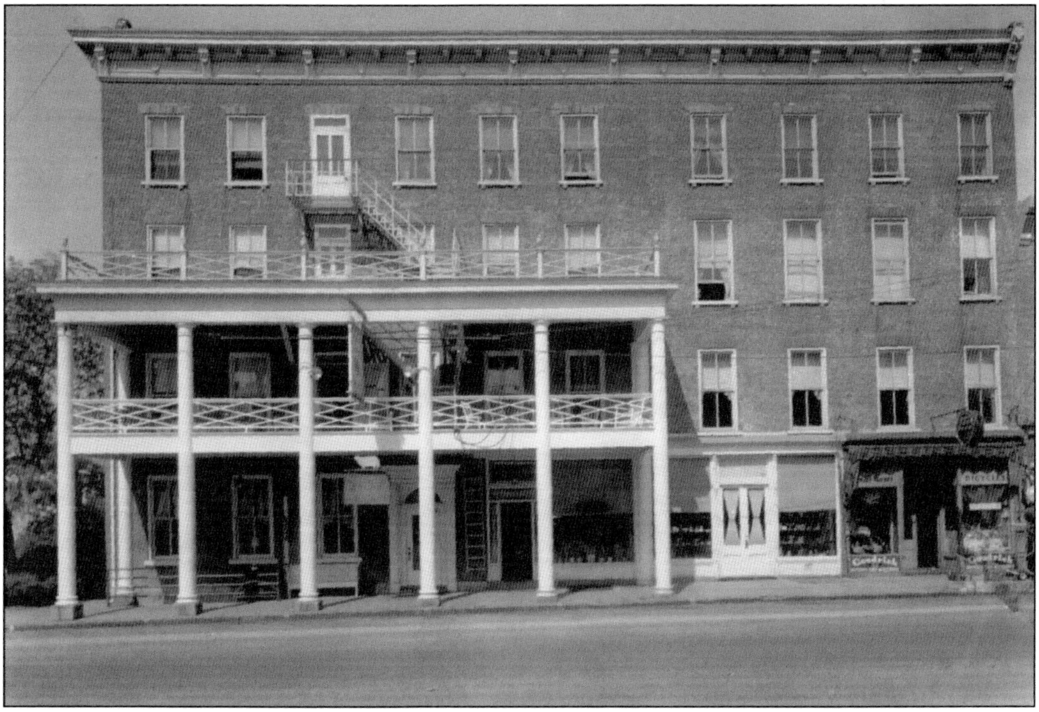

This 1950s image of the Golden Lamb shows the hotel after an extensive renovation in the mid-1930s. The wrought-iron balcony and the heavily decorated window casings were gone, and in their place was a two-story Colonial-style balcony that architecturally did not belong on a Federal-style building and plain unadorned windows. The restaurant was expanded to three dining rooms, and the auto repair shop still occupied what would eventually be dining room space. (Courtesy of WCHS Museum.)

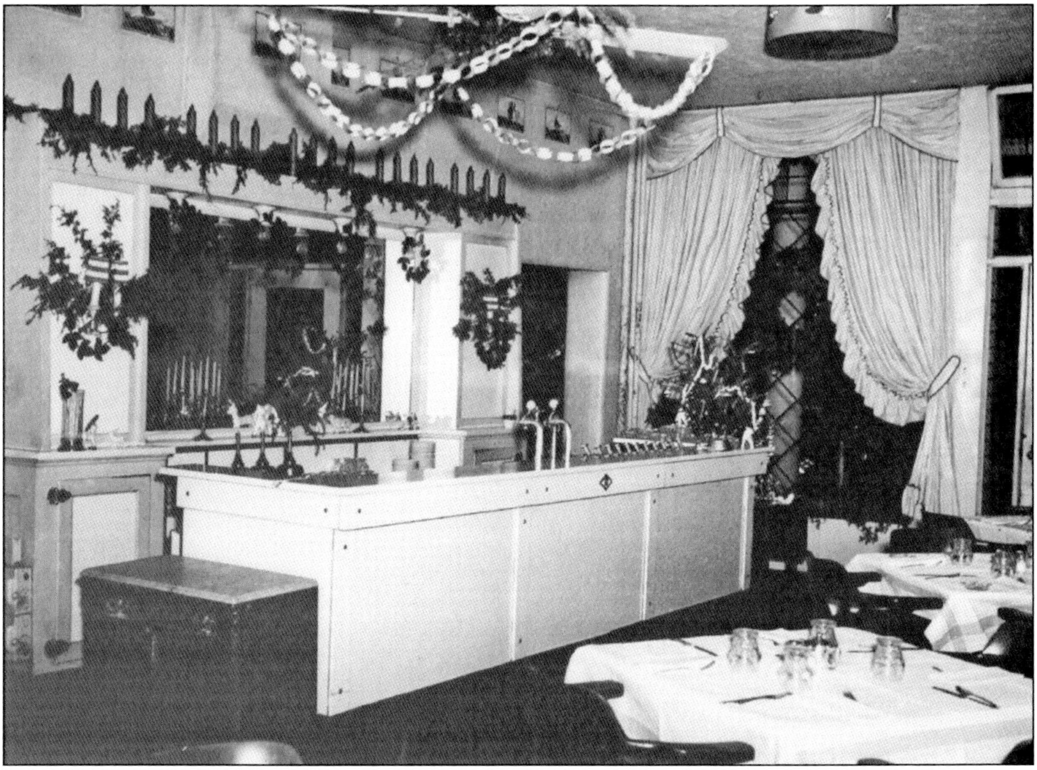

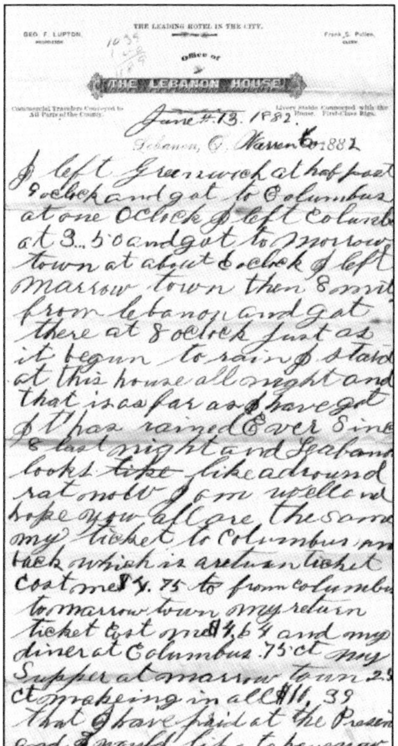
THE LEADING HOTEL IN THE CITY.

GEO. F. LUPTON, Proprietor. Frank S. Pullen, Clerk.

Office of THE LEBANON HOUSE

Commercial Travelers Conveyed to All Parts of the County. Livery Stable Connected with the House. First-Class Rigs.

June #13. 1882.

Lebanon, O. Warren Co. 1882

I left Greenwich at haf past
9 oclock and got to Columbus
at one Oclock I left Columb
at 3.. 50 and got to Morrow
town at about 6 oclock I left
Marrow town then 8 mil
from lebanon and got
there at 8 oclock just as
it begun to rain I staid
at this house all night and
that is as far as I have got
It has rained Ever Since
last night and Leabanon
looks ~~like~~ like a drownd
rat now I am well and
hope you all are the same
my ticket to Columbus an
back which is a return ticket
cost me $4.75 to from columbu
to marrow town my return
ticket Cost me $4.64 and my
diner at Columbus .75 ct my
Supper at marrow town 25
ct makeing in all $11, 39
that I have paid at the Presen
and I would like to have you

This 1940s image is of what is now the Golden Lamb's Dickens Dining Room. At this time, the inn had only two dining rooms, a formal dining room (now the Lebanon Room) and this room, which was a more casual coffee shop. The soda fountain lasted until the mid-1950s. (Courtesy of the Portman family collection.)

This unique letter, dated June 1882, is on stationary advertising the Lebanon House as "The Leading Hotel In The City." The text of the letter describes a stranded traveler in Lebanon who needs money to get to Morrow, Ohio, some 12 miles away. The letterhead advertises livery stables and the conveyance of guests to all parts of the county. (Author's collection.)

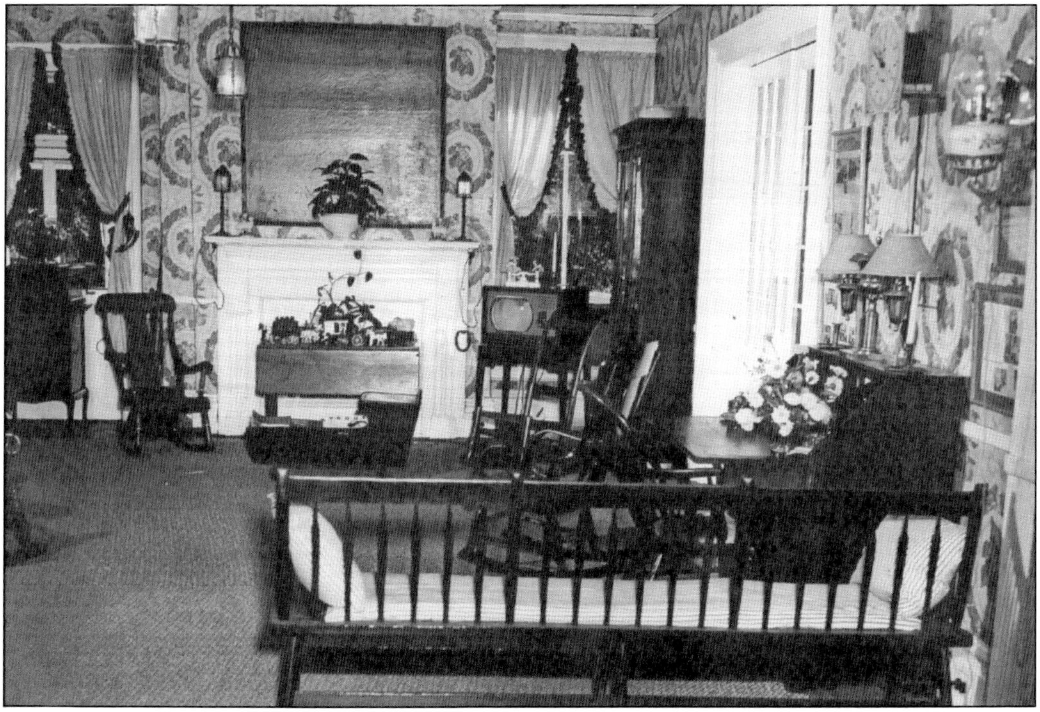

This is a rare 1950s photograph of the lobby at the Golden Lamb. Of particular note is the small intrusion of modern technology within the hotels antique-filled lobby. In the background on the right, a television set has been placed in the hotel's lobby amongst the collection of 19th-century furniture and artifacts. (Courtesy of the Portman family collection.)

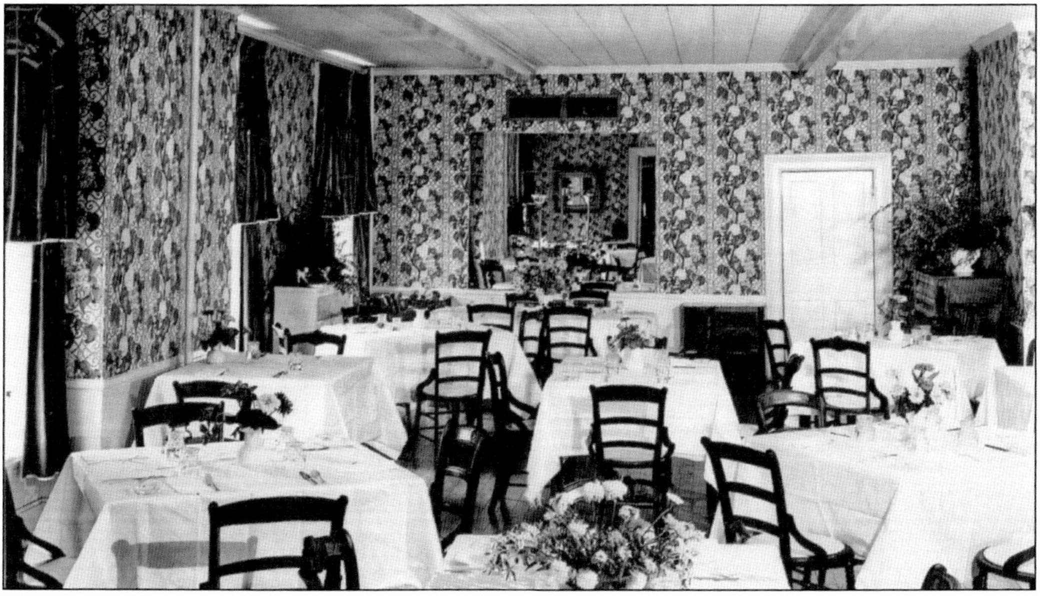

This is a 1950s image of the Golden Lamb's "formal dining room," now the Lebanon Room. Floor-to-ceiling glass doors separated this room from the lobby, and local residents speak lovingly of a red piano that sat in the room. In 1965, this room was extensively remodeled to accommodate the addition of the newly built tavern and gift shop. (Courtesy of the Portman family collection.)

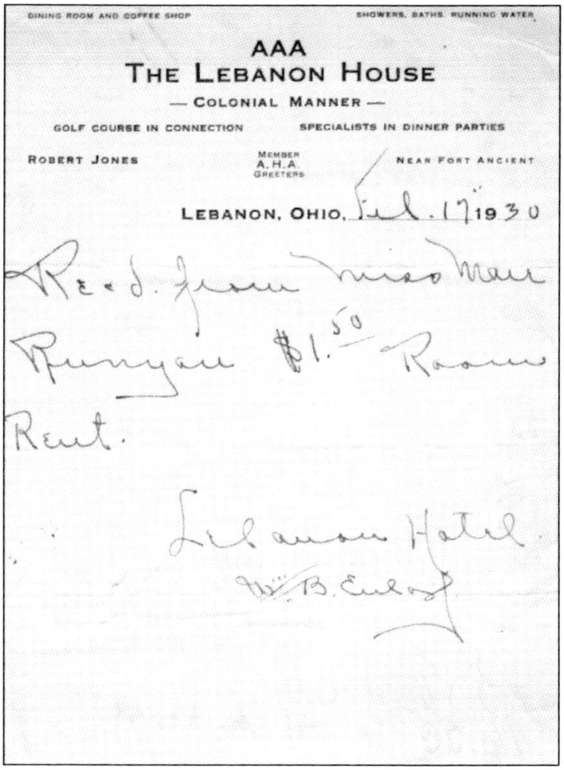

DINING ROOM AND COFFEE SHOP — SHOWERS, BATHS, RUNNING WATER

AAA
THE LEBANON HOUSE
— COLONIAL MANNER —

GOLF COURSE IN CONNECTION — SPECIALISTS IN DINNER PARTIES

ROBERT JONES — MEMBER A.H.A. GREETERS — NEAR FORT ANCIENT

LEBANON, OHIO, Feb. 17 1930

Rec'd. from Miss Mary Runyan $1.50 Room Rent.

Lebanon Hotel
W. B.

This receipt, dated February 1930, advertises the Lebanon House, one of the many names the Golden Lamb was known by throughout the years. At this period in the inn's history, owner Robert Jones had not started the restoration and collection leading to the modern-day Golden Lamb. The letterhead merely advertises two dining rooms, "showers and baths," and "running water." (Author's collection.)

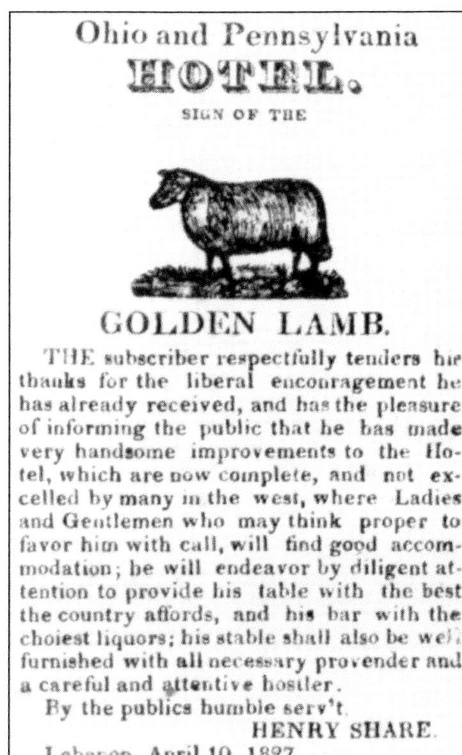

Ohio and Pennsylvania
HOTEL.
SIGN OF THE

GOLDEN LAMB.

THE subscriber respectfully tenders his thanks for the liberal encouragement he has already received, and has the pleasure of informing the public that he has made very handsome improvements to the Hotel, which are now complete, and not excelled by many in the west, where Ladies and Gentlemen who may think proper to favor him with call, will find good accommodation; be will endeavor by diligent attention to provide his table with the best the country affords, and his bar with the choiest liquors; his stable shall also be well furnished with all necessary provender and a careful and attentive hostler.

By the publics humble serv't.
HENRY SHARE.

Lebanon, April 10, 1827.

This 1827 advertisement for "The Ohio and Pennsylvania Hotel Sign of the Golden Lamb" is probably the most iconic of all Golden Lamb images. This early advertisement, placed by innkeeper Henry Share, touts "handsome improvements" and a hotel "not excelled by many in the west." The handsome improvements Share advertises are the removal of Jonas Seaman's original log tavern (replaced by a brick addition) and a partial second-floor addition over the original 1815 structure. Share's advertisement appeared not in a local newspaper but in the *Cincinnati Enquirer*, probably in an attempt to lure travelers arriving in Cincinnati and traveling north. (Courtesy of WCHS Museum.)

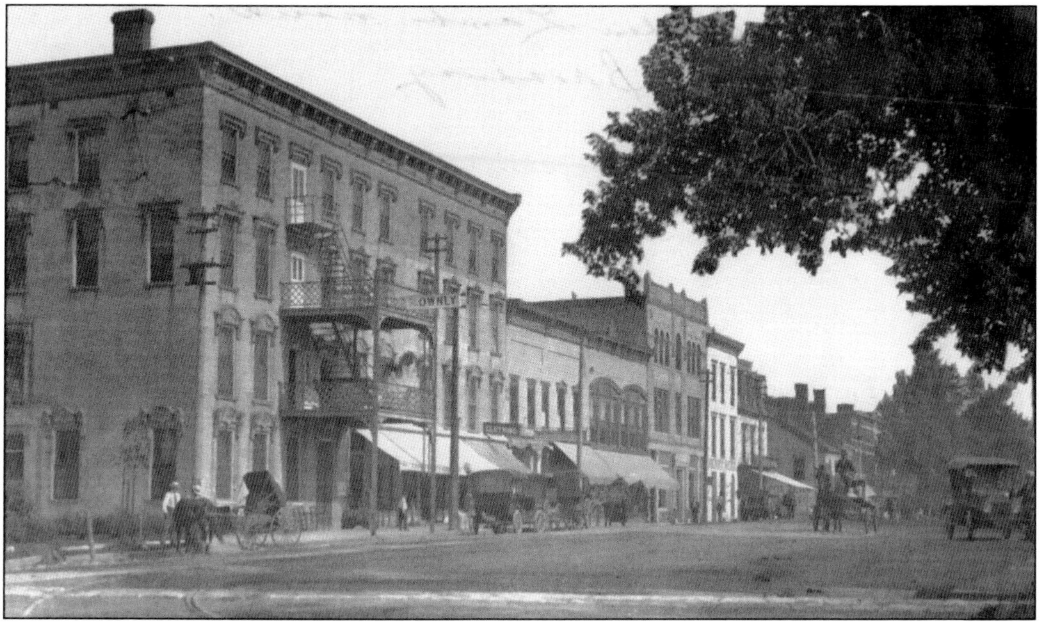

This c. 1917 image of the Golden Lamb shows it operating as the Ownly Hotel. Throughout the inn's history, it was customary for the innkeeper to incorporate his or her own name into that of the hotel. Notable examples in advertisements are the Stubbs House, Mrs. Shares Hotel, and the Bradley House, all "at the sign of The Golden Lamb." In 1914, when Ownly Furman purchased the business, he promptly hung a sign outside advertising the Ownly Hotel. (Author's collection.)

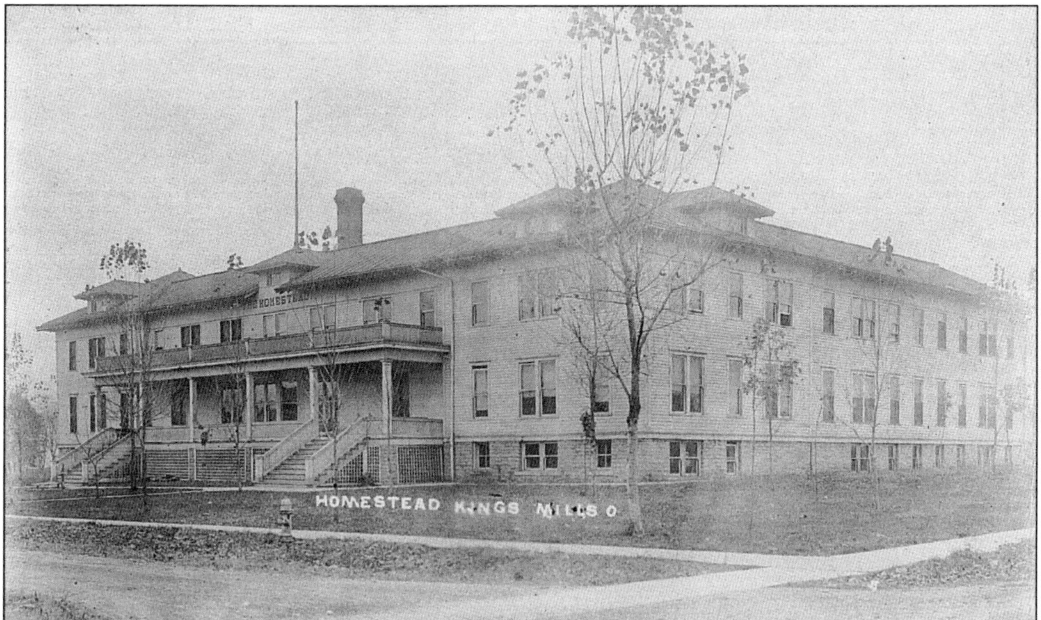

In 1915, the King Powder Company built its own hotel, the Homestead, in Kings Mills, Ohio. This two-story rambling structure was used to house unmarried company employees, visitors to the powder plant, and visitors to Kings Mills. Its unique connection to the Golden Lamb is revealed on the following page. (Courtesy of WCHS Museum.)

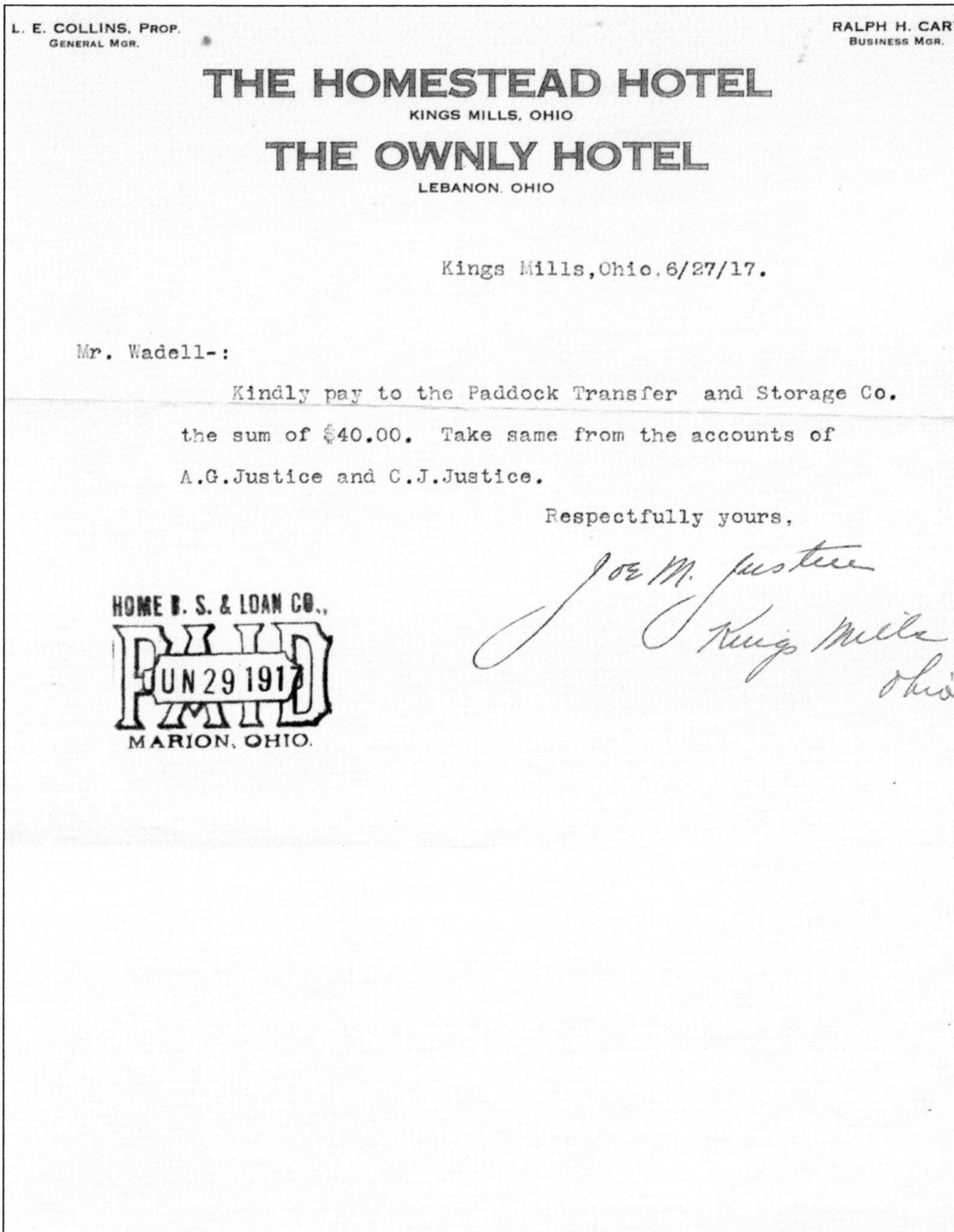

L. E. COLLINS, PROP.
GENERAL MGR.

RALPH H. CARY
BUSINESS MGR.

THE HOMESTEAD HOTEL
KINGS MILLS, OHIO

THE OWNLY HOTEL
LEBANON, OHIO

Kings Mills, Ohio, 6/27/17.

Mr. Wadell-:

Kindly pay to the Paddock Transfer and Storage Co. the sum of $40.00. Take same from the accounts of A.G.Justice and C.J.Justice.

Respectfully yours,

Joe M. Justice
Kings Mills
Ohio

HOME B. S. & LOAN CO.,
PAID
JUN 29 1917
MARION, OHIO.

This recently discovered piece of letterhead, dated June 1917, indicates that the Golden Lamb (then known as the Ownly Hotel) and the Homestead Hotel, 12 miles away in Kings Mills, were apparently operated by the same person. L. E. Collins, whose name is shown in the upper left-hand corner of the letterhead, was a well-known operator of the Golden Lamb for a number of years and the person responsible for the "chicken dinners" in the image on page 74. (Author's collection.)

Six

From Canals to Kings
Lebanon's Transportation History

From its very beginning, Lebanon has always been a destination. Throughout the 19th century, the little town, located just one-day's ride from Cincinnati, was a frequent and often necessary stopping point for travelers heading north, south, east, or west.

Travel in the 19th century was tiresome, rigorous, and sometimes dangerous. A long journey by coach was not for the faint of heart. Travelers, if they could afford the cost of a ticket, usually arose well before dawn and trusted their well-being to an itinerant driver who probably could neither read or write. This was not a problem since there was only one road from Cincinnati, the current U.S. Route 42, which still runs through the center of Lebanon.

Travelers sat cramped, back to back, for the long dusty, drafty, and sometimes wet ride from Cincinnati. For the sum of $1.25, they were guaranteed an eight-hour trip with a "sober and honest driver" and a stop in Sharonville to change horses.

In 1840, canal traffic commenced in Lebanon, albeit for a short time. Built in sections, the Warren County Canal was constructed on the broad depression between the two Miami Rivers, which would eventually link to the Miami and Erie Canal. Unfortunately the canal proved financially disastrous. Local commerce could not support it, and seven years after its inception the canal was abandoned.

Within five years after the demise of the Warren County Canal, work began on the Cincinnati, Lebanon, and Xenia Railroad. It would be almost 30 years before the first engine came steaming into Lebanon. With various owners, including the Cincinnati and Lebanon Northern Railroad, the Pennsylvania Railroad, and the Dayton, Lebanon, and Cincinnati Railroad, regular rail service was provided to Lebanon until the late 1930s. Lebanon's earliest railroad station still stands at the base of Broadway Street as a testament to the resilience and foresight of Lebanon's residents well over a century ago. But by the 1940s, improved roads and automobiles brought travelers to Lebanon, where less than a century ago they were carried by wagon and horseback.

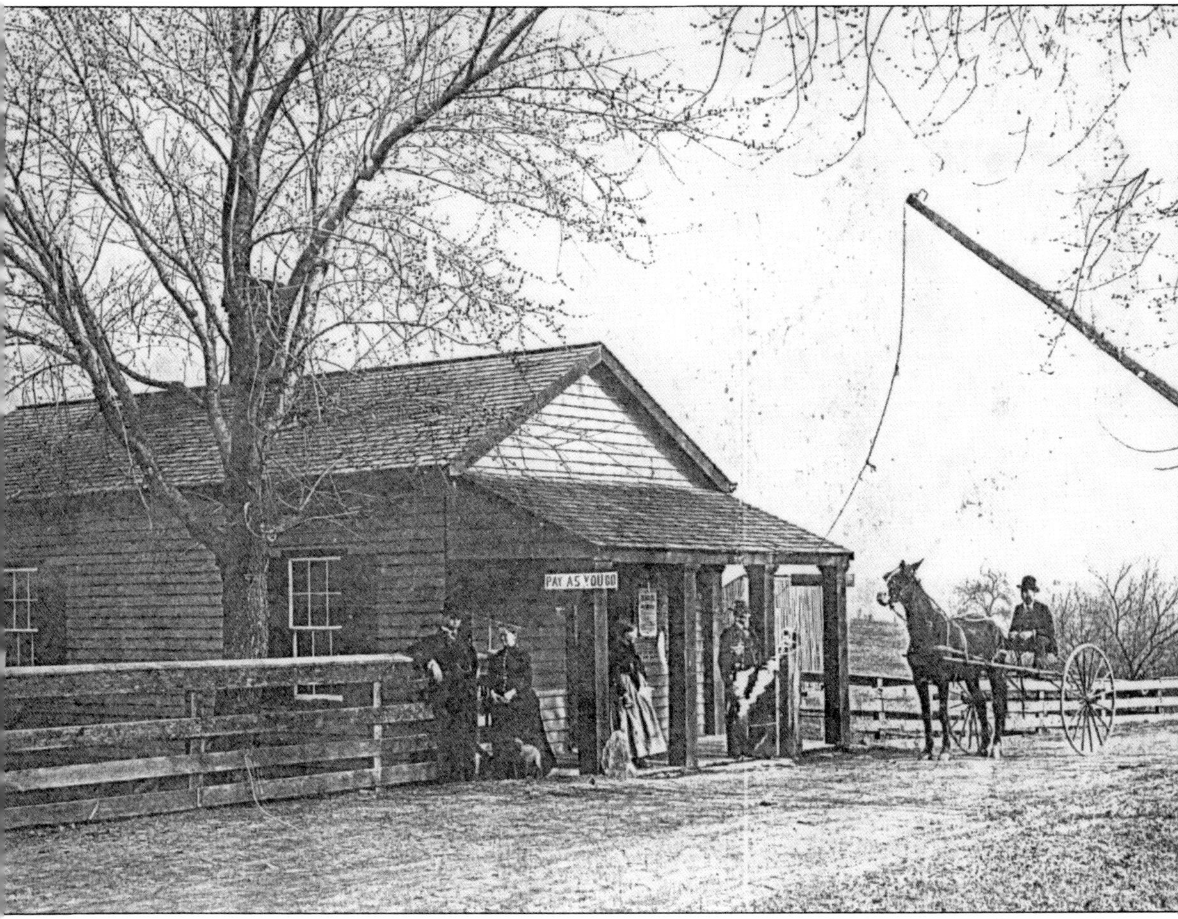

The earliest travelers to Lebanon came either on foot or on horseback. Most traffic came from the south on what is now U.S. 42, which is Lebanon's Broadway Street. This mid-19th-century image was taken on Deerfield Road in Lebanon and shows one of the original tollhouses where owners charged the public for use of a portion of the road. The large pike on the right-hand side was raised and lowered as tolls were paid. This particular tollhouse is still standing. (Courtesy of WCHS Museum.)

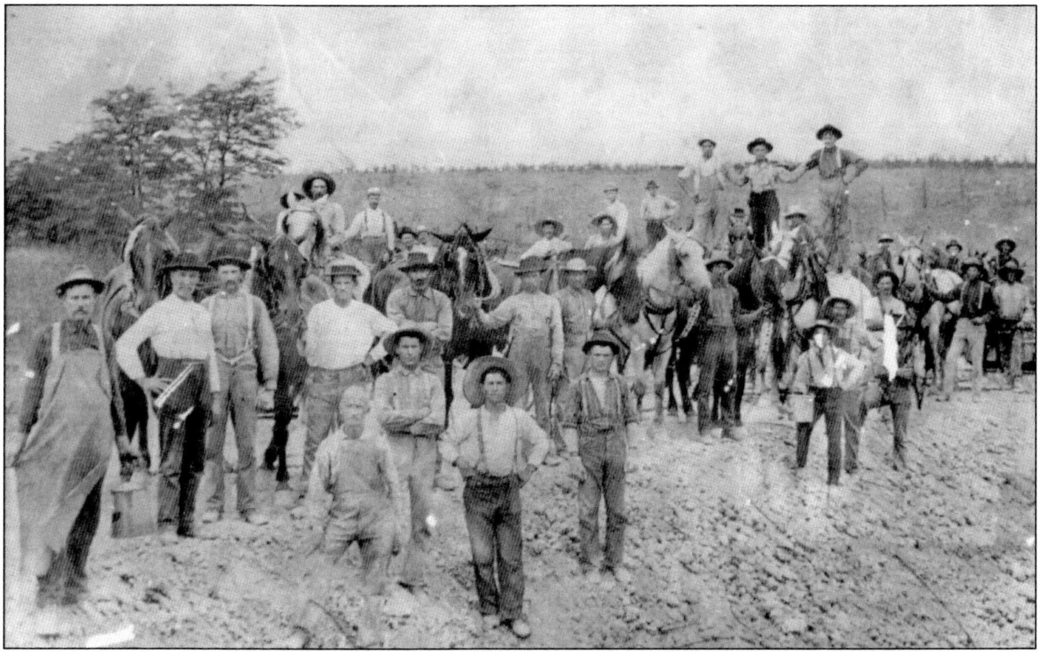

The Interurban, or traction line, flourished in southwestern Ohio from 1903 to 1922. Electrically powered "streetcars" wound their way from as far south as Cincinnati to Mason, Lebanon, and Franklin. The traction line was built by workers, many of them farmers, who hired themselves and their teams out by the day to help clear land. (Courtesy of WCHS Museum.)

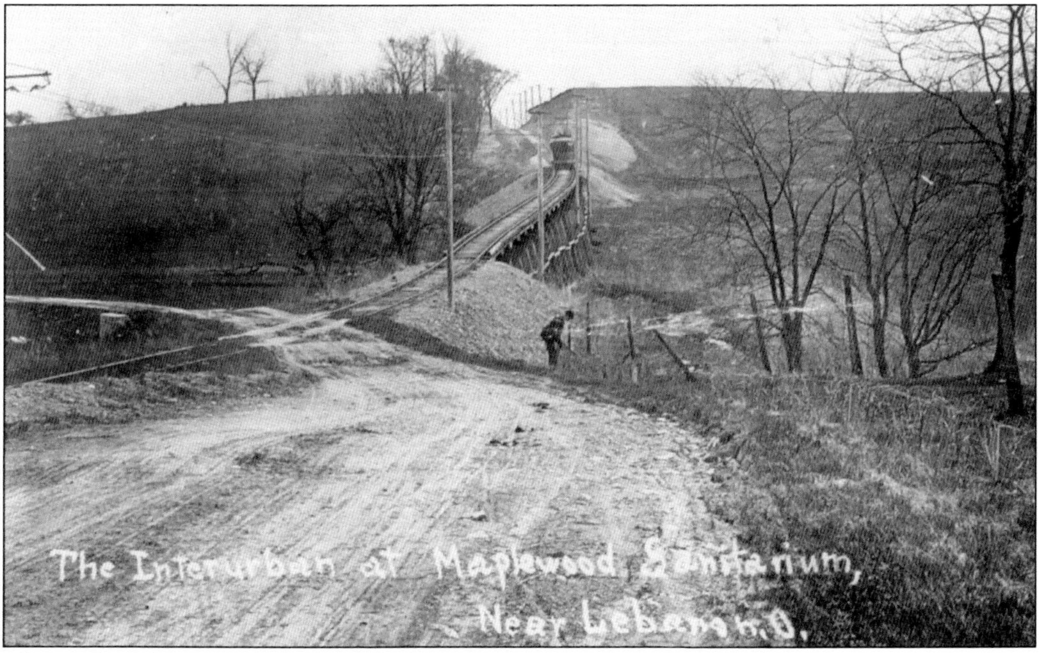

This early-19th-century photograph shows a typical traction line car slowly going up the hill on Deerfield Road in the southern part of Lebanon. The electrical lines on either side were powered by a substation in South Lebanon. Interior lights in the cars were left on, with their dimness or brightness an indication of how much power was available. (Courtesy of WCHS Museum.)

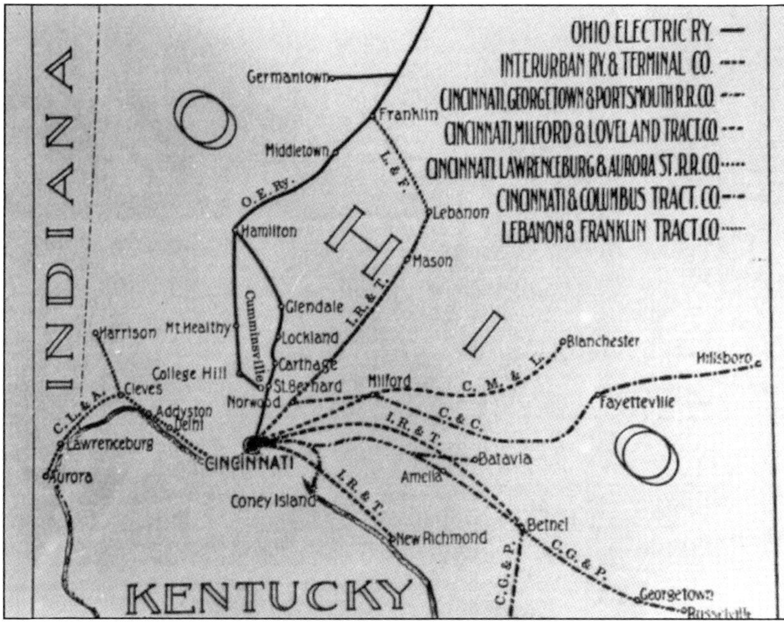

This early map of the interurban line shows the extant of the electrically powered vehicles in southwestern Ohio. Starting as far east as Georgetown, Ohio, the cars could travel through Hamilton County, Clermont County, Warren County, and Montgomery County, which was close to Dayton. (Courtesy of WCHS Museum.)

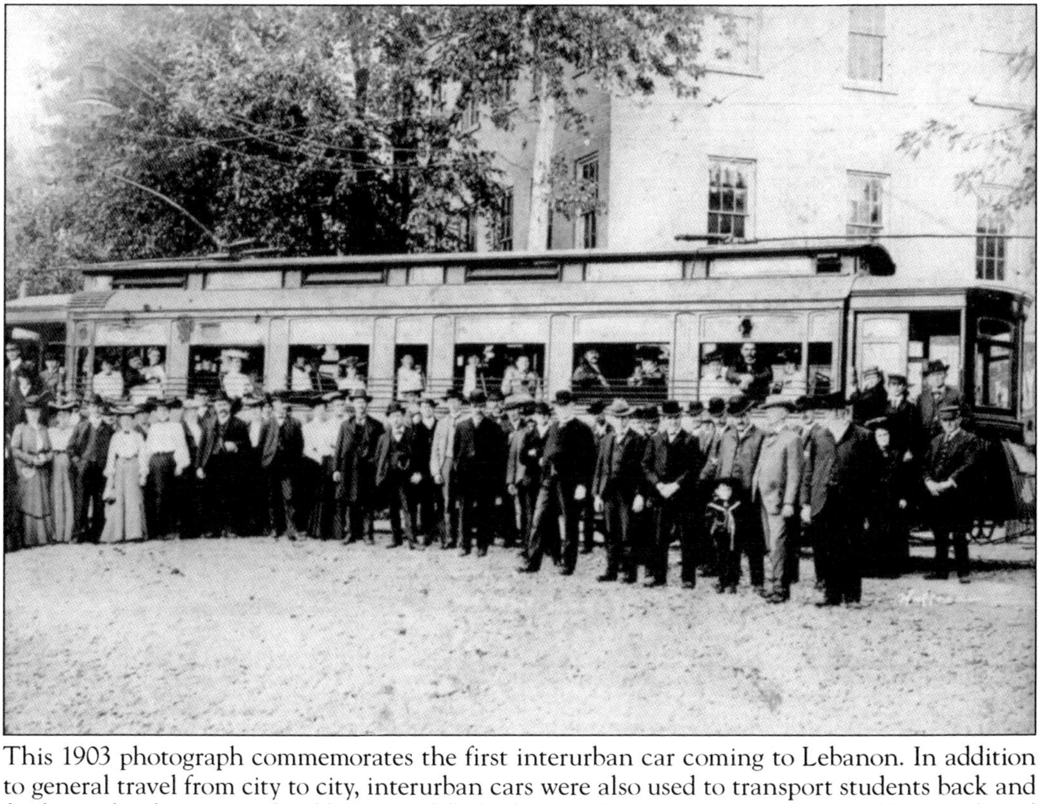

This 1903 photograph commemorates the first interurban car coming to Lebanon. In addition to general travel from city to city, interurban cars were also used to transport students back and forth to school prior to school buses, and flatbed interurban cars were used to haul livestock and merchandise. (Courtesy of WCHS Museum.)

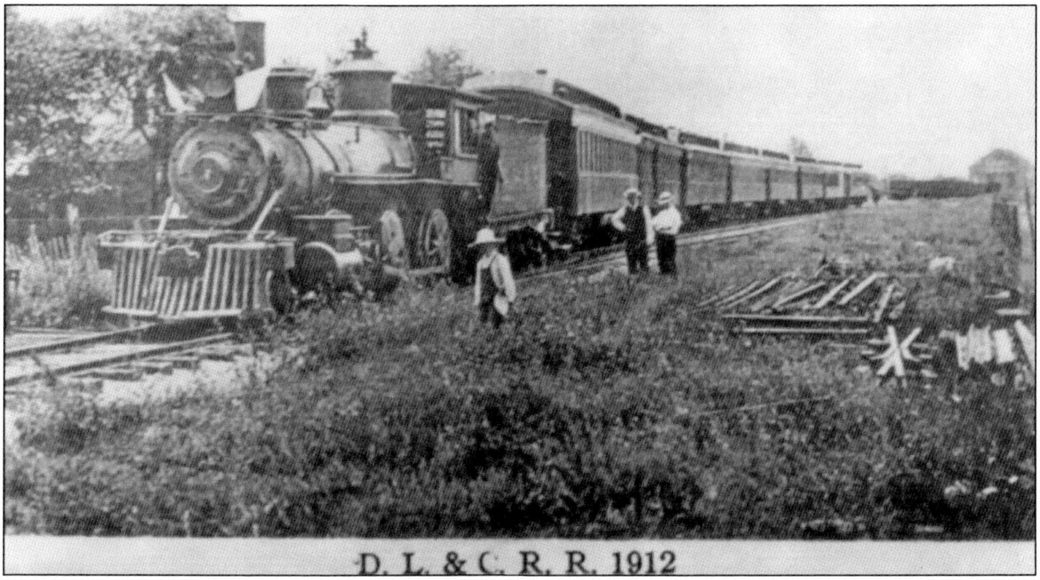

The railroads were somewhat late in coming to Lebanon with the first train steaming into the Lebanon Station in 1881. Lebanon was in fact the last town in Warren County to receive rail service. Regular rail service continued until about 1930, when individual motorized transportation gained in popularity. This 1912 photograph illustrates a typical train of the Dayton, Lebanon, and Cincinnati Railroad, which had been organized in 1889. (Courtesy of WCHS Museum.)

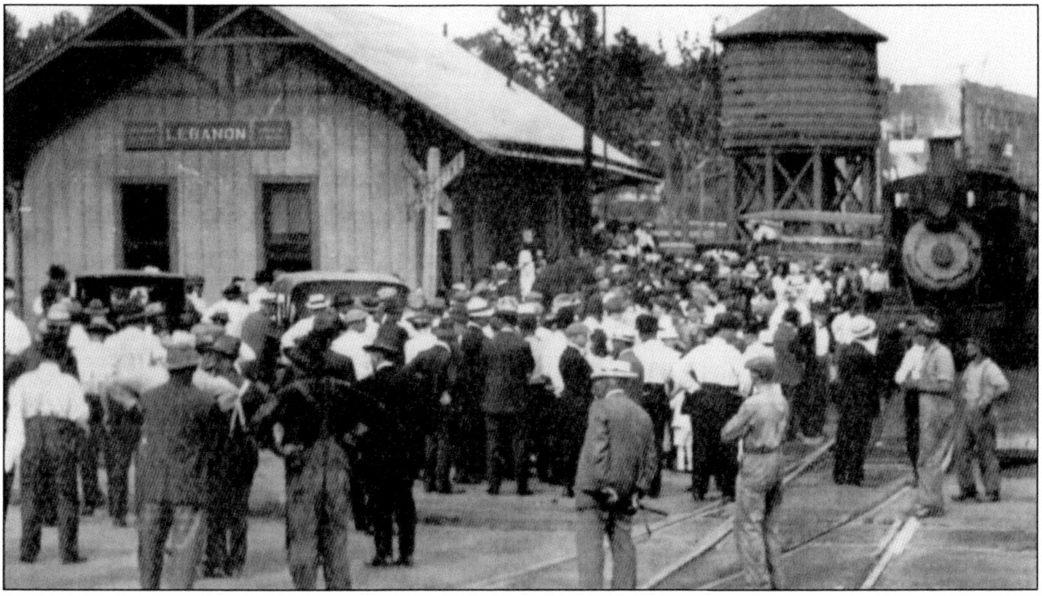

This early image of Lebanon Station at the base of Broadway Street illustrates a group of citizens awaiting the arrival of a train from the south. The station, at the corner of Broadway and South Streets, is standing to this day, serving as a home to the local garden clubs and a staging area for excursion trains departing Lebanon. (Courtesy of WCHS Museum.)

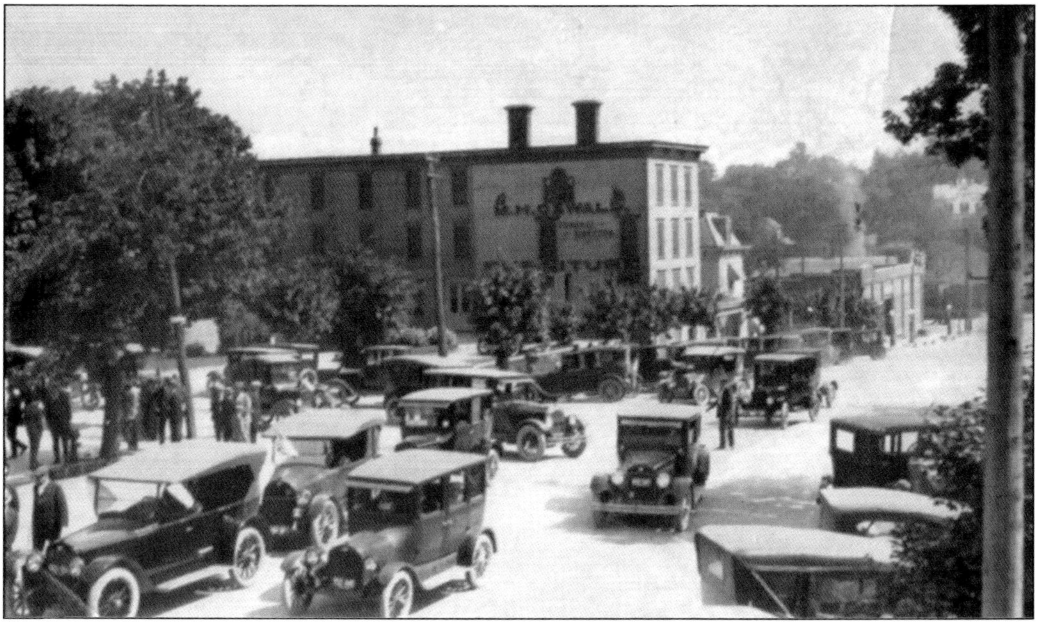

As automobiles became more commonplace, Lebanon streets became more crowded. This 1920s photograph of the intersection of Broadway and Main Streets shows the effect the automobile had on a small town. Visible in this image is the Oswald Building on the left and the Roll Building at the base of Broadway. (Courtesy of WCHS Museum.)

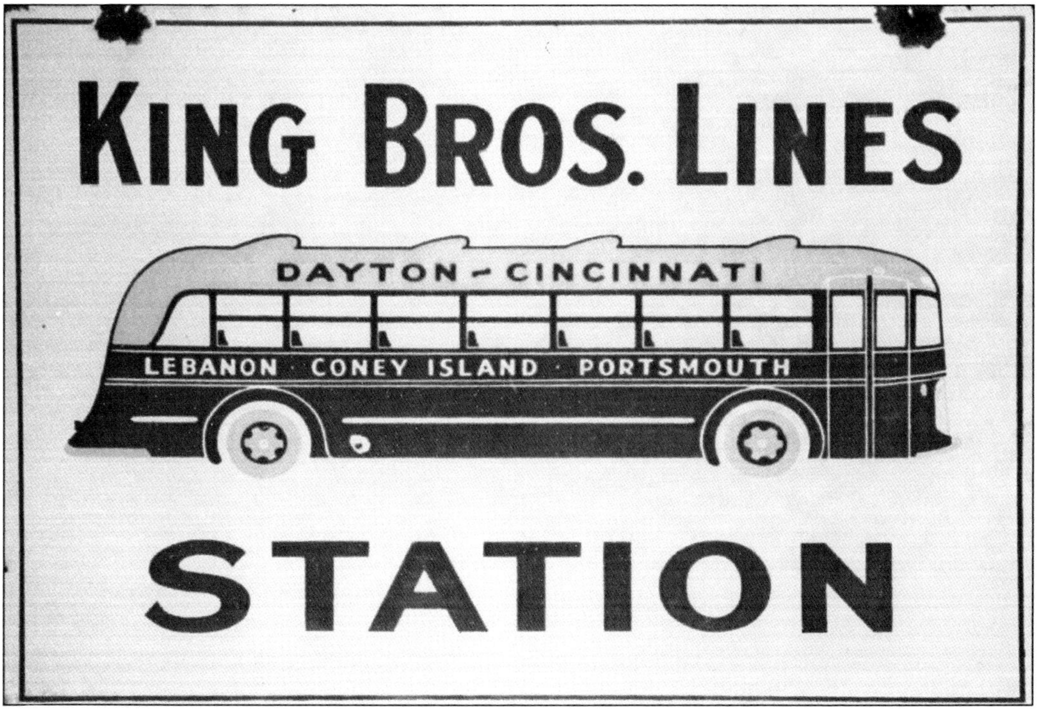

The King Brothers Lines operated in Lebanon from 1921 until 1950. Initially two seven-passenger touring cars shuttled passengers between Lebanon and Dayton. In later years, service expanded south to Cincinnati. (Courtesy of WCHS Museum.)

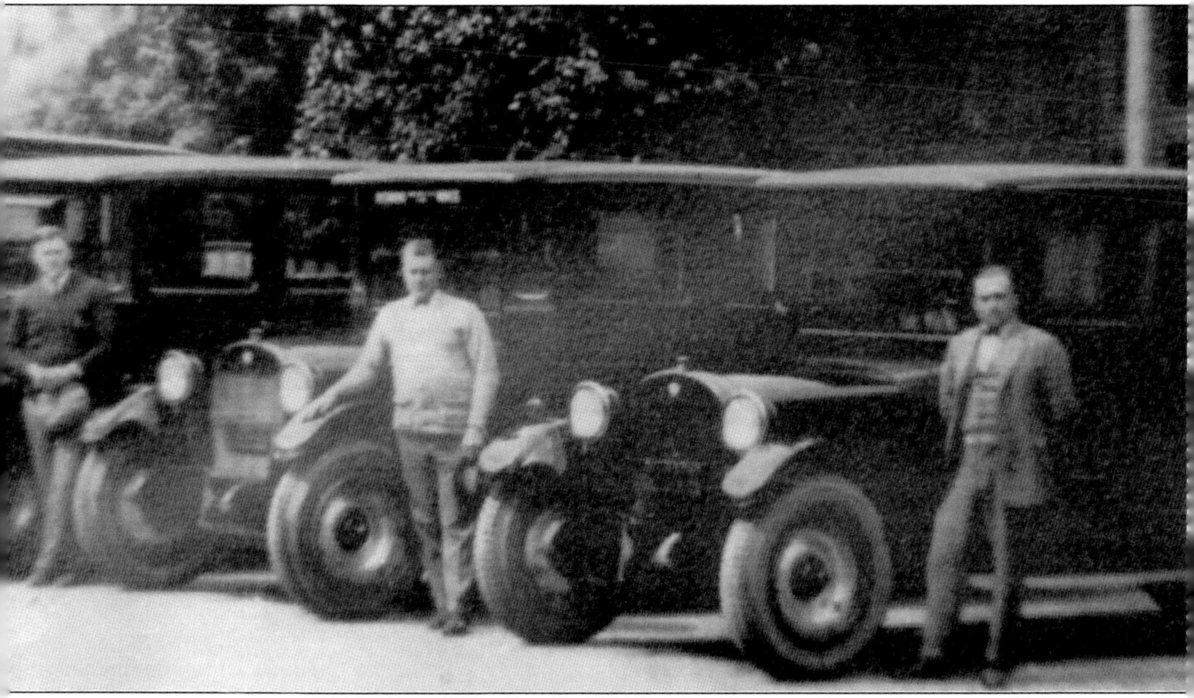

Pictured here from left to right are brothers Robert, Firman, and Fred King, owners and operators of the King Brothers Lines. By 1928, the brothers had expanded the line to include hourly trips between Cincinnati and Dayton at a cost of $1.75. Baggage, up to 150 pounds, was carried for free. The bus depot was located within the Decker Hotel at Broadway and Silver Streets. King Brothers Lines was absorbed by Greyhound around 1950. (Courtesy of WCHS Museum.)

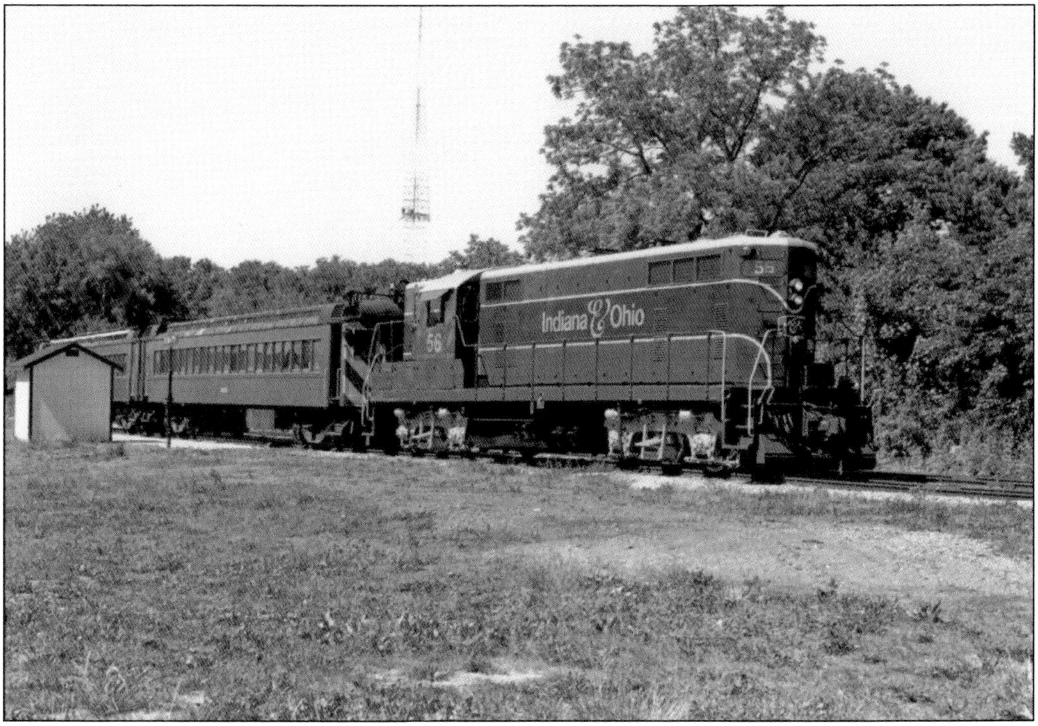

Rail travel returned to Lebanon in the 1980s in the form of the Turtle Creek Valley Scenic Railway, which offered excursion train rides between Lebanon and Mason. The restored 1940s passenger rail cars, some open-air for better viewing, provided riders a leisurely tour through the countryside. The trains, now operated by the Lebanon, Mason, and Monroe Railroad (LM&M), depart seasonally from Lebanon's historic railway station at the base of Broadway Street. (Courtesy of WCHS Museum.)

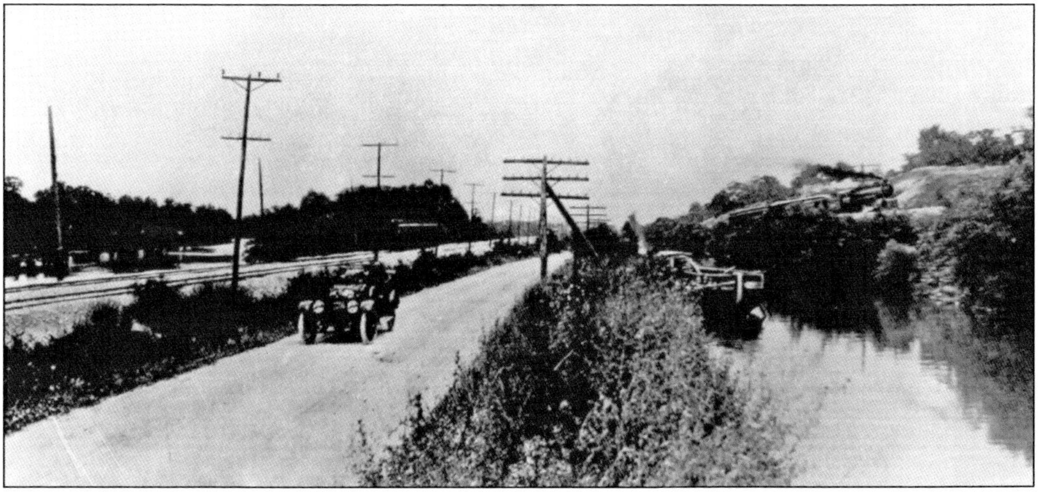

This 1920s photograph shows the four modes of Lebanon's transportation history together: to the far left is an interurban car following along a series of electric poles necessary for power; in the left center is a paved road for use by automobiles; to the right of the road is part of the canal system that served Lebanon for a short time; and to the far right is a steam engine. (Courtesy of WCHS Museum.)

Seven

Anything May Be Called Perfect
Lebanon's Union Village

Though it ceased to be a formal entity almost 100 years ago, Lebanon's Shaker community, Union Village, lives on today in the hearts and minds of local residents and anyone interested in the Shaker religion. This once thriving "western" Shaker village was the largest, oldest, and richest Shaker community west of the Allegheny Mountains.

Union Village was founded in 1805 by three missionaries from New Lebanon, New York—John Meachem, Benjamin S. Youngs, and Issacher Bates. The three reportedly walked 1,000 miles in the dead of winter to fulfill a prophecy of their founder and leader, Mother Ann Lee.

In March 1805, they made their earliest converts in the form of Malcolm Worley and Richard McNemar, who was then pastor of the Turtle Creek Church. Worley and McNemar both deeded their farms to the United Society of Believers (Shakers), giving the society an agricultural beginning that would grow to over 4,000 acres in the newly formed community of Lebanon. The primary site of Union Village was located approximately 3 miles west of Lebanon on what is now State Route 63 on the northwest side of the road.

Almost totally self-sufficient, Union Village, like all Shaker communities, practiced celibacy, strict separation of the sexes, sexual equality, and furious industry. Shaker dictum taught that "anything may be called perfect which perfectly answers the purpose for which it was designed." People often forget the simple inventions that the Shakers readily gave to the world. Cut nails, the common clothespin, flat brooms, permanent press fabrics, and circular saws were but a few of the innovations credited to the Shakers—simple ideas but outstanding in their functionality and necessity.

By 1830, the population of Union Village had passed the 500 mark, making it the largest Shaker community in the West. In 1913, the last of the true believers returned to eastern villages, leaving only their leader James Fennessey behind to dispose of the community's vast land holdings, livestock, and belongings.

Only one of the Shakers' 40 or 50 buildings remains today as a testament to their presence in Lebanon almost a century ago. The building is owned by the Otterbein Retirement Community.

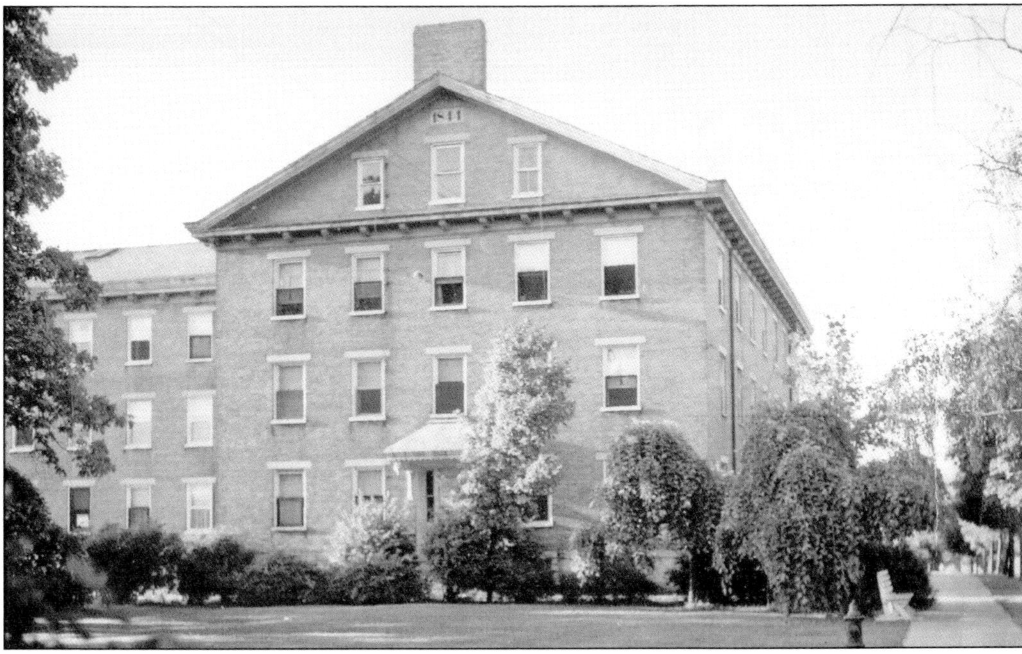

This image illustrates the massive Grand Center House, which was begun in 1842, completed in 1846, but for some reason bears a stone plaque with the date 1844. This building provided living quarters for 112 people, a meeting room, and a large communal dining hall. The building was demolished in 2010. (Courtesy of WCHS Museum.)

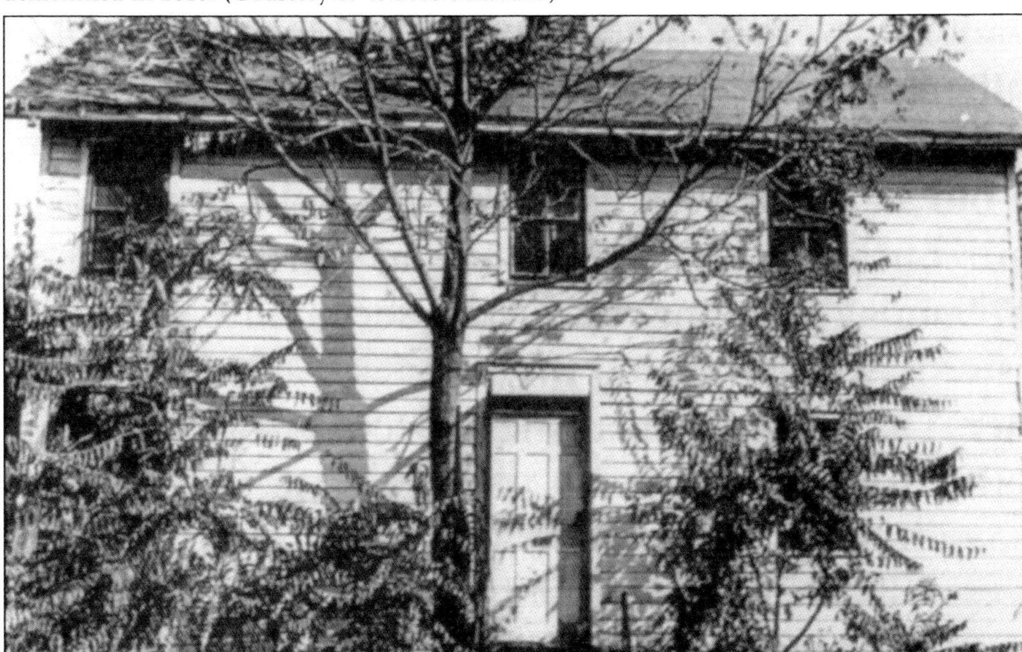

This rare photograph is of the home of Malcolm and Peggy Worley, who gave shelter to the three original Shaker missionaries in 1805. Worley and his wife became two of the earliest Shaker converts and were prominent members of the society. (Courtesy of WCHS Museum.)

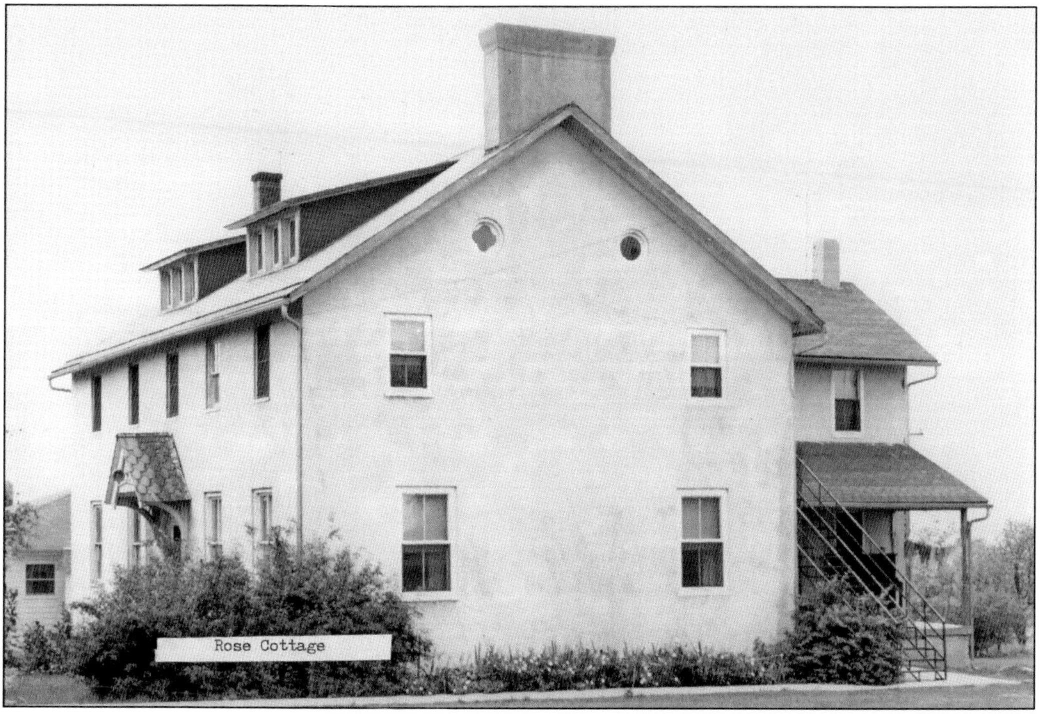

Rose Cottage was one of the many buildings in Union Village that was systematically destroyed after the sale of Union Village in 1913. Though the building was razed, many of the hand-fired bricks, which were "burned" at the site, were preserved by the Warren County Historical Society. (Courtesy of WCHS Museum.)

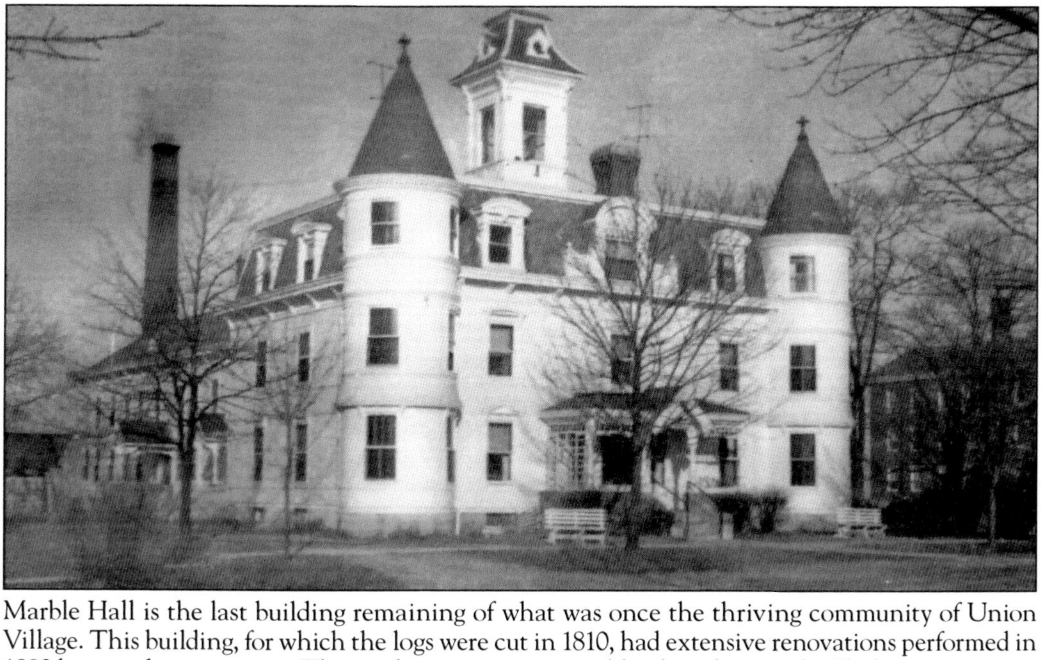

Marble Hall is the last building remaining of what was once the thriving community of Union Village. This building, for which the logs were cut in 1810, had extensive renovations performed in 1892 by outside contractors. The result was a structure unlike the others in the Shaker community. It is now owned by Otterbein Retirement Community. (Courtesy of WCHS Museum.)

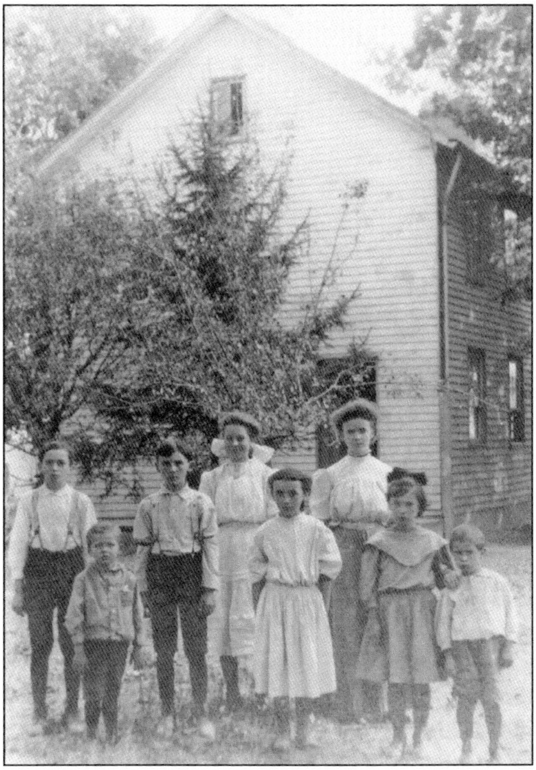

This early image of Shaker schoolchildren illustrates the equality in Shaker education. Union Village established its first school in 1808. Though all children, both male and female, were required to attend classes, males were typically taught in the winter and females in the summer. (Courtesy of WCHS Museum.)

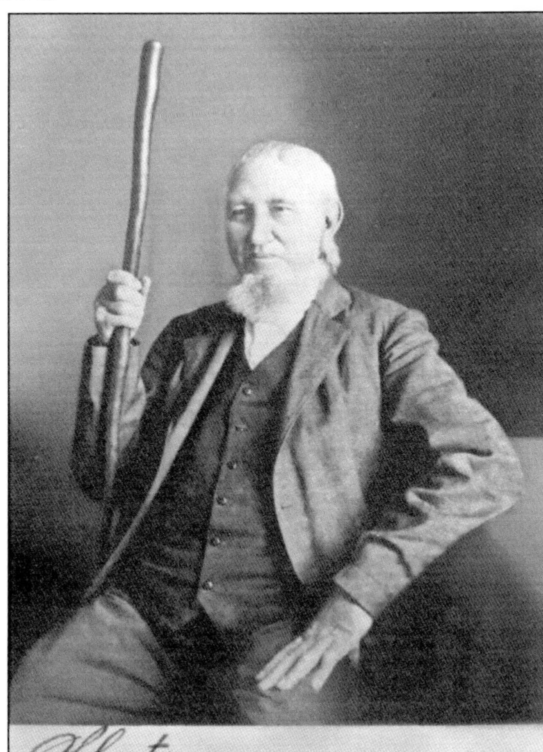

A Shaker his entire life, Peter Boyd was a leading member of Union Village and entrusted with the marketing of all Shaker products to the outside world. Boyd's image even appeared on labels for numerous Shaker syrups and herbal medicines as a testament to their quality and authenticity. (Courtesy WCHS Museum.)

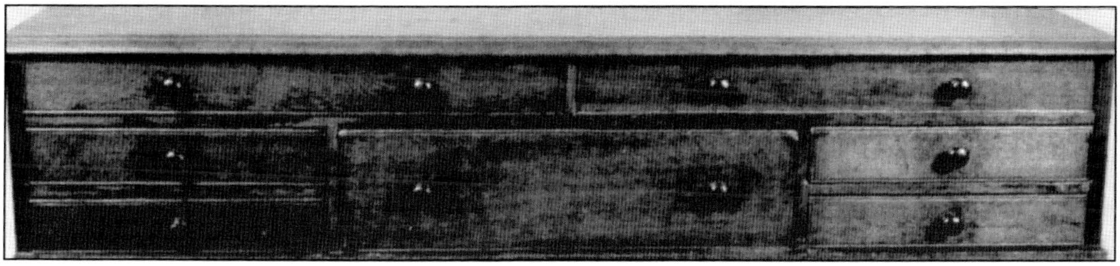

This small tool chest, part of the collection of the Warren County Historical Society, was built in Union Village by Richard McNemar for his son Benjamin. McNemar is famous for allegedly putting a "curse" on Lebanon for its treatment of the Shakers and blessing Dayton, Ohio, which was much more tolerant. (Courtesy of WCHS Museum.)

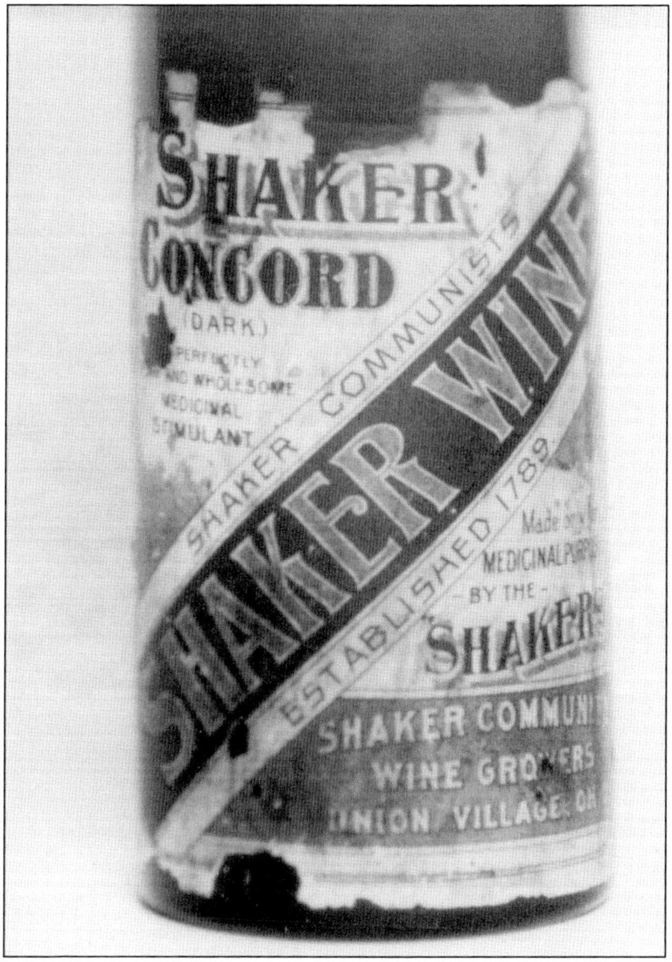

Though temperate by nature, the Shakers did produce some spirits at Union Village. Though wine production was much greater in the northern Ohio settlements around Cleveland, Union Village did produce a small amount of commercial wine for "medicinal purposes." (Courtesy of WCHS Museum.)

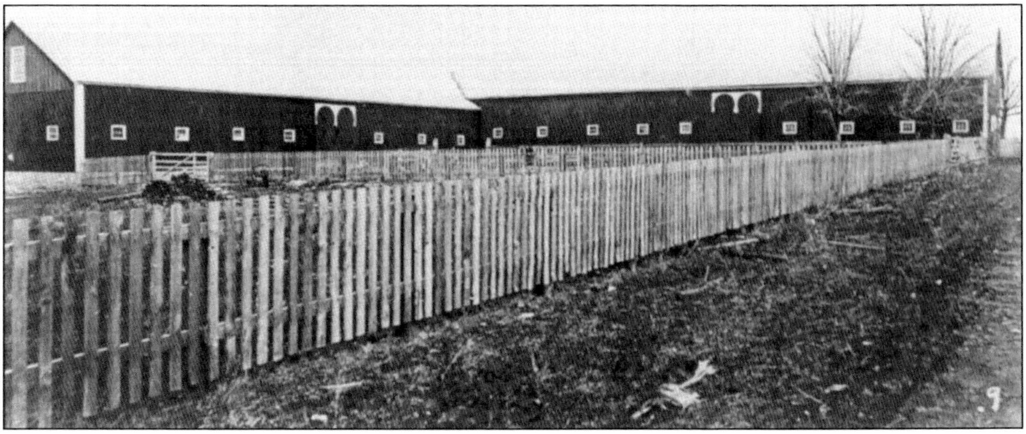

This early photograph of a milking barn and fence line serves to illustrate the immense size of the Shaker holdings at Union Village. At one time, the Shakers controlled over 4,000 acres of farm and pastureland, which they either farmed themselves or leased out to other individuals. (Courtesy of WCHS Museum.)

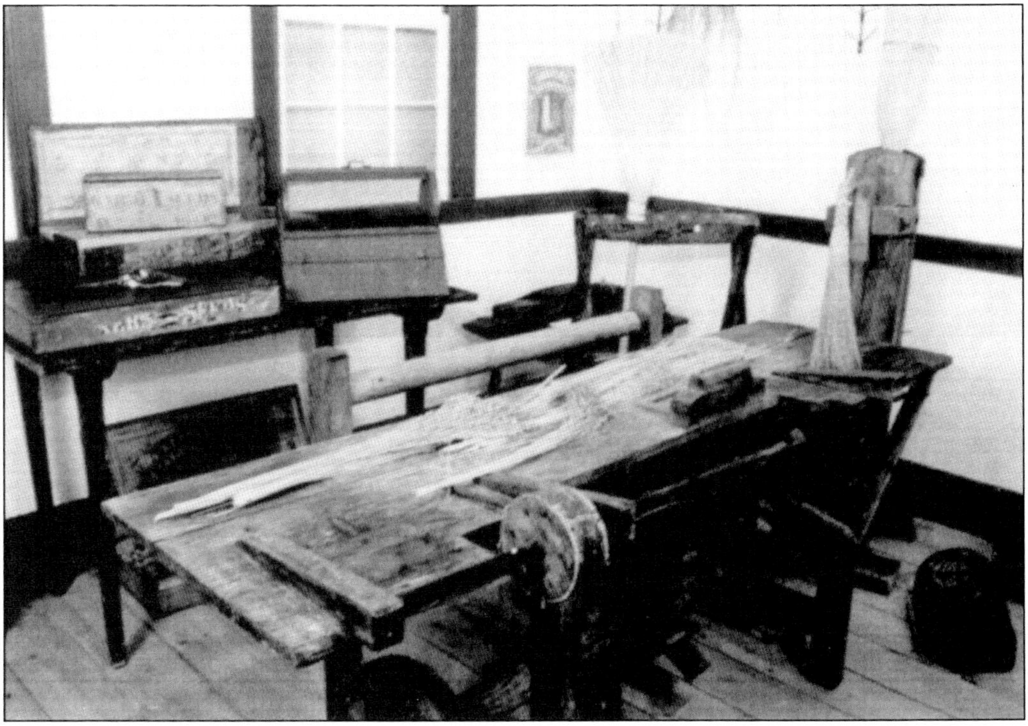

Though known primarily for their highly collectible furniture, one of the primary products in Union Village was not furniture but brooms. The Shakers are credited with the invention of the flat broom at their village in Watervliet, New York. This display, at the Warren County Historical Society, is recreated from authentic broom-making equipment in Union Village. (Courtesy of WCHS Museum.)

This photograph is of a young James Fennessey, the last Shaker in Union Village. It was Fennessey's task to dispose of all the Shaker land and personal property in 1913, when the last of the true believers began returning to the eastern settlements. After selling the property, Fennessey remained in Lebanon and taught in the Lebanon school system. (Courtesy of WCHS Museum.)

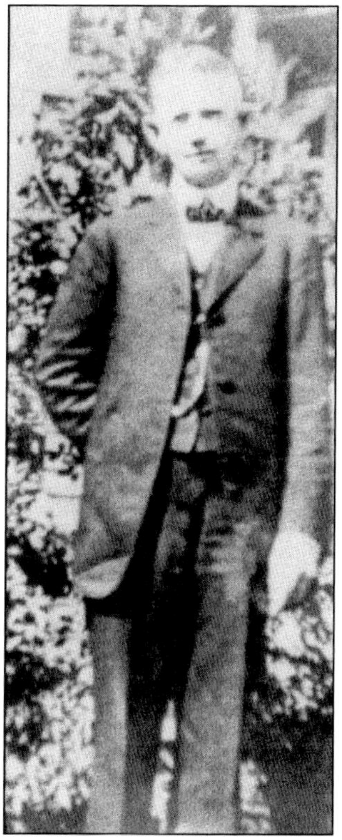

This unusual view of the center family house, or Bethany Hall, shows over 30 windows in this massive construction and a two-level porch. Also noteworthy are the double chimneys on both ends of the building. (Courtesy of WCHS Museum.)

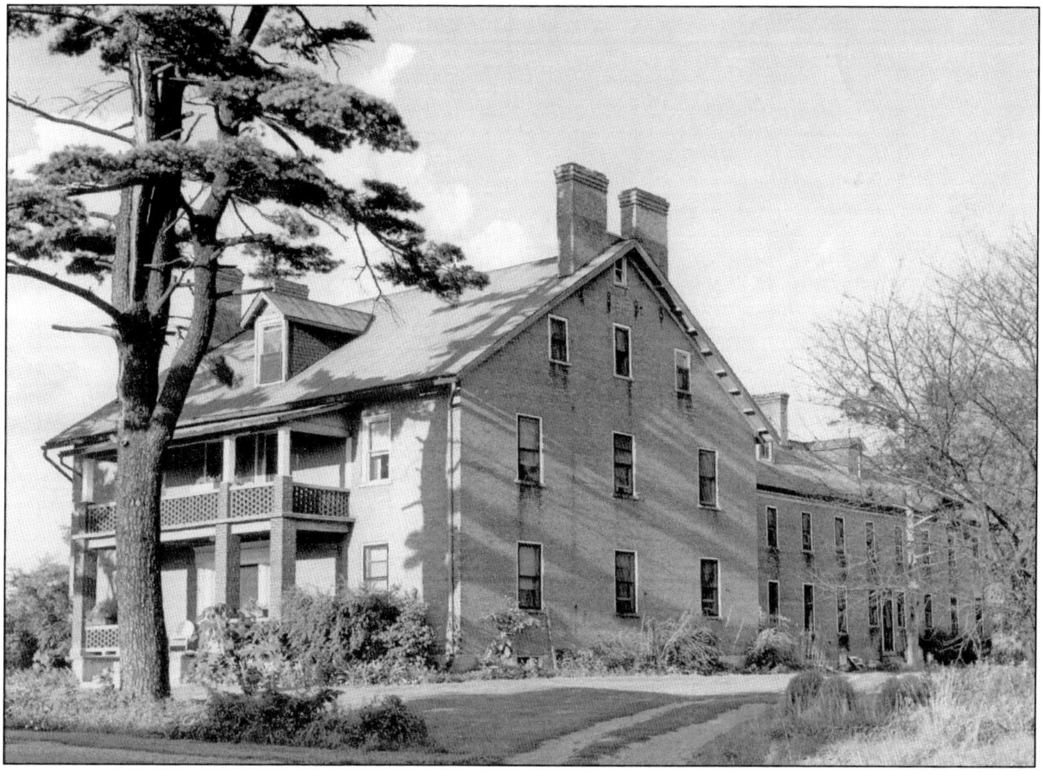

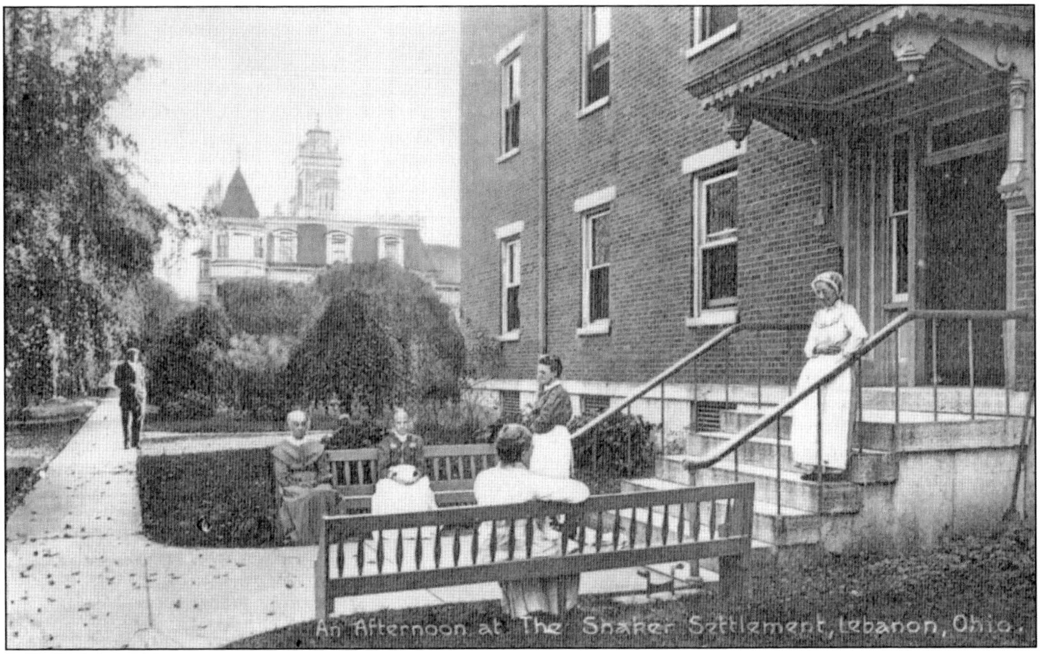

This early postcard scene is of a group of Shaker sisters relaxing outside of what is possibly Bethany Hall around 1900. In the background to the left is the very ornate Marble Hall. (Courtesy of WCHS Museum.)

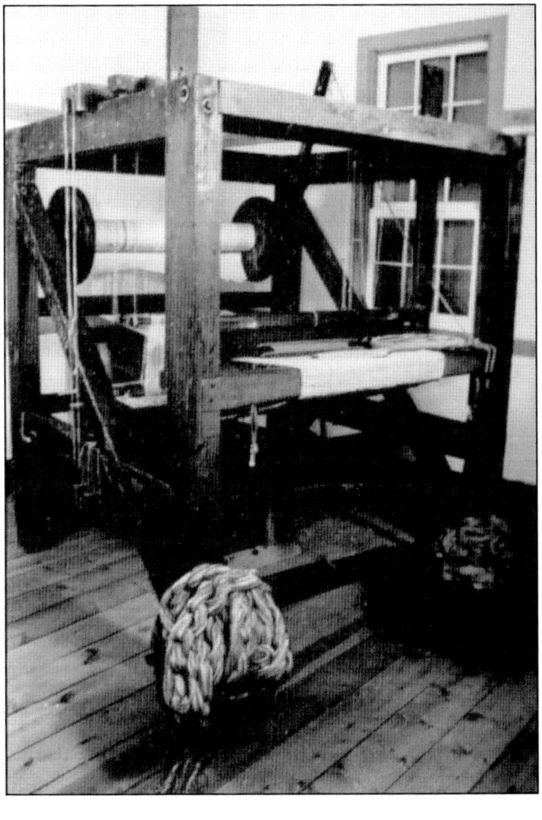

This large Shaker loom was made in Union Village and is part of the collection of the Warren County Historical Society. After the demise of Union Village in 1913, this particular loom was used for many years at Cincinnati's Clovernook School for the Blind. (Courtesy of WCHS Museum.)

Eight

FROM LUCILLE BERRY TO HARPER VALLEY
LEBANON'S SCHOOLS AND CHURCHES

Though taverns were usually the first buildings erected in a new community, churches and schools soon followed. *Beer's History of Ohio* states that the first church close to Lebanon was built in 1798, just 1 mile east of Lebanon. The Turtlecreek Church, constructed with logs and a dirt floor, listed among its members Mathias Corwin (father of future governor Thomas Corwin and brother to Ichabod Corwin), Judge Francis Dunlevy, and Col. Lewis Drake, all well-known family names still familiar in Lebanon. Five years later, in 1803, the church had a roster of 53 members. This church lasted for eight years until a substantial brick meetinghouse was erected in Lebanon and it became known as the Baptist Church at Lebanon. This church stood until 1860, when it was razed and replaced with the old West Baptist Church. The 19th-century churches still standing in Lebanon include St. Patrick's Episcopal (which started life as a Presbyterian church) on east Main Street, the Lebanon United Methodist Church on Silver Street (built in 1863), and the current Presbyterian church on north East Street (built in 1859).

The only vestige left of 19th-century education in Lebanon is the original Academy Building on New Street near the current post office. Once part of National Normal University, the academy building served as an educational institution until the 1960s, when it was replaced by larger, more modern schools. Lebanon's Romanesque-inspired Pleasant Street School, just one street away from the academy building, served Lebanon students until the 1960s, when it too was replaced by more up-to-date facilities.

Local schools today honor those teachers and educators who made a difference in the educational lives of their students. Current schools are named for Lebanon educators such as Louisa Wright, Lucille Berry, Alfred Holbrook, Francis Dunlevy, and William and Margaret Donovan. Though the great 19th- and early-20th-century educators are all gone, the memory of them and their accomplishments live on in the schools named in their honor.

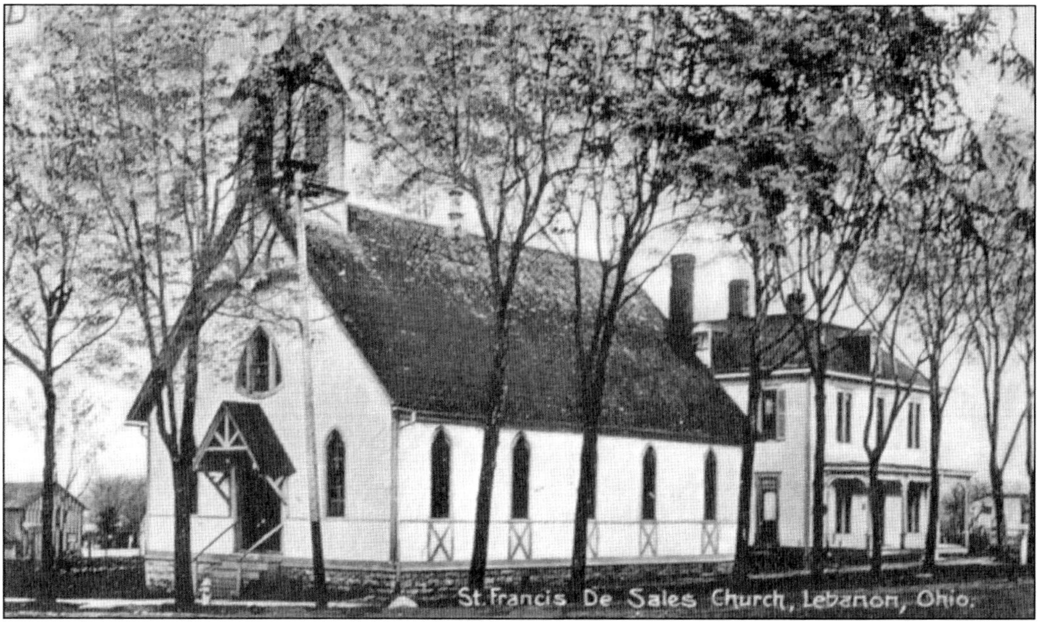

The original Catholic church, St. Francis DeSales, was located at the opposite end of town from where it is today. This simple, one-story structure, built in 1883, stood at the corner of east Orchard and South Mechanic Streets in what was then a residential neighborhood. The current church is located on North Broadway Street. This building was eventually razed in the 20th century. (Courtesy of the Sally Foster collection.)

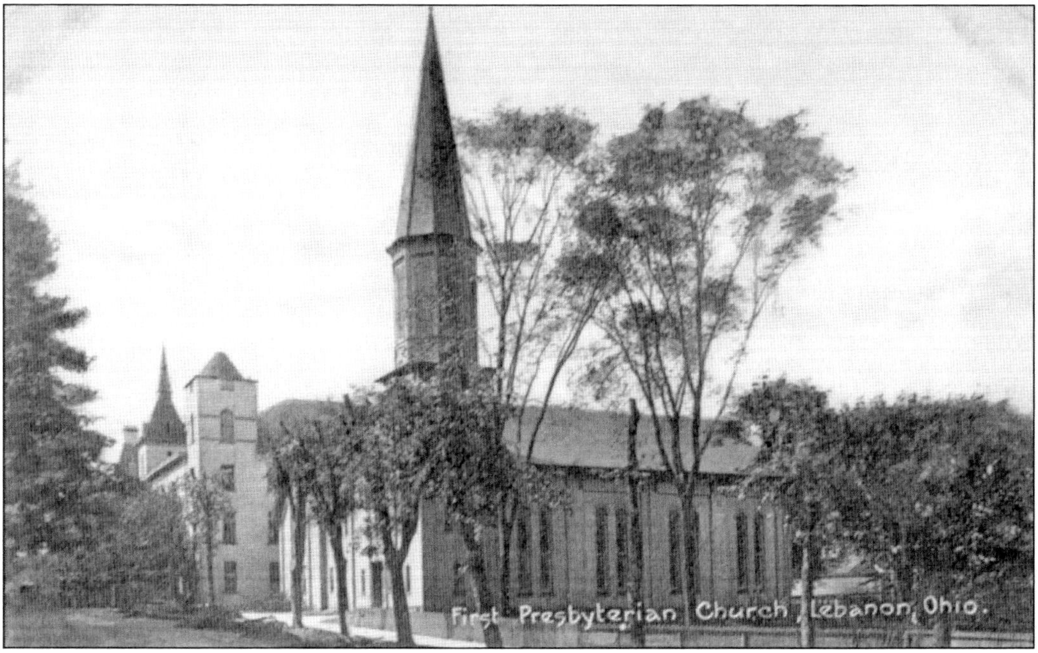

This early image is of the First Presbyterian Church built in 1859. Prior to the construction of this church, meetings were held in the old courthouse on Silver Street in Lebanon. Located adjacent to National Normal University, the church purchased the old Lyceum Building and added an addition in the latter part of the 20th century. (Courtesy of the Sally Foster collection.)

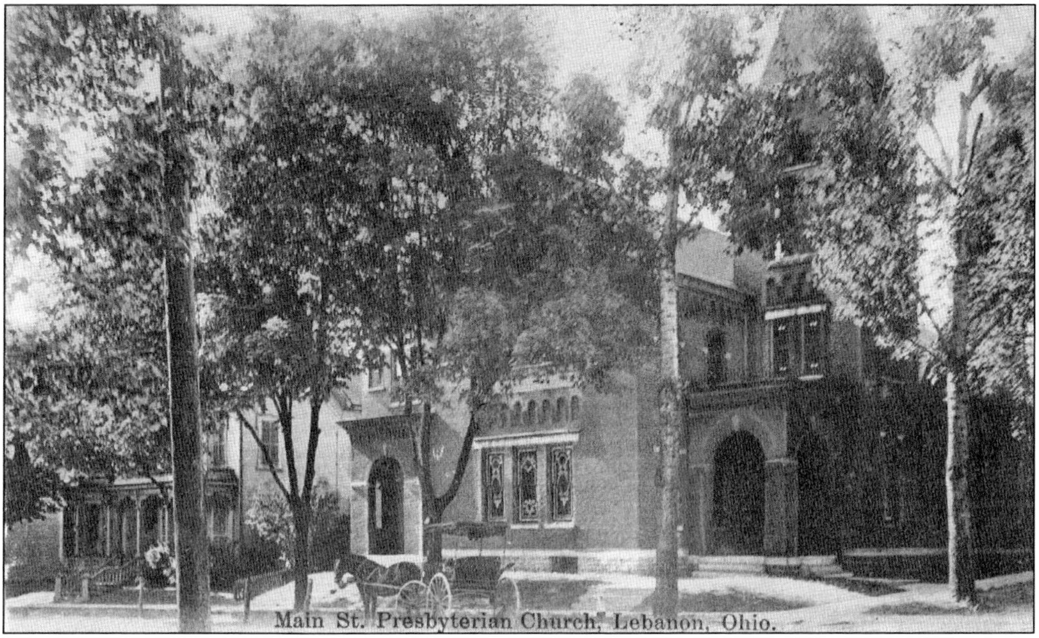

This 19th-century image of the Main Street Presbyterian Church vividly illustrates the Romanesque Revival style of architecture so prevalent in Lebanon. This church, still standing at the corner of Main and East Streets, is now home to St Patrick's Episcopal Church. (Courtesy of the Sally Foster collection.)

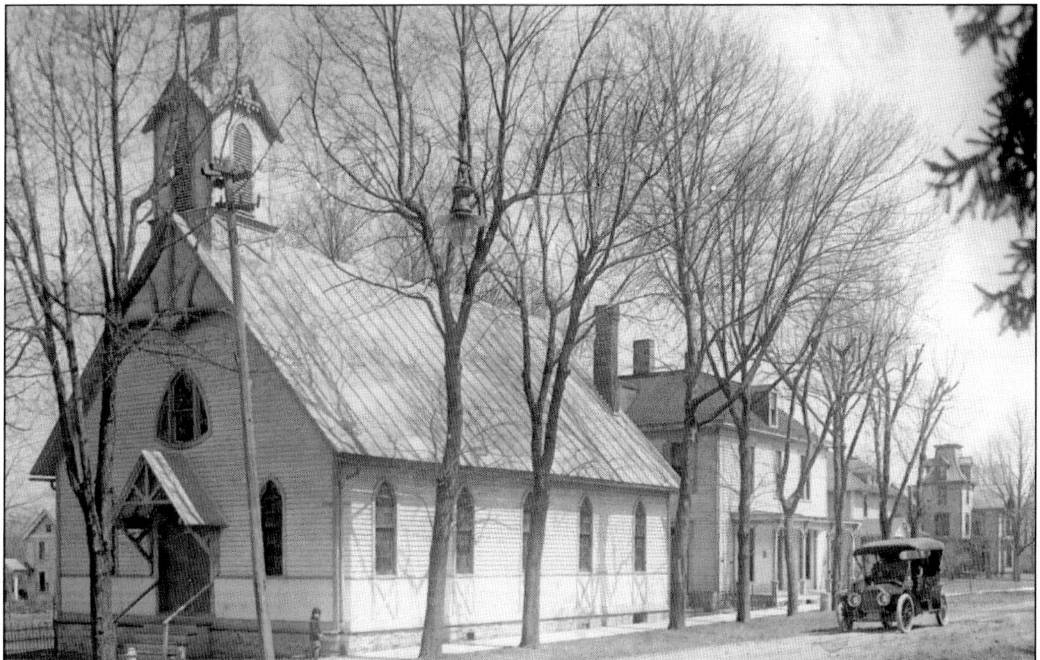

This photograph of the original St. Francis DeSales Church shows its original location in a strictly residential neighborhood. This simple one-story structure illustrates the 1880s trend in Gothic architecture but on a much smaller scale. (Courtesy of WCHS Museum.)

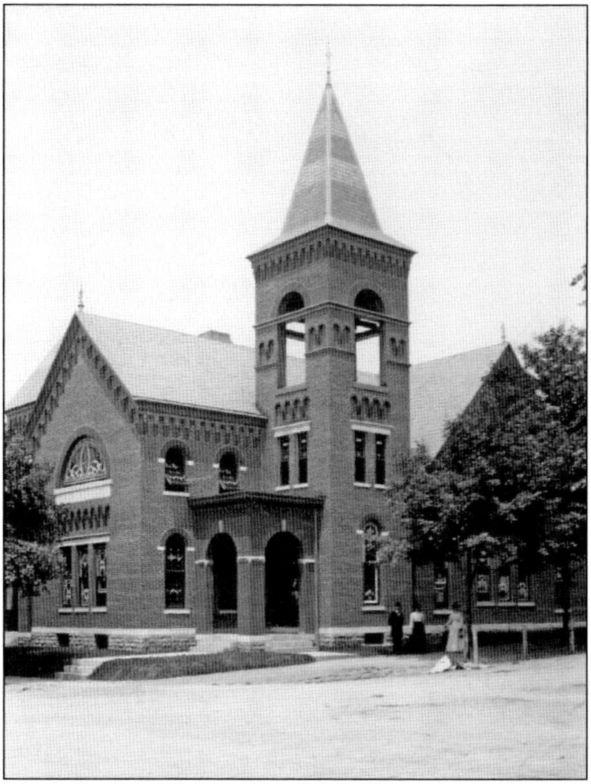

This view of the Main Street Presbyterian Church shows the strict Romanesque Revival architectural style. The towers flanking the facade are at different heights, and the structure features the use of semicircular arches for window and door openings. (Courtesy of WCHS Museum.)

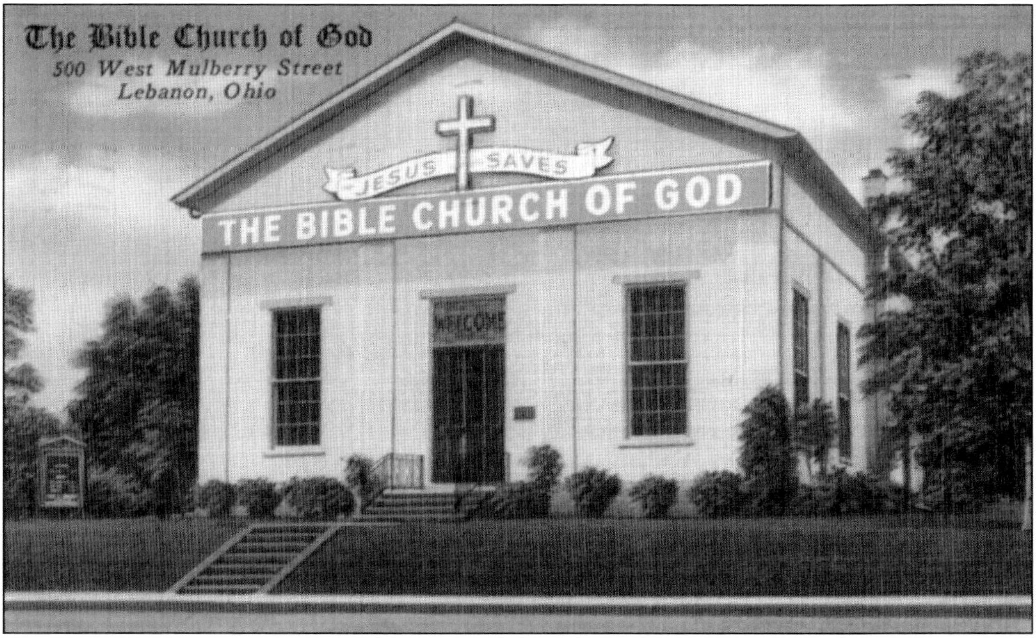

This postcard image of the Bible Church of God illustrates perhaps Lebanon's only church with a neon sign. Located on West Mulberry Street, for decades it was home to the ministry of Rev. Kash Amburgey. The 1940s building is still standing and home to the Possibilities Church. (Courtesy of the Sally Foster collection.)

This postcard interior view of the Main Street Presbyterian Church illustrates the original sanctuary before numerous 20th-century renovations. The interior, with its massive organ on the altar and semicircular arches, shows the Romanesque theme was carried out in the church as well as on the outside. Also of particular note is the theater-style seating as opposed to traditional church pews. (Courtesy of the Sally Foster collection.)

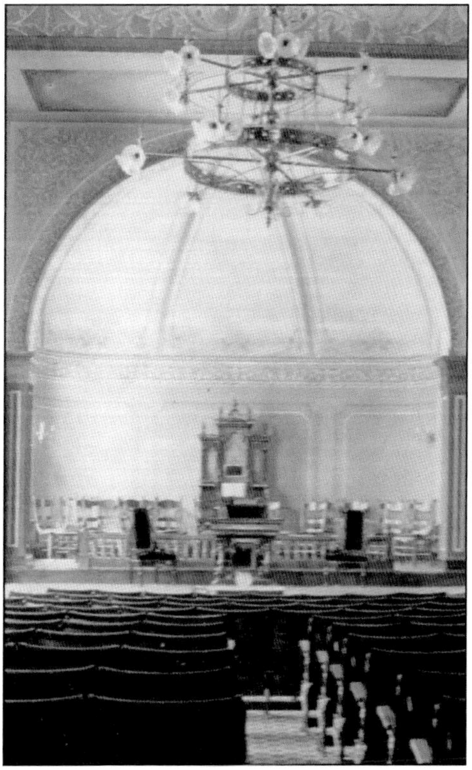

This early image is of Union School, the first public schoolhouse built in Lebanon, Ohio. Prior to Union School, classes had been held in basements of several local churches. In 1847, taxpayers voted a levy, which would provide $7,000 for the construction of what would become Union School. Seven years later, an additional school was built, just a short distance from Union School, for African American children. African Union School would remain in operation until around the turn of the century. In April 1862, a fire destroyed much of Union School, including its library. A new building was constructed on the same site. (Courtesy of WCHS Museum.)

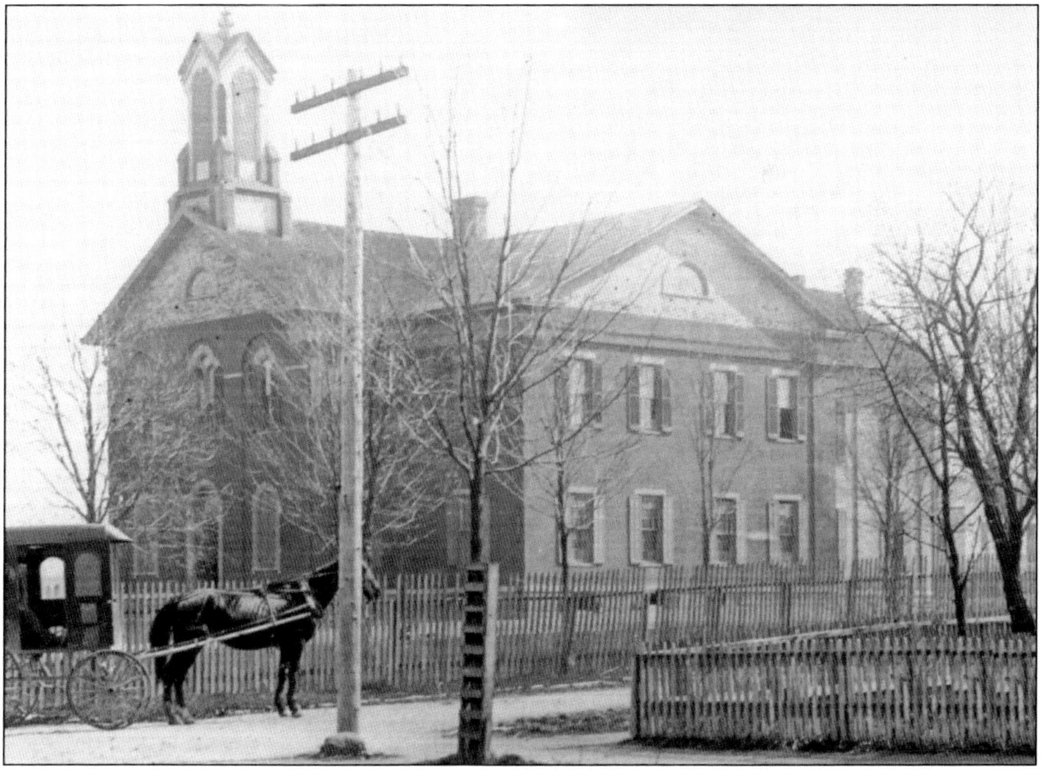

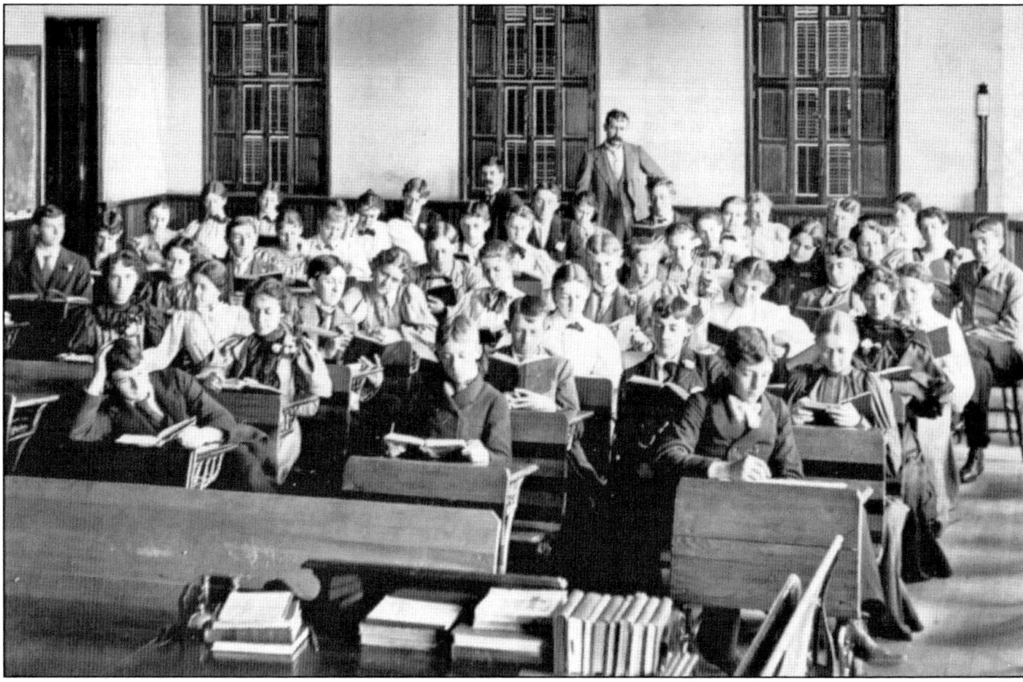

This 1880s image of a classroom in Union School illustrates the need for a larger facility for Lebanon's growing student population. In this classroom, 44 students are under the watchful eye of one stern teacher. (Courtesy of WCHS Museum.)

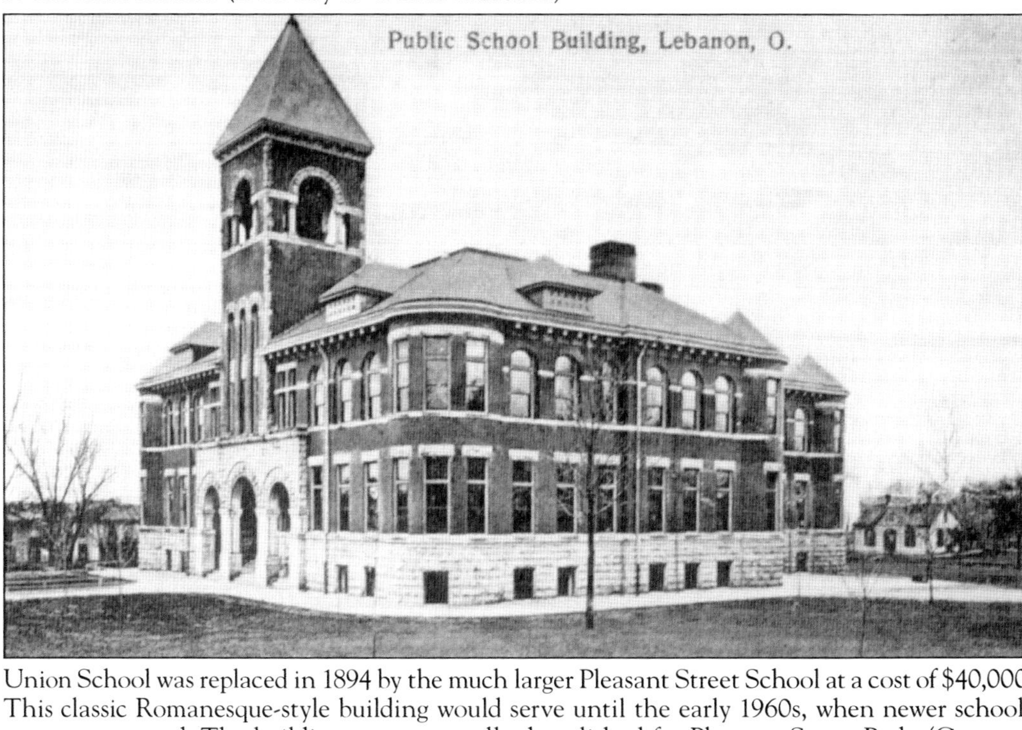

Union School was replaced in 1894 by the much larger Pleasant Street School at a cost of $40,000. This classic Romanesque-style building would serve until the early 1960s, when newer schools were constructed. The building was eventually demolished for Pleasant Street Park. (Courtesy of the Sally Foster collection.)

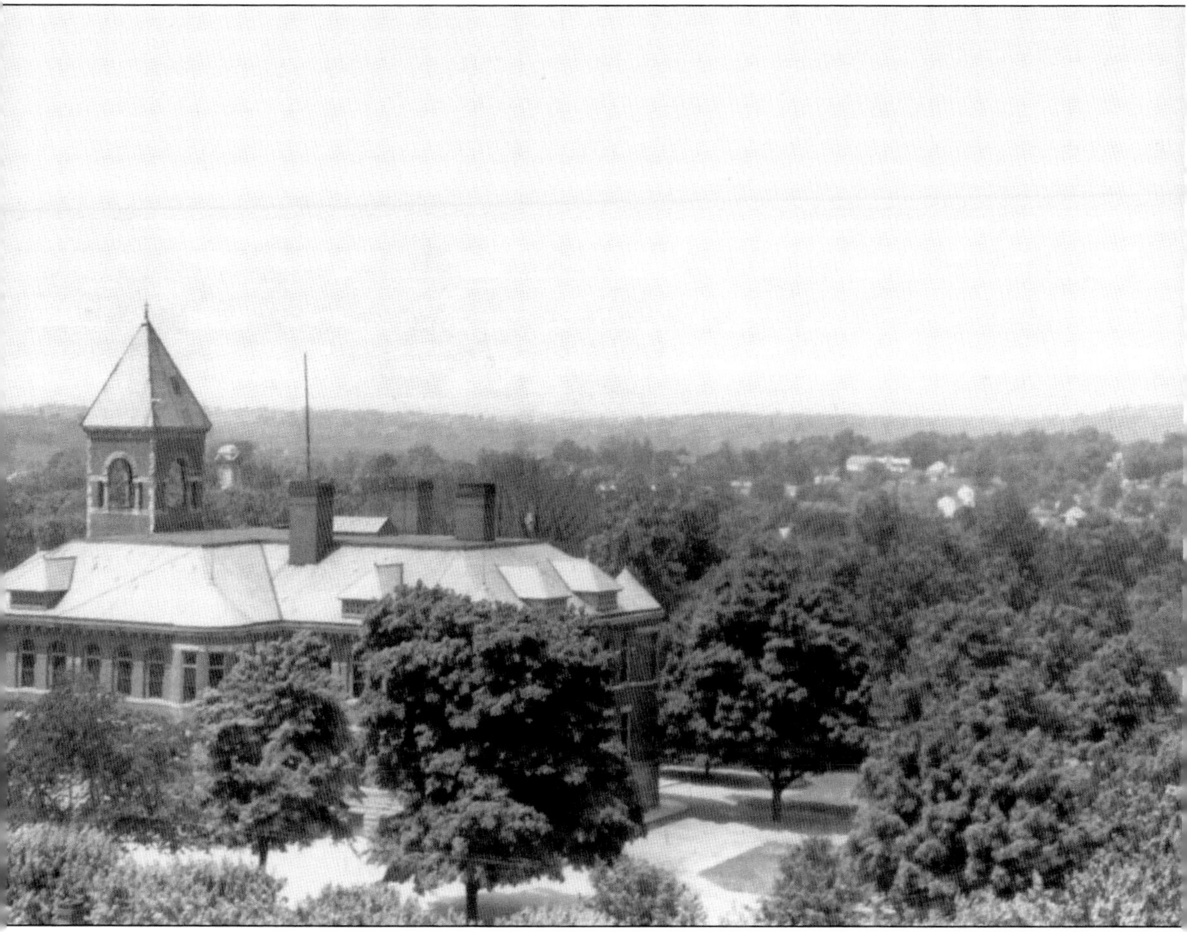

This bird's-eye view of Pleasant Street School illustrates the sheer expanse of Lebanon's then newest school building. This photograph was probably taken from the tower of the Presbyterian church on Silver Street. (Courtesy of WCHS Museum.)

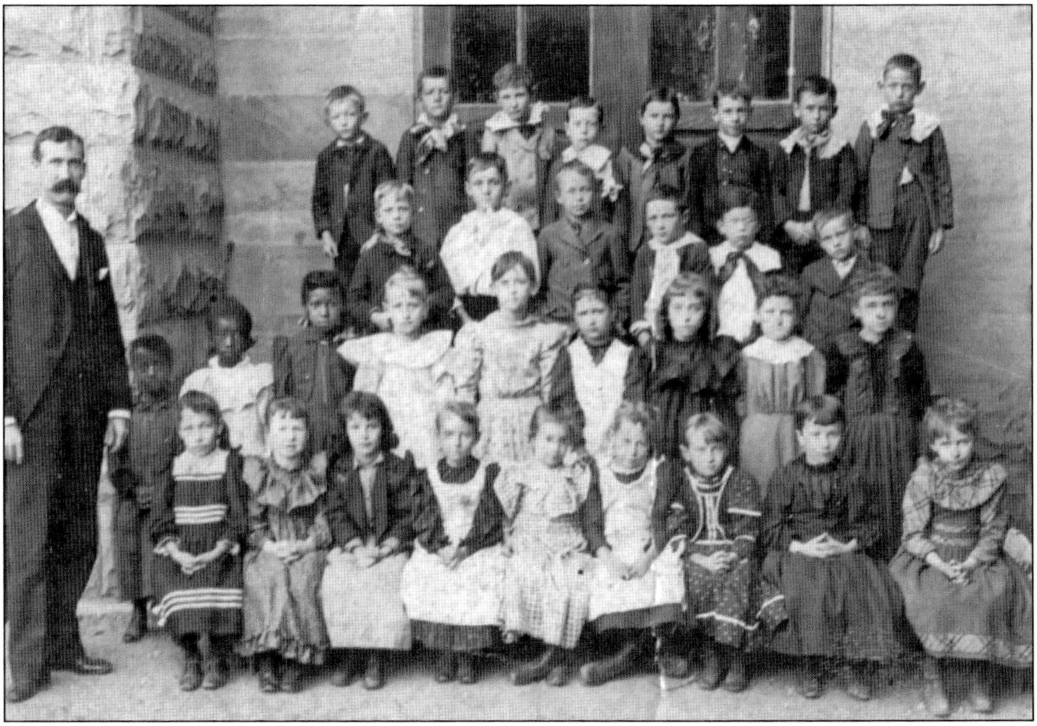

This 1860s photograph was taken outside of Union School. It shows an integrated group of students despite the fact that African Union School was in operation at the time. (Courtesy of WCHS Museum.)

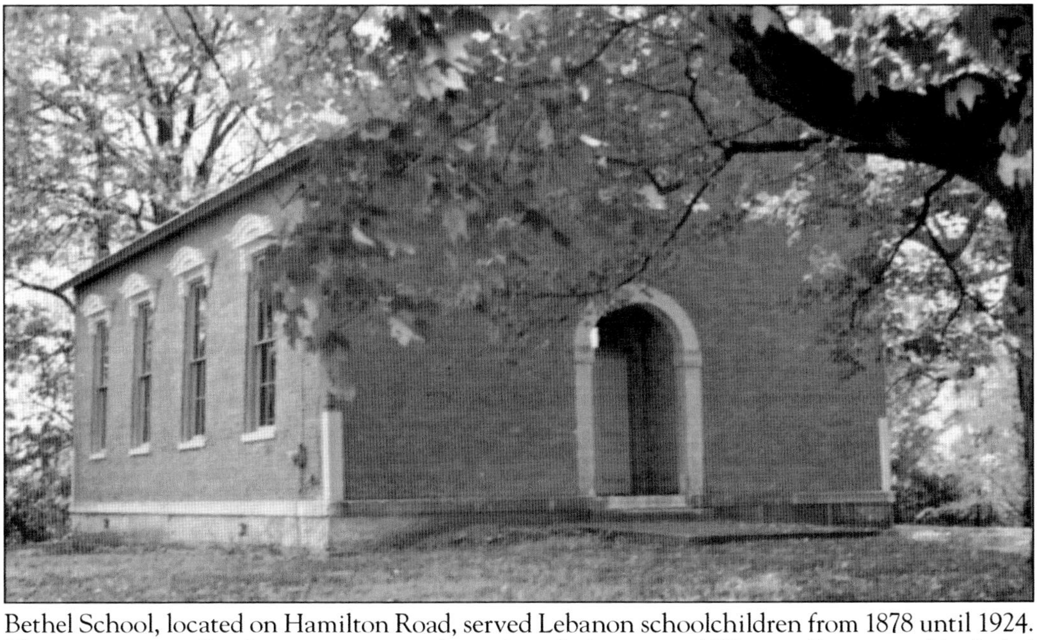

Bethel School, located on Hamilton Road, served Lebanon schoolchildren from 1878 until 1924. These one-room schools were common throughout Lebanon and Warren County and included not only Bethel School, but also Shaker Hill School, Hart School, and Utica School. (Courtesy of WCHS Museum.)

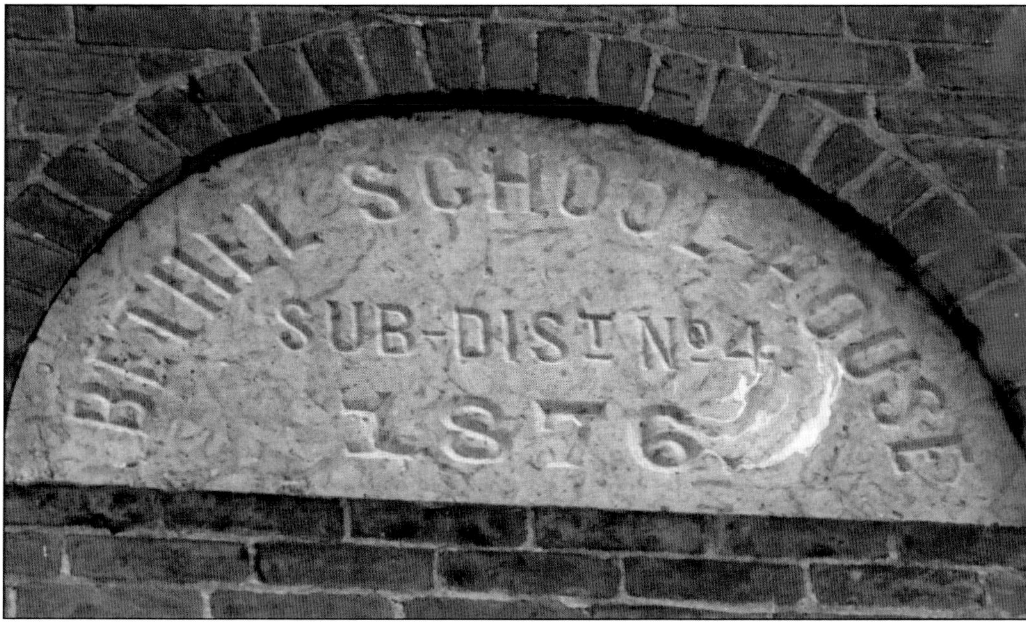

This detail photograph of Bethel School shows the inset plaque commemorating the date of 1874, the year the school was built. After closing in 1924, the school sat vacant for decades. Late in the 20th century, the building was purchased by local resident Russell Horn and restored. (Courtesy of WCHS Museum.)

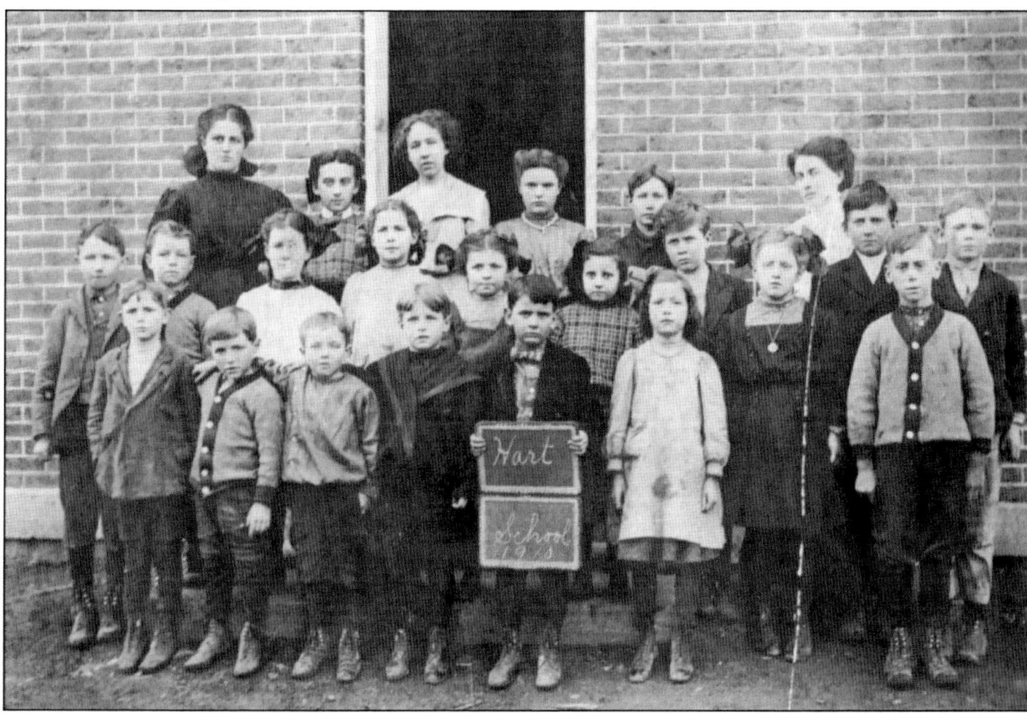

This 1910 image of schoolchildren was taken outside of Hart School, which was northwest of downtown Lebanon. This building, which is still standing, is owned privately, has not been restored, and is unused. (Courtesy of WCHS Museum.)

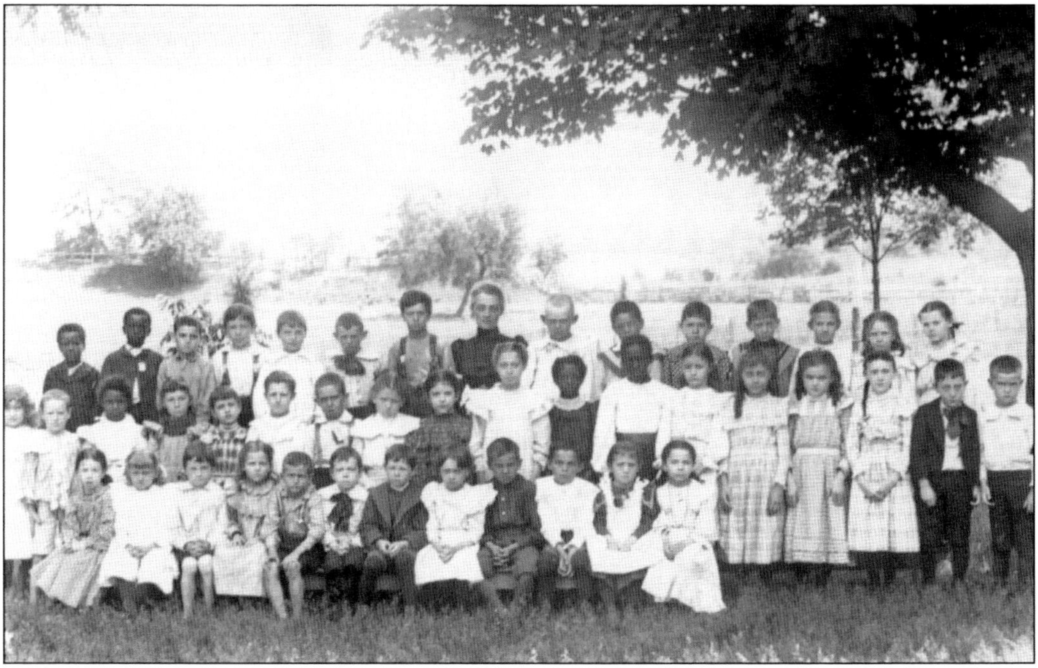

This 1890s image of an unidentified group of schoolchildren once again shows the early integration of classes in the Lebanon school system. Due to the sheer number of students and varying age ranges, it must be assumed these children attended one of the many one-room schools scattered throughout the area. (Courtesy of WCHS Museum.)

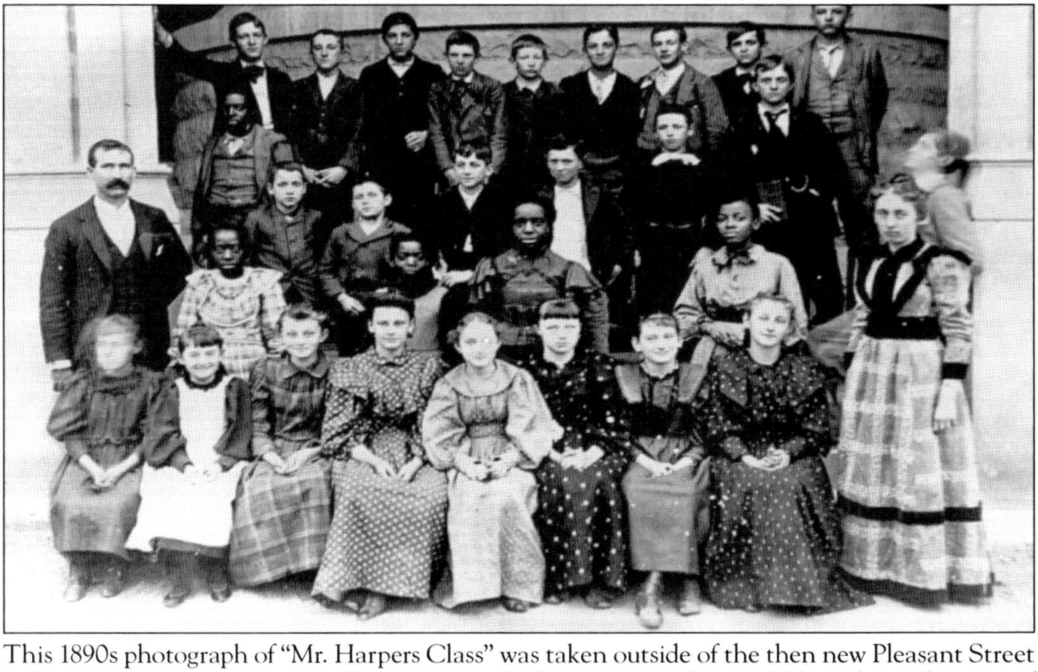

This 1890s photograph of "Mr. Harpers Class" was taken outside of the then new Pleasant Street School. Since the students are all approximately the same age, this would have been the start of Lebanon's school system dividing classes by age groups as opposed to teaching all students together in one room. (Courtesy of WCHS Museum.)

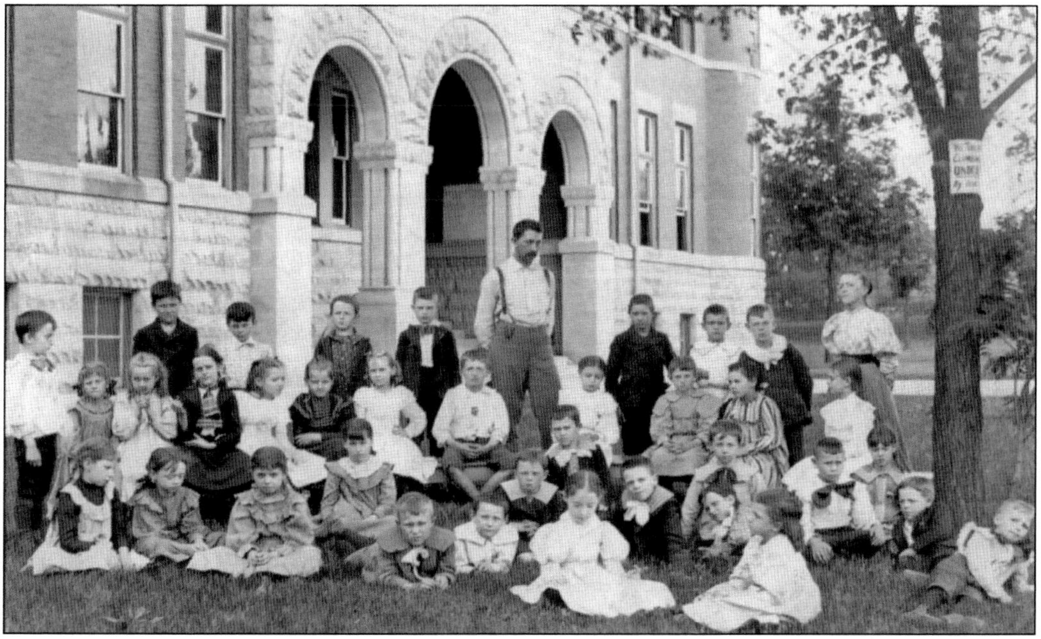

This image is of another group of younger students, again with Mr. Harper, taken outside of Pleasant Street School. The school was the third and last educational building constructed on this site: the first in 1854, the second in 1862, and this school in 1893. (Courtesy of WCHS Museum.)

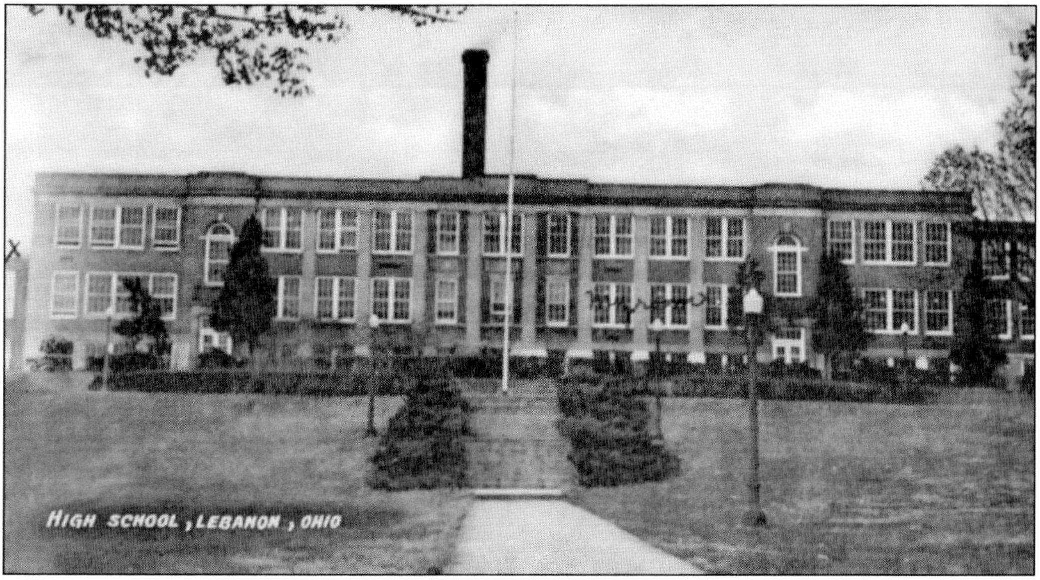

What is now Lucille Berry Middle School was originally Lebanon's first dedicated high school. In 1917, the Lebanon Board of Education purchased the old Maple Farm Hotel property on North Broadway Street with every intention of building a new high school. The 17-acre location, close to downtown, had ample room for not only a building but athletic fields as well. The United States involvement in World War I delayed construction for approximately 10 years. In 1928, the board set aside $250,000 for construction of the new school. In September 1930, the first formal Lebanon High School was opened to students. This school was featured prominently in the movie *Harper Valley PTA*, which was filmed in Lebanon in 1978. (Courtesy of WCHS Museum.)

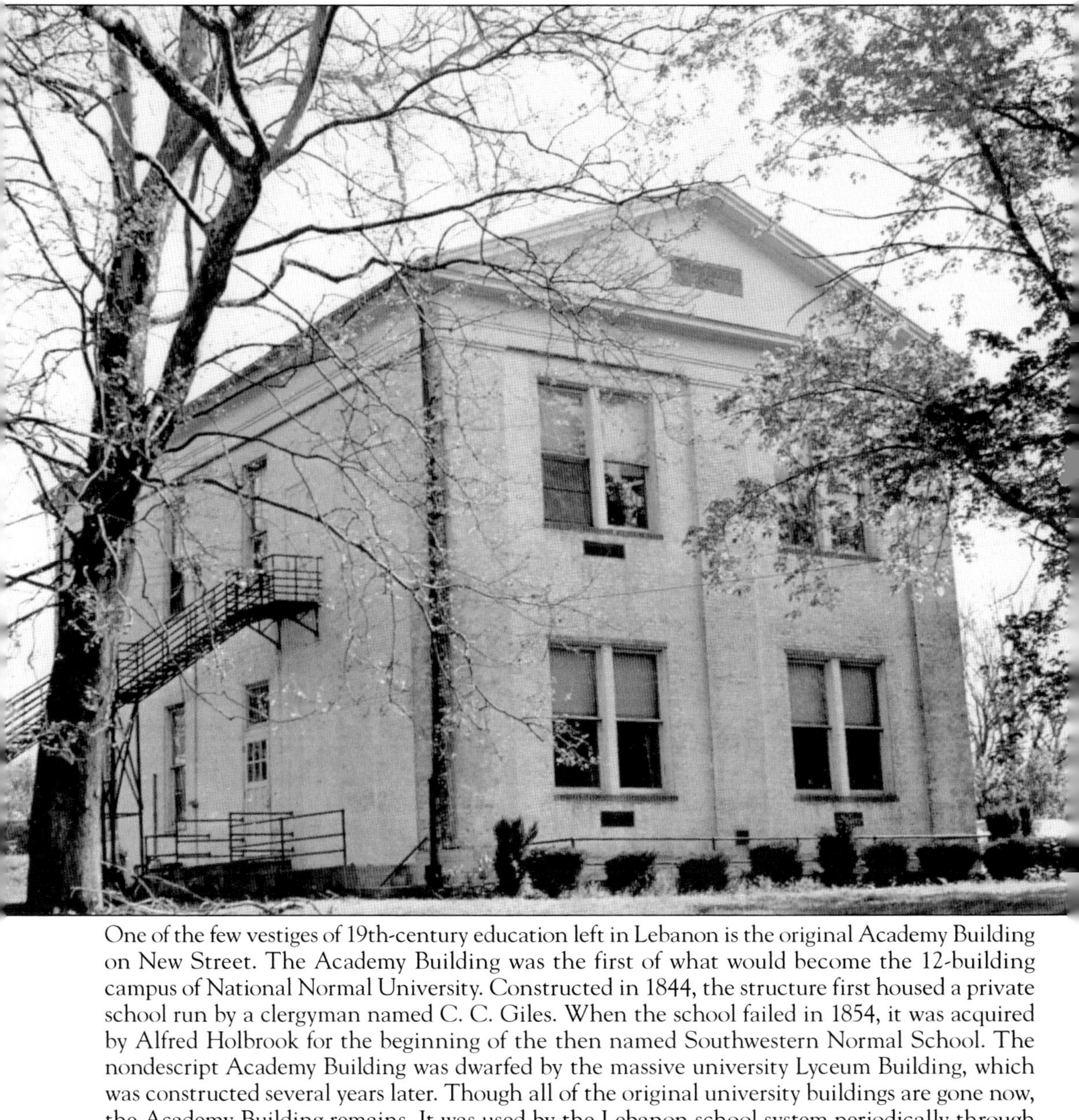

One of the few vestiges of 19th-century education left in Lebanon is the original Academy Building on New Street. The Academy Building was the first of what would become the 12-building campus of National Normal University. Constructed in 1844, the structure first housed a private school run by a clergyman named C. C. Giles. When the school failed in 1854, it was acquired by Alfred Holbrook for the beginning of the then named Southwestern Normal School. The nondescript Academy Building was dwarfed by the massive university Lyceum Building, which was constructed several years later. Though all of the original university buildings are gone now, the Academy Building remains. It was used by the Lebanon school system periodically through the 1960s and now houses a local food pantry. (Courtesy of WCHS Museum.)

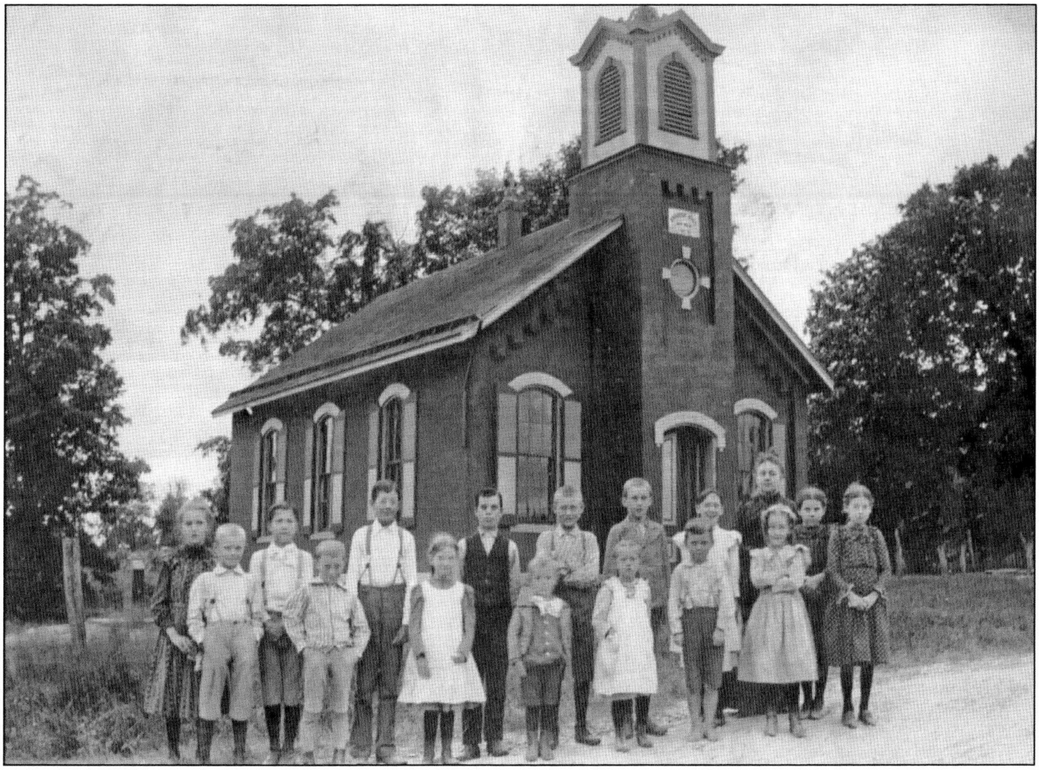

This 1880s image was taken near Shaker Hill School, just outside of Lebanon. Constructed in 1873, this was another of the one-room schoolhouses that dotted the countryside in Lebanon. It is interesting to note the wide range of ages of the students attending the same school, from what could be kindergarten up to high school age. (Courtesy of WCHS Museum.)

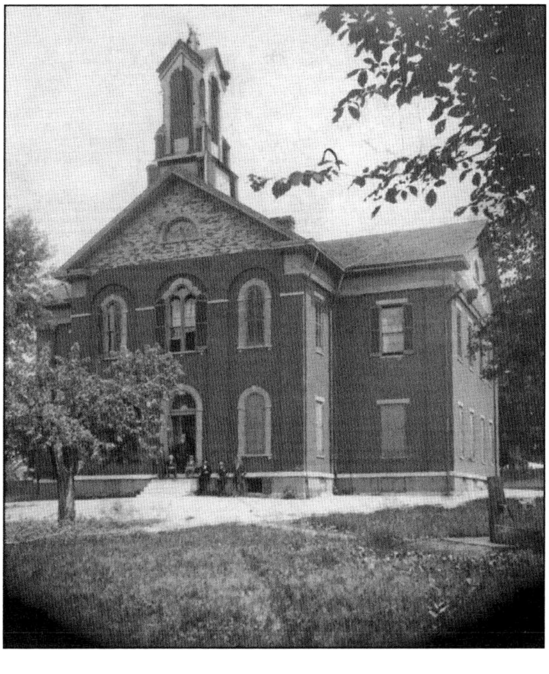

This photograph of Lebanon Union School was taken shortly before it was replaced by the Pleasant Street School in 1893, which was the second educational facility built on this site. Constructed around 1863, this school served Lebanon students until 1893. Pictured here from left to right are "Bud" Hinkle, Charles Eulass, J. F. Lukens, David Greeley, Dr. Frank Frost, Leonidas Simonton, and George Carey. (Courtesy of WCHS Museum.)

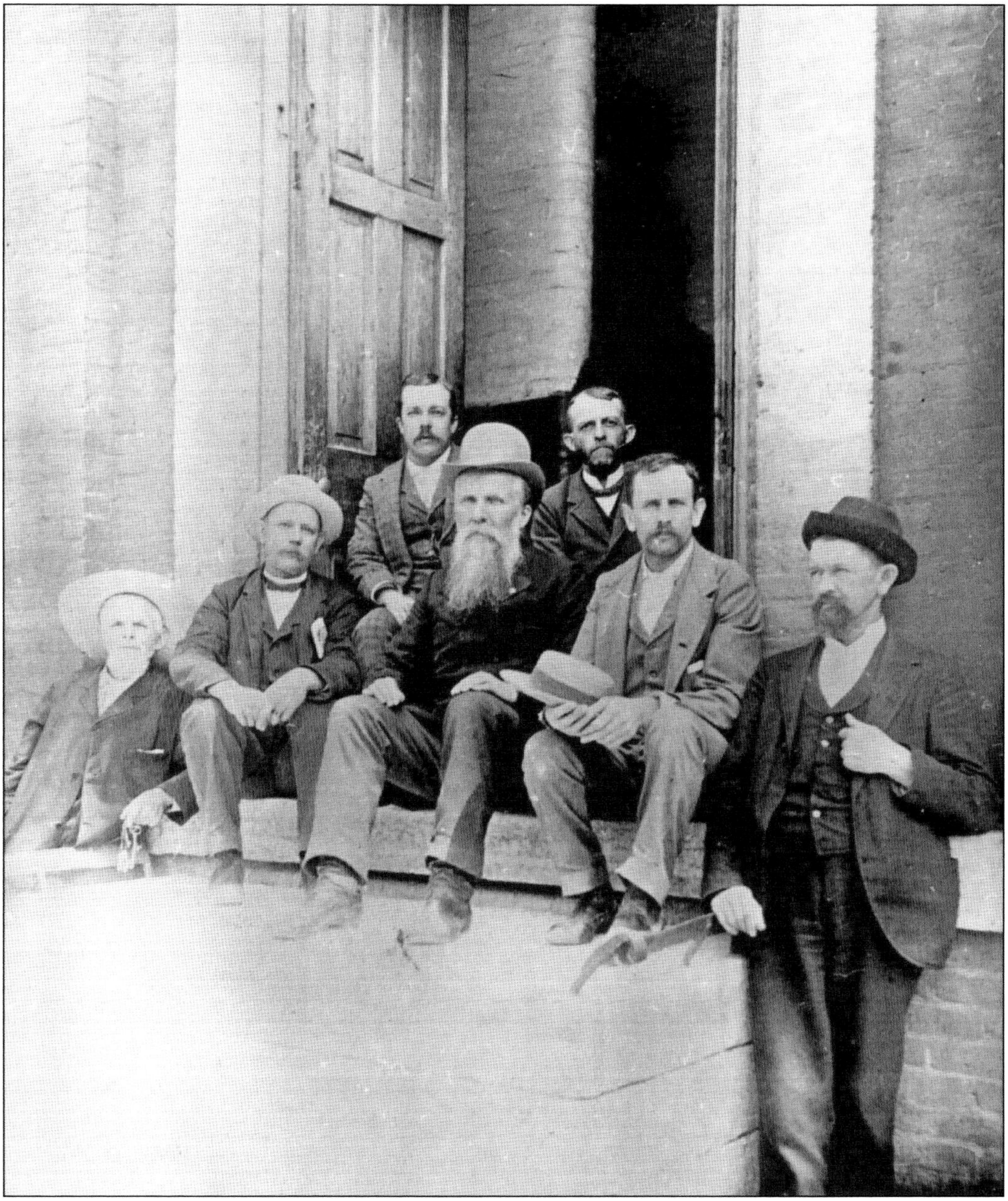

This late-1890s image shows the Lebanon School Board posing on the steps of the Union School. Pictured from left to right are (first row) janitor Bud Hinkle, Charles Eulass, superintendent of schools J. F. Lukens, David Greeley, and (standing) George Carey; (second row) Dr. Frank Frost and Leonidas Simonton. (Courtesy of WCHS Museum.)

Nine

From the Mexican War to Modern Living
Lebanon's Famous Residents

Many visitors to Lebanon question the lack of monuments in such a historic town. Where are the statues and the plaques honoring the accomplishments and triumphs of 19th- and early-20th-century citizens who left their mark on the town and its history?

Citizens will quickly respond that the monuments are there but not in the form of a resting place for pigeons or a brass plaque that has to be polished and maintained. The monuments for the accomplishments of Lebanon's citizens are living monuments that benefit the lives of local citizens every day.

Noted philanthropist and Lebanon resident William Harmon once said, "I have a very deep conviction that one owes something to the place of his nativity. One should not lay out expenditures for public ends without taking into consideration the needs of his birthplace." Even though Harmon died in 1928, the Harmon Civic Trust that he established in the early 1900s still meets once a month to "take into consideration" the needs of Lebanon.

Other notable Lebanon citizens such as John McClean have their monuments not in the form of statues but in a local weekly newspaper, the *Western Star*, that has been published continuously since 1807. Alfred Holbrook, Louisa Jurey Wright, and Lucille Blackburn Berry have their monuments in the generations of schoolchildren that have benefited from the educational standards they established.

Lesser-known citizens such as Ichabod Corwin, Ephraim Hathaway, Silas Hurin, and Samuel Manning have their monuments in Lebanon's "Four Corners," which form a city square at the intersection of Broadway and Main Streets. In the early 19th century, shortly after Lebanon was founded, these four citizens donated the lots "to be used only for the public good." Two of the corners house public parks, one corner the city building, and the other corner is anchored by one of the original Carnegie Libraries.

Lebanon's monuments are indeed there, just not in the usual sense. The institutions, organizations, and values put in place by citizens well over a century ago serve as much better monuments than any statue or plaque.

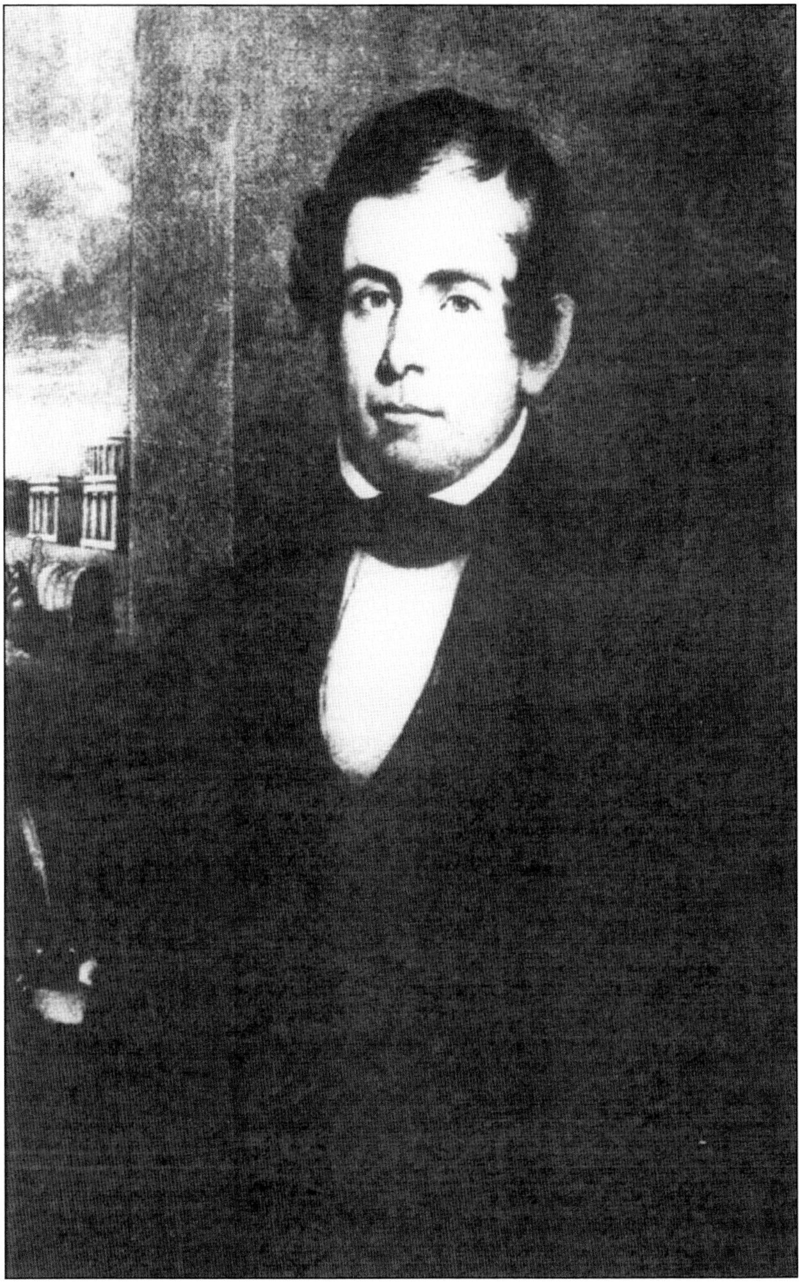

Perhaps Lebanon's most well-known 19th-century resident was Thomas Corwin. Born in Bourbon County, Kentucky, in 1794, Corwin's family came to Lebanon in 1798. According to one story, Thomas was familiar with the entire alphabet and its function by age four. Corwin began studying law in 1814, and by 1818 he was the prosecuting attorney for Warren County. Beginning in 1821, his political career would take him to the governor's mansion, the U.S. House of Representatives, and the U.S. Senate. Corwin's 1847 speech speaking out against the Mexican War is still regarded as one of the greatest ever given on the floor of the Senate. Corwin was secretary of the treasury under Millard Fillmore and ambassador to Mexico under Abraham Lincoln. (Courtesy of WCHS Museum.)

This bust of Gov. Thomas Corwin is part of the collection of the Warren County Historical Society. Sculpted by Thomas Dow Jones sometime in the 19th century, Corwin is represented in the Grecian style—an homage to his well-known oratory skills. (Courtesy of WCHS Museum.)

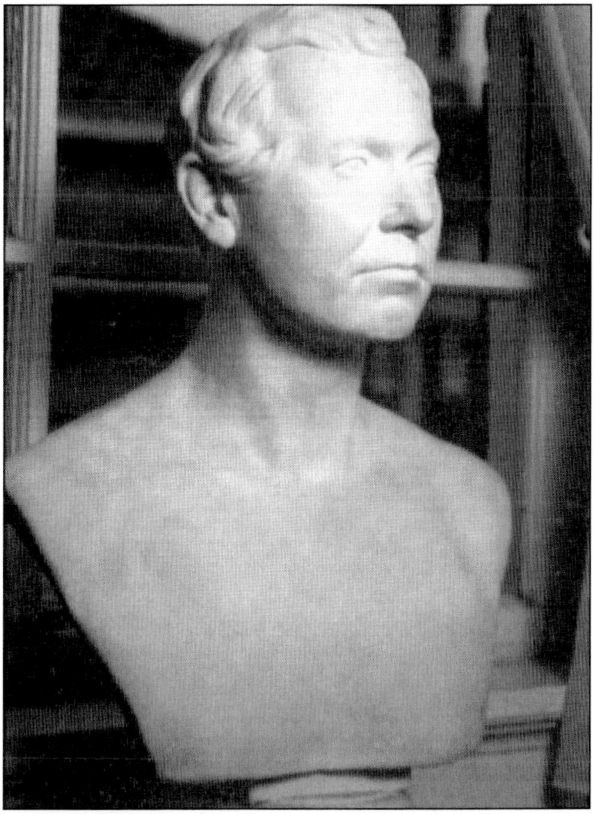

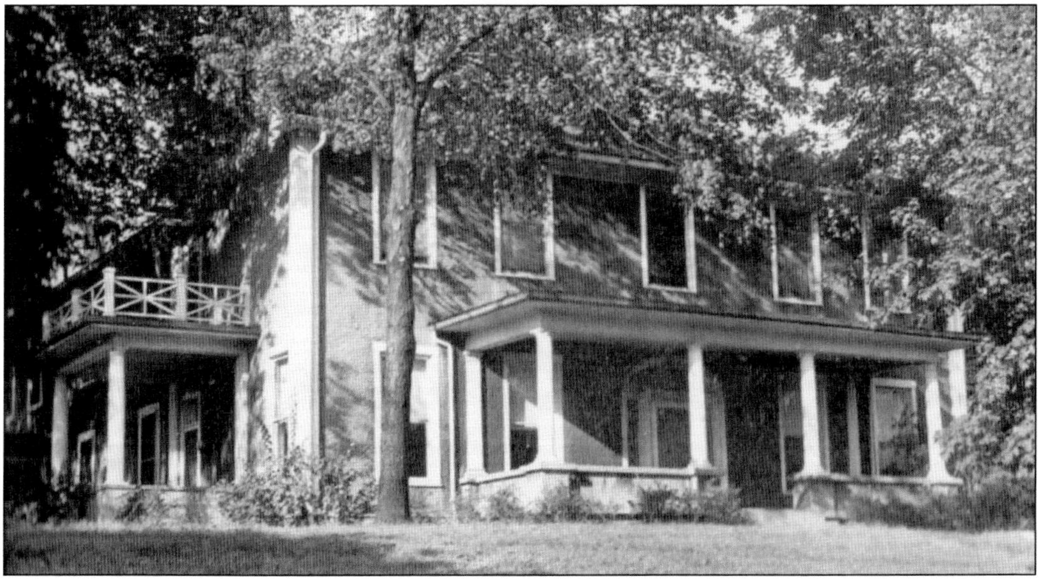

This photograph of the Thomas Corwin home on West Main Street was probably taken in the late 1960s or early 1970s. The home unfortunately was not maintained or restored, with much of the original woodwork stripped out when the building was converted into apartments. It was extensively remodeled in the late 20th century and is now used as an office building. (Courtesy of WCHS Museum.)

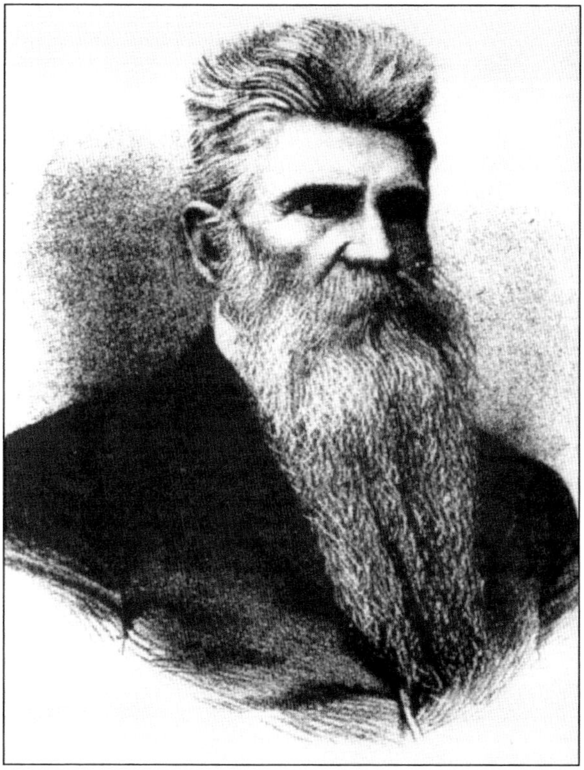

Andrew Graham McBurney came to Lebanon in 1830 as a cabinetmaker. In 1840, he began his study of law and was admitted to the bar in 1843. McBurney went on to become state senator for two terms and lieutenant governor of Ohio from 1866 to 1868. His family owned McBurney Farms, which would later become a large Lebanon residential development called McBurney Hills. (Courtesy of WCHS Museum.)

This 1920s photograph of "Belles and Bows," a local theatrical troop, was taken in the home of Andrew McBurney. The home, which stood on the corner of Broadway Street and Orchard Avenue, had 22-foot ceilings and a center hall with a freestanding staircase. Notable in the photograph is the portrait of McBurney that appears at left. (Courtesy of WCHS Museum.)

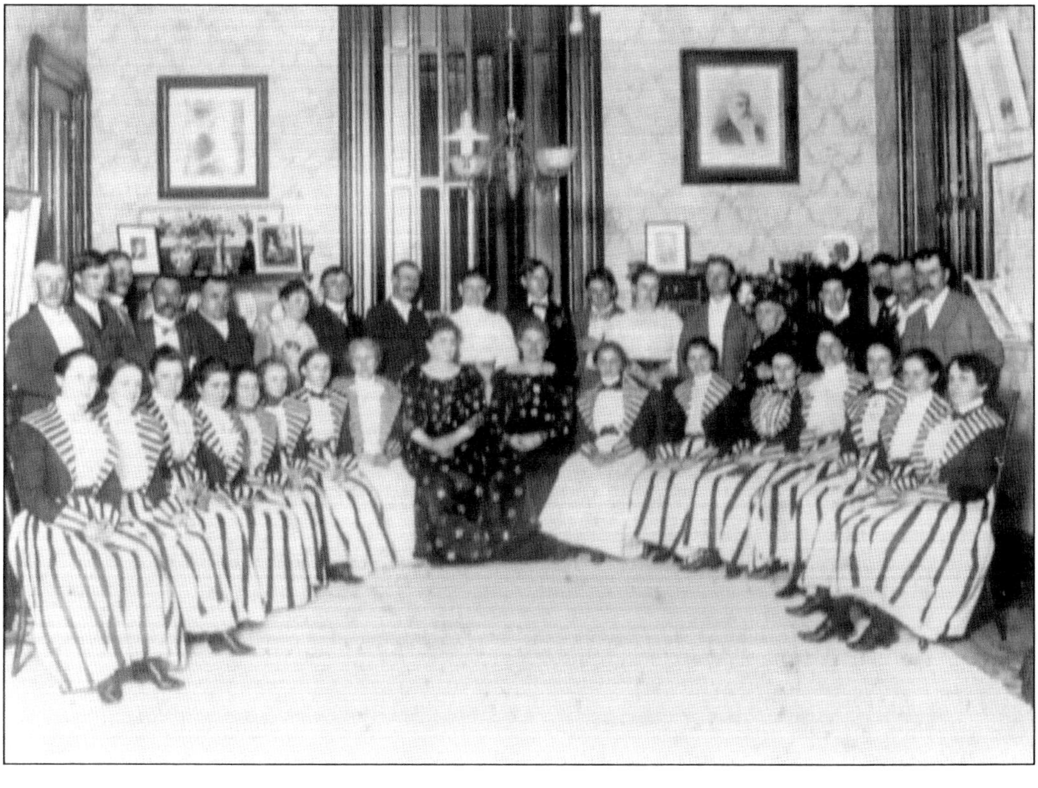

Ormsby McKnight Mitchel was a distinguished military hero and an astronomer. Mitchel graduated from West Point in 1829 and taught at the school for a number of years. He resigned from the army in the late 1830s, only to be recalled to serve in the Civil War where he was given the rank of major general. Mitchel also helped found the first Naval Observatory and later the Cincinnati Observatory. (Courtesy of WCHS Museum.)

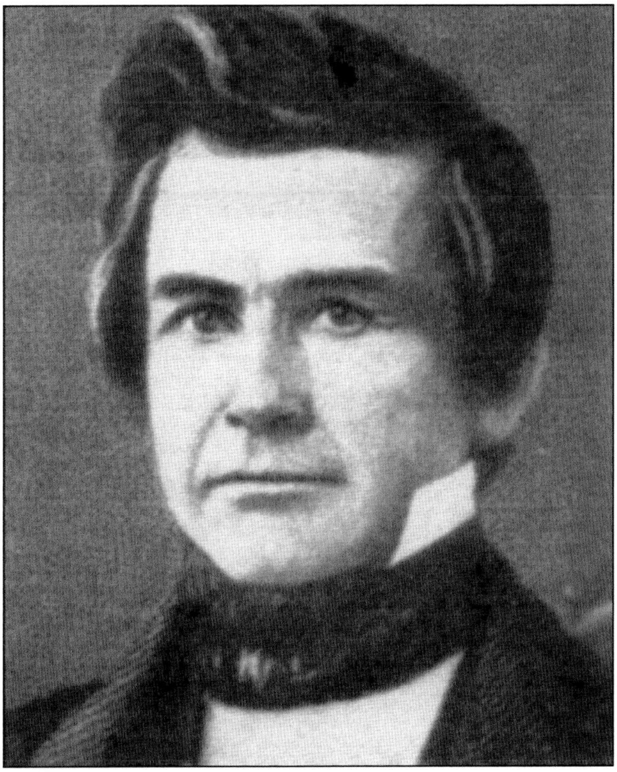

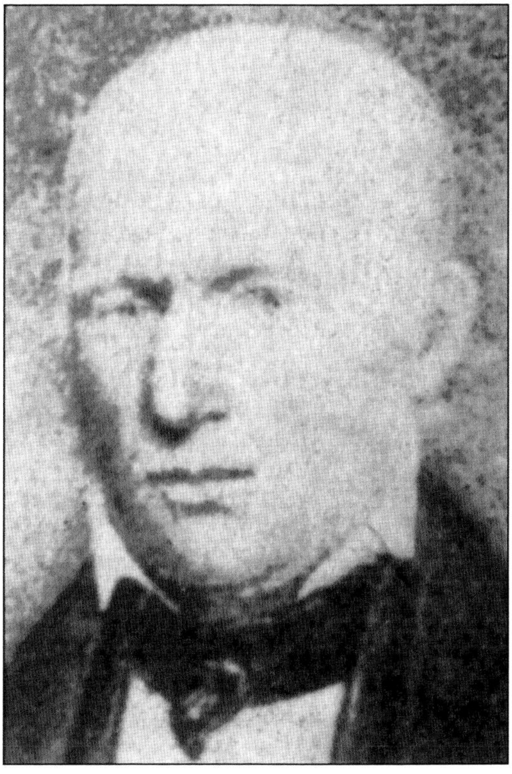

Ichabod Corwin has been called Lebanon's first citizen. In 1796, Corwin cleared 12 acres of land and built a cabin on the site of what is now Lucille Berry Middle School on North Broadway Street. Corwin would later build a two-story cabin on North Broadway in town, which would eventually become Lebanon's famous Black Horse Tavern. Corwin's daughter Lucinda was born on December 8, 1800, and was the second child born in the future village of Lebanon. (Courtesy of WCHS Museum.)

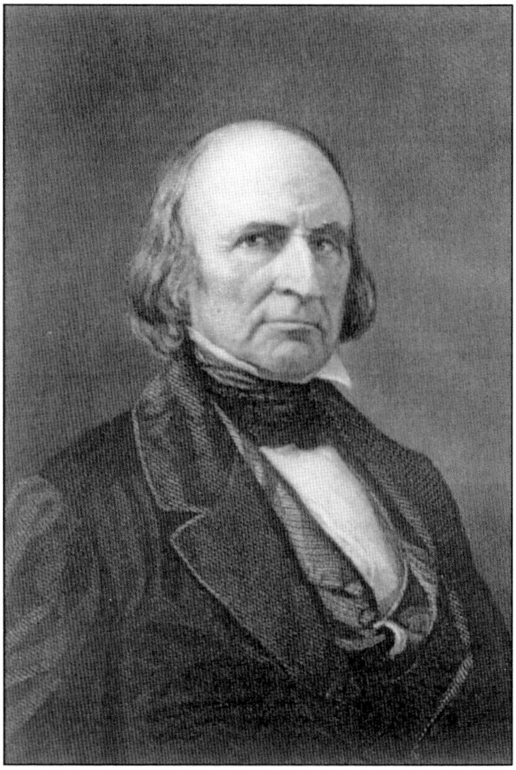

In 1807, Lebanon resident John McLean began publishing the *Western Star*, which at the time was the oldest continuous weekly newspaper west of the Allegheny Mountains. The newspaper still appears every Thursday on Lebanon doorsteps. McLean also went on to become justice of the Ohio Supreme Court, postmaster general of the United States, and from 1829 until 1861 justice of the U.S. Supreme Court. (Courtesy of WCHS Museum)

Pictured here with his children, William Elmer Harmon is a name that appears throughout Lebanon. Born on Mechanic Street in 1862, Harmon went on to amass a fortune in real estate holdings and spent most of his life giving it away. The Harmon Civic Trust, established in the early 1900s, still meets monthly to dispense Harmon's benevolence. Harmon Hall (home of the Warren County Historical Society) and Lebanon's Harmon Park are but two of Harmon's lasting achievements. (Courtesy of WCHS Museum.)

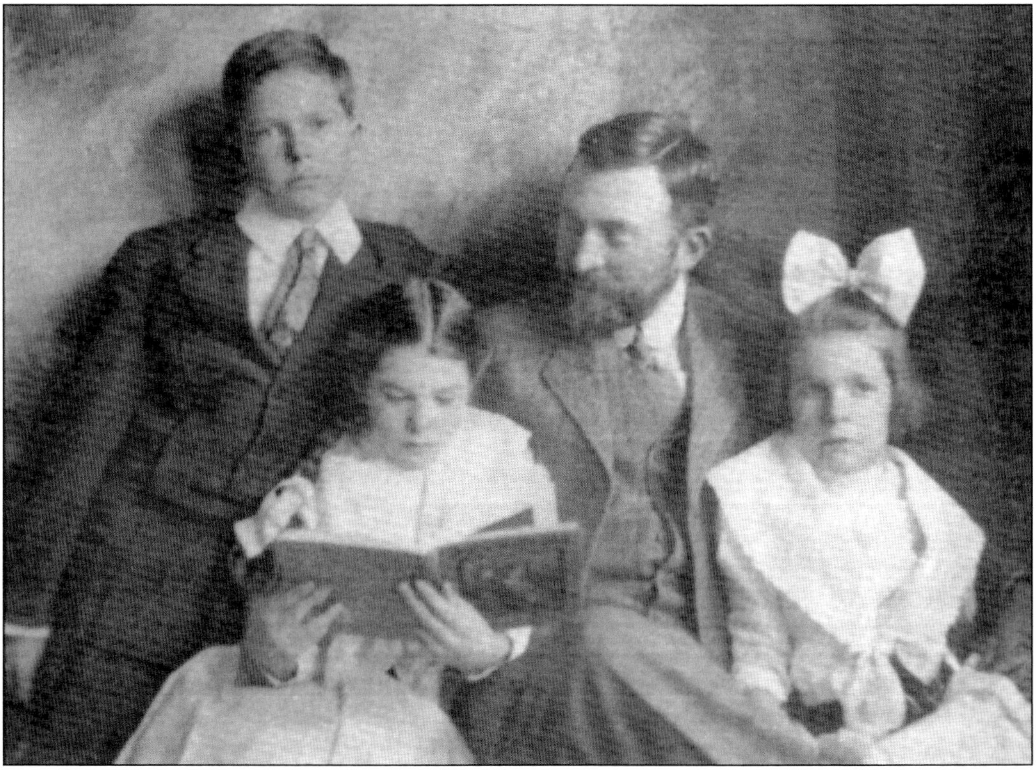

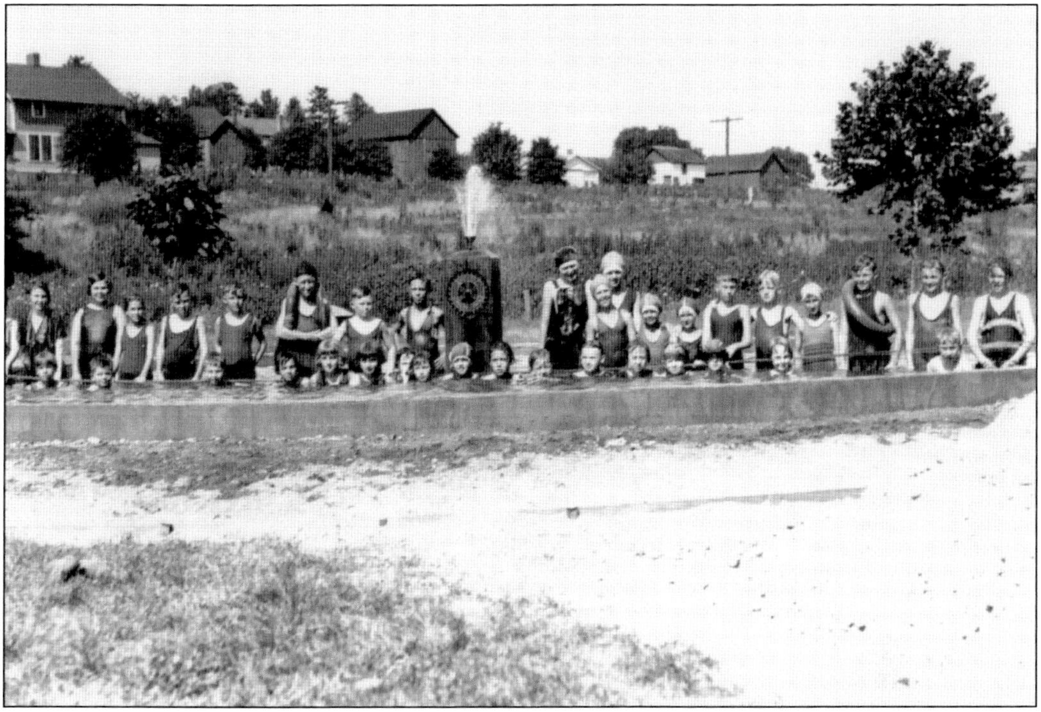

This *c.* 1915 image is of a small swimming pool in Harmon Park built by the Lebanon Rotary Club. The concrete pool, removed from the park decades ago, was a constant reminder Harmon said of "the old swimming hole" he had enjoyed in Lebanon as a youth. (Courtesy of WCHS Museum.)

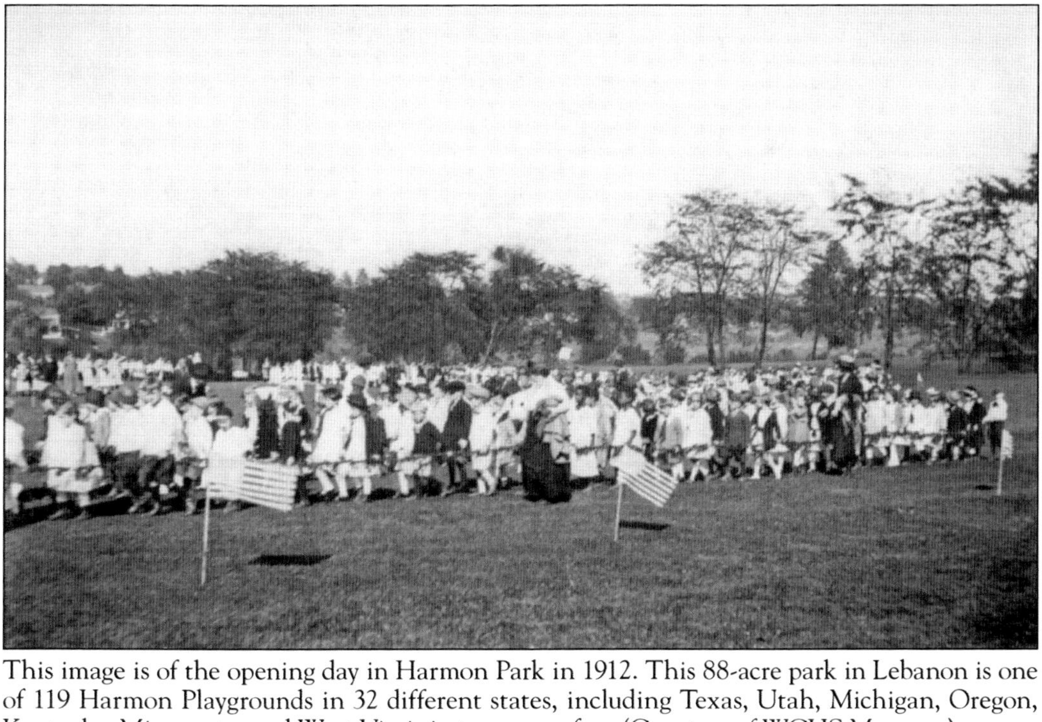

This image is of the opening day in Harmon Park in 1912. This 88-acre park in Lebanon is one of 119 Harmon Playgrounds in 32 different states, including Texas, Utah, Michigan, Oregon, Kentucky, Minnesota, and West Virginia to name a few. (Courtesy of WCHS Museum.)

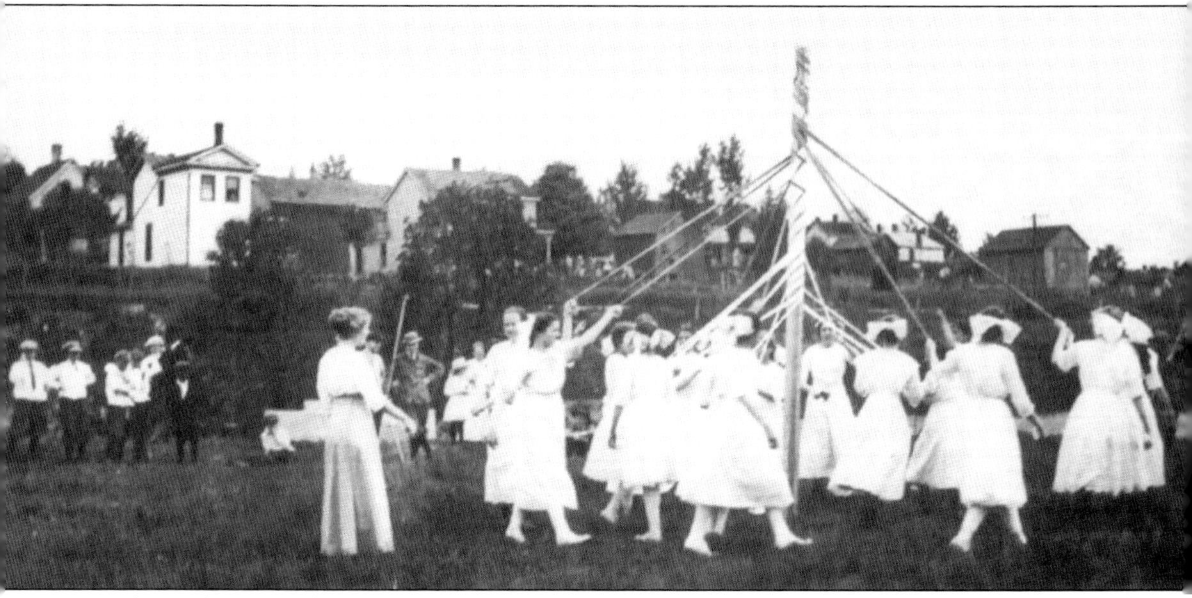

This early image shows a group of students doing a maypole dance in Harmon Park. Maypole dancing was popular in the United States for about 75 years beginning around 1850. The students pictured here are doing the less traditional form of dancing by merely circling the pole while holding onto a ribbon. (Courtesy of WCHS Museum.)

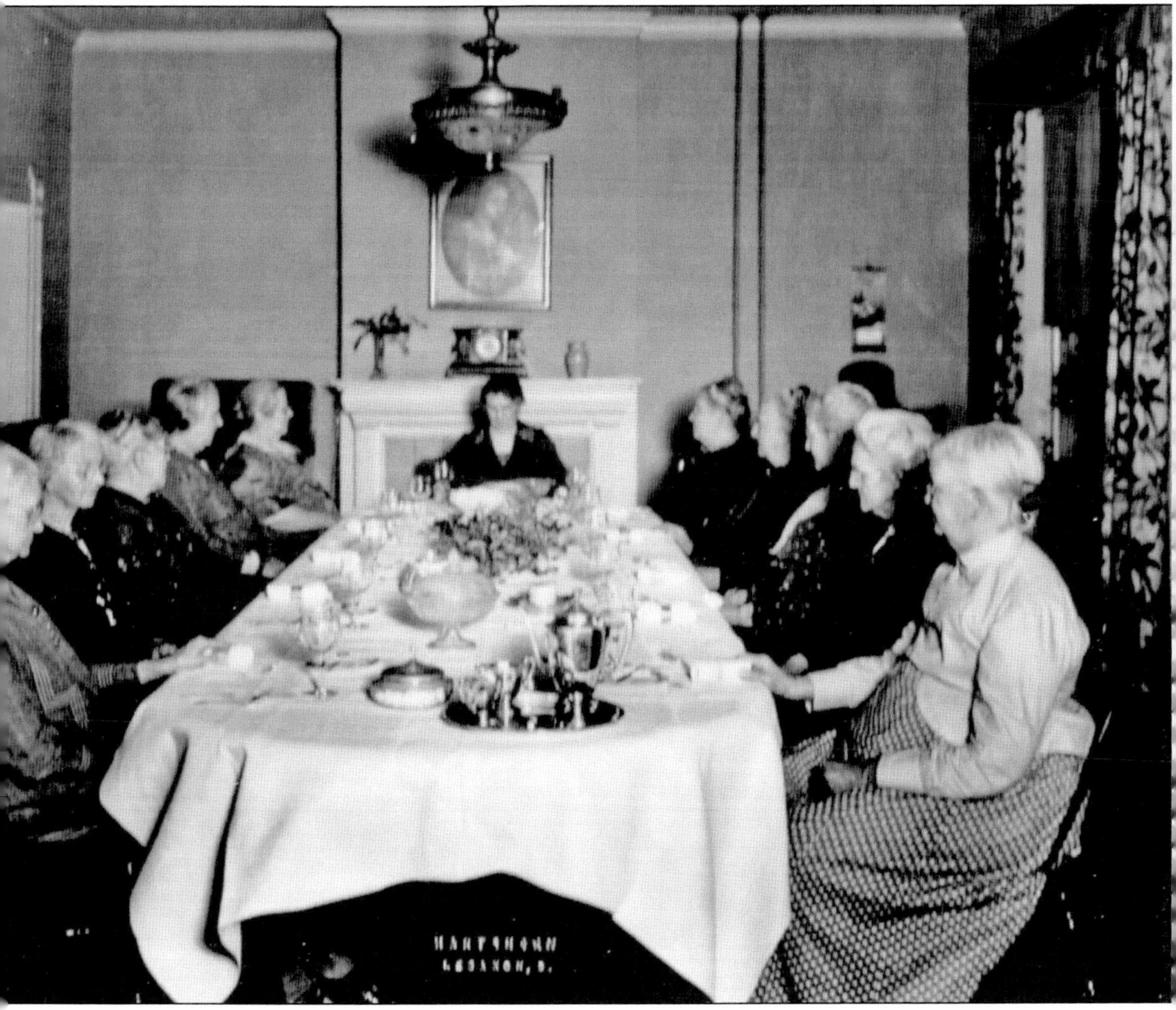

The Molly Harmon Home for Aged Gentlefolk was another monument to Harmon's generosity to, as he called it, "his place of nativity." Named after his mother, this spacious brick home was put under the control of the Harmon Civic Trust. The project preceded modern retirement homes by decades. The home was sold after it was no longer practical to be operated for its original purpose. (Courtesy of WCHS Museum.)

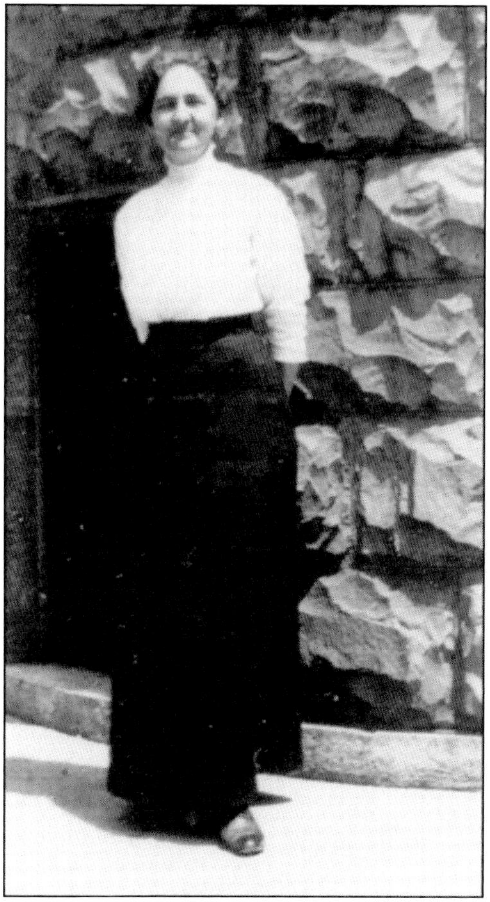

Lucille Blackburn Berry, born in 1872, was a graduate of National Normal University. She spent almost 50 years educating Lebanon students. First teaching at Pleasant Street School, where this photograph was taken, in 1930 she moved to the newly constructed Lebanon High School on Broadway Street. Lucille Berry spent the last 12 years of her teaching career there. In 1963, at age 91, she was present when the school was renamed Lucille Berry Junior High School in her honor. (Courtesy of WCHS Museum.)

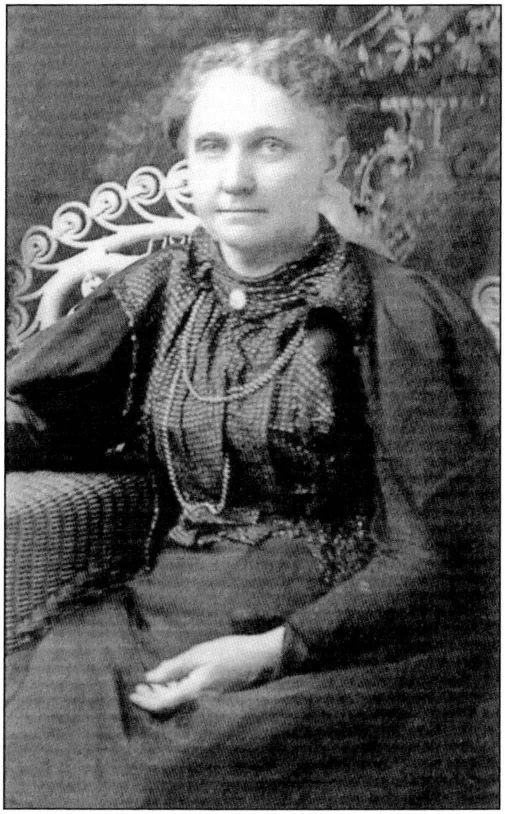

Another graduate of Southwestern Normal School, Louisa Jurey Wright holds the distinction of being the first female school superintendent in Lebanon's history. Louisa had been a teacher at Lebanon Union School and had been married only a few months when she was appointed superintendent in the fall of 1867. Under her leadership, the Lebanon school system had its first high school graduates. There were three members, and all of them were female. (Courtesy of WCHS Museum.)

Lebanon resident Russel Wright, born in 1904, went on to become one of the foremost industrial designers in America and the first to popularize the modern and informal lifestyle in design. Wright attended the Art Academy of Cincinnati while still in high school and studied at the Columbia School of Architecture and the New York University School of Architecture. Wright was credited as most responsible for the shift toward modern design in the 1930s. (Courtesy of WCHS Museum.)

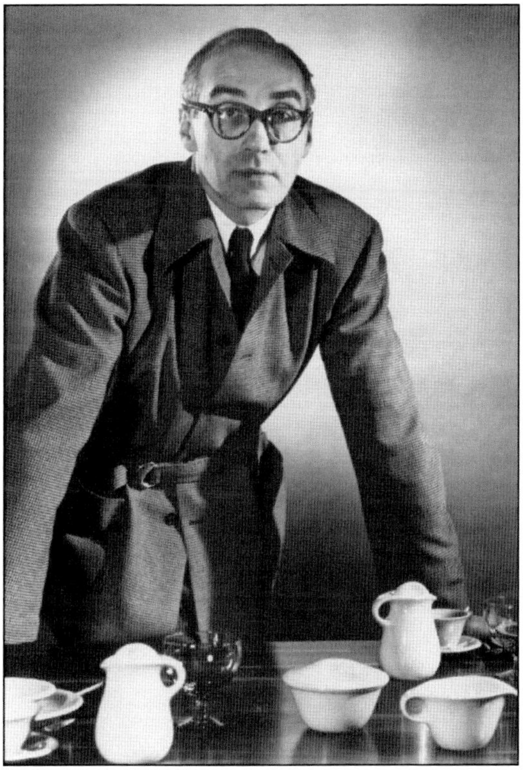

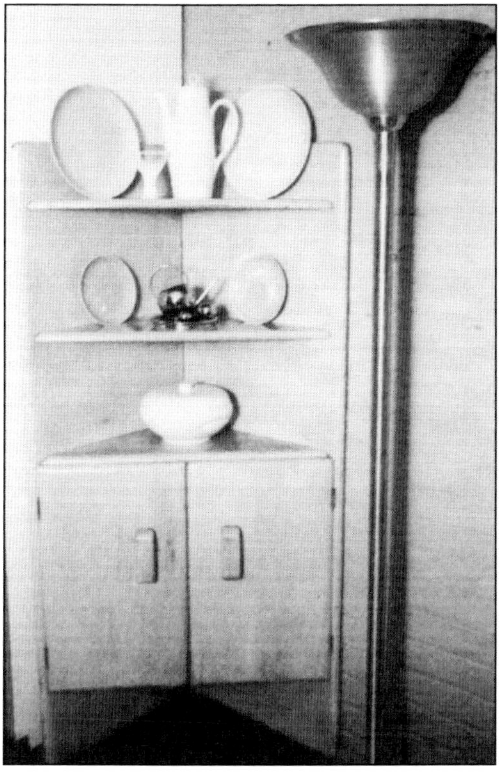

This image, part of the Russel Wright collection at the Warren County Historical Society, shows Wright's furniture line called American Modern that was introduced in 1935. The corner cabinet is made of solid maple and in a finish called "Blonde," a term coined by Russel Wright. The spun aluminum floor lamp is also an iconic Russel Wright design. (Courtesy of WCHS Museum.)

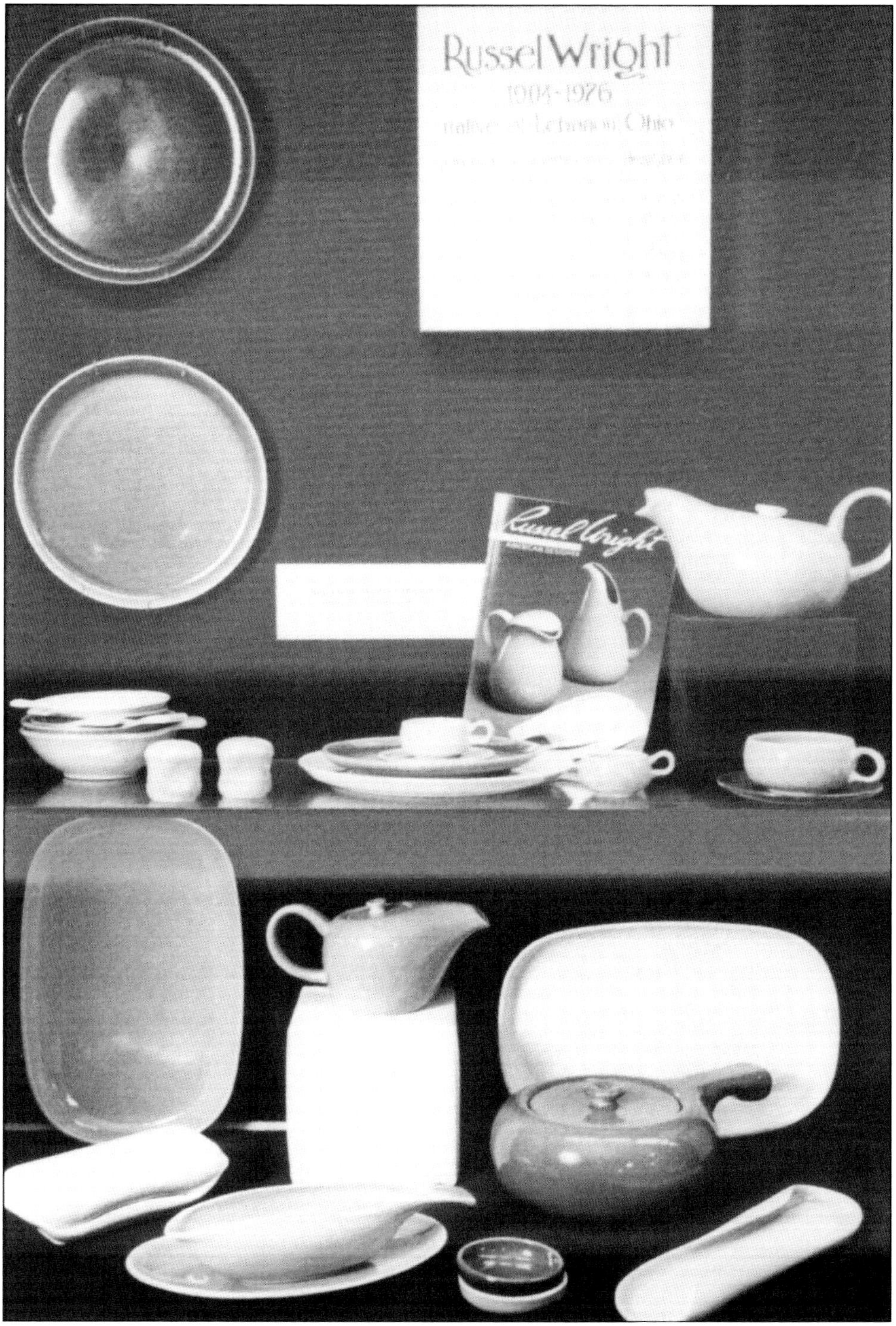

This image, more of the Russel Wright collection of the Warren County Historical Society, highlights Wright's modern and forward-thinking china designs. This collection, called American Modern Dinnerware, was manufactured in Steubenville, Ohio, from 1939 until 1959. (Courtesy of WCHS Museum.)

Lebanon resident Dr. Robert H. Blair, along with his brother Edward, established Blair Brothers Hospital in Lebanon in 1921 on the east side of Broadway Street between Main and Mulberry Streets. The tiny nine-room facility admitted patients from as far away as Dayton and Cincinnati. (Courtesy of WCHS Museum.)

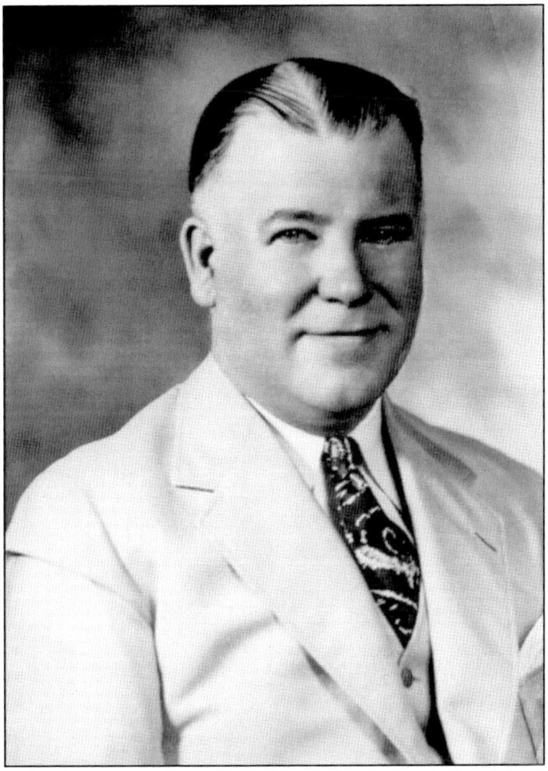

The Blair Brothers Hospital was located on the second floor of the building where the awnings are evident in this image. The hospital was the first in the county to have x-ray equipment and could accommodate as many as 15 patients. The hospital at one point had 13 newborns in residence. It closed in 1947 for economic reasons. (Courtesy of WCHS Museum.)

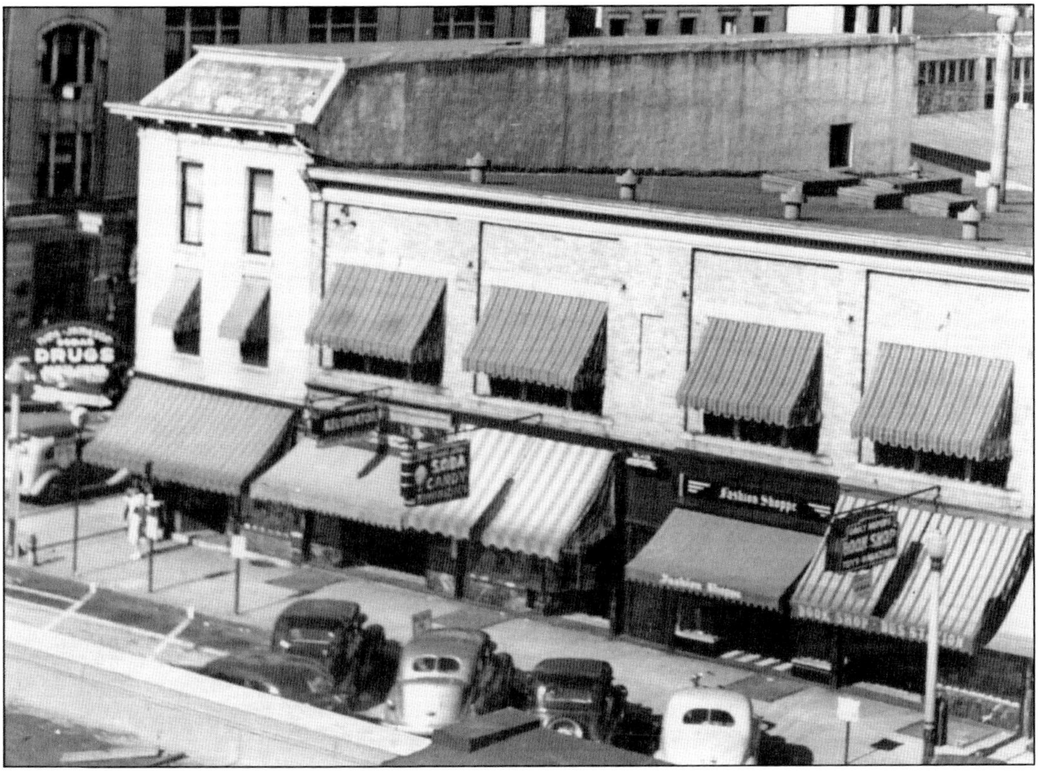

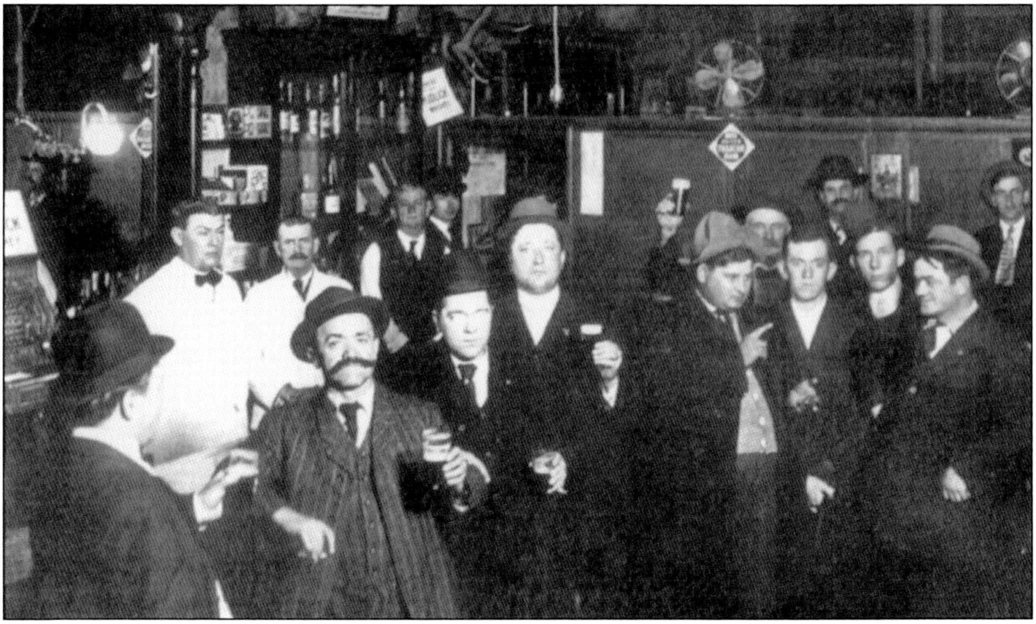

This image was taken in an unidentified saloon that was on the ground floor of the Blair Brothers Hospital on the Mulberry Street side. According to local folklore, when ambulances came to the Mulberry Street entrance, patrons were often asked to assist in carrying stretchers to the second-floor hospital. (Courtesy of WCHS Museum.)

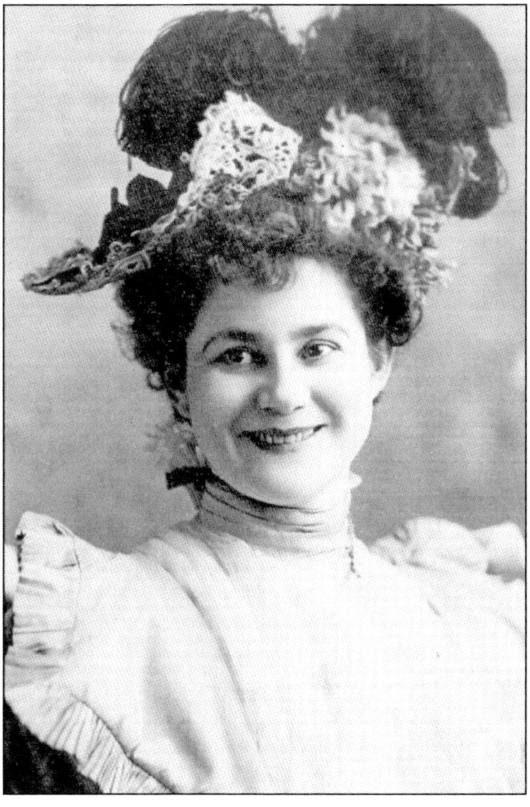

Lebanon sisters Dolly Nobles (pictured) and Laura Bellini were the daughters of Lebanon residents William and Rebecca Woolwine. Laura was born in 1851, while sister Dolly was born in 1861. Dolly married actor William Nobles at age 19 and appeared with her husband not only in Shakespearian tragedies, but also on Broadway Street and in vaudeville. (Courtesy of WCHS Museum.)

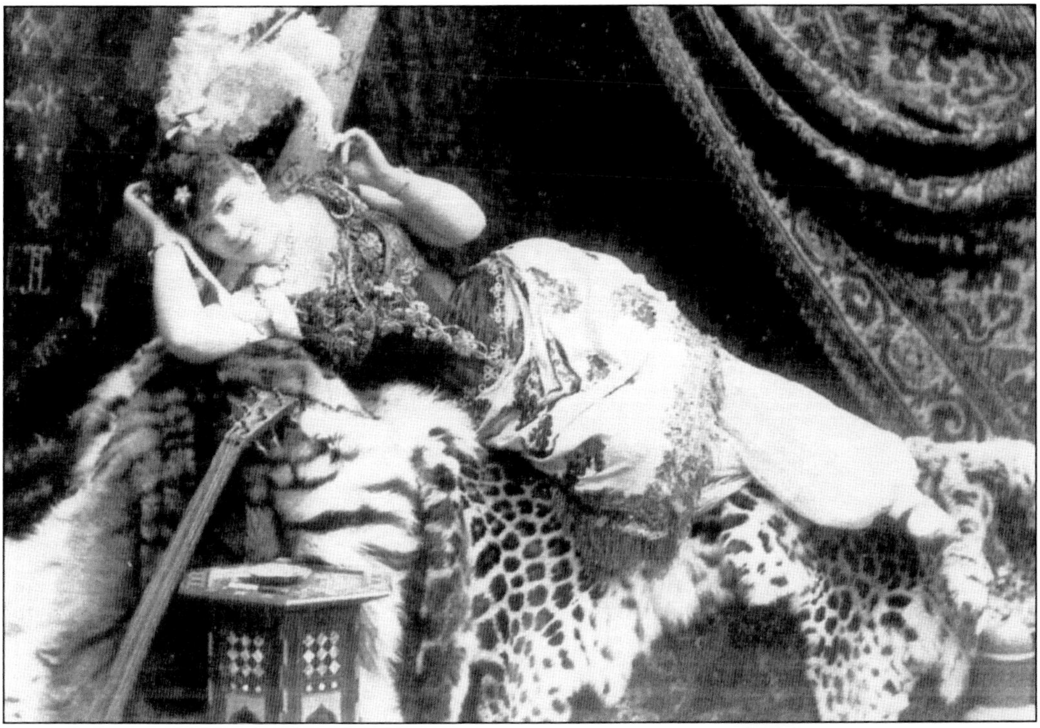

Laura Bellini studied opera in Italy. She made her debut at La Scala, appearing in *Rigoletto.* During the latter part of the 19th and early 20th centuries, she performed at the greatest opera houses in Italy, France, and England. She returned to Lebanon for a centennial concert and sang at the Lebanon Opera House. Laura died in 1931 and is buried in the Lebanon Cemetery. (Courtesy of WCHS Museum.)

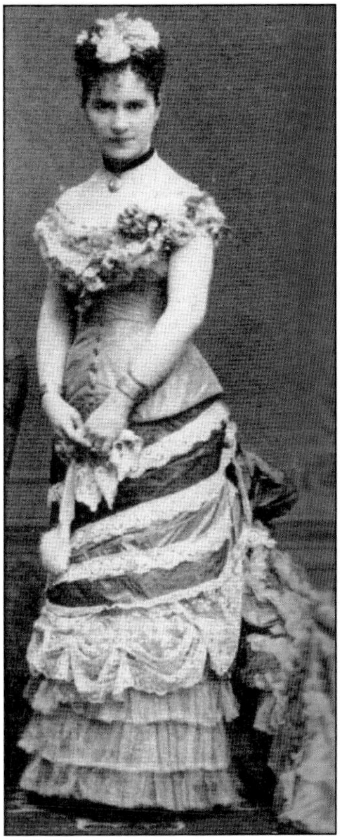

This early-1900s image of Laura Bellini shows her in costume for one of her many theatrical performances. After this picture was taken, the photographer used a pencil to disguise her décolletage for modesty's sake. (Courtesy of WCHS Museum.)

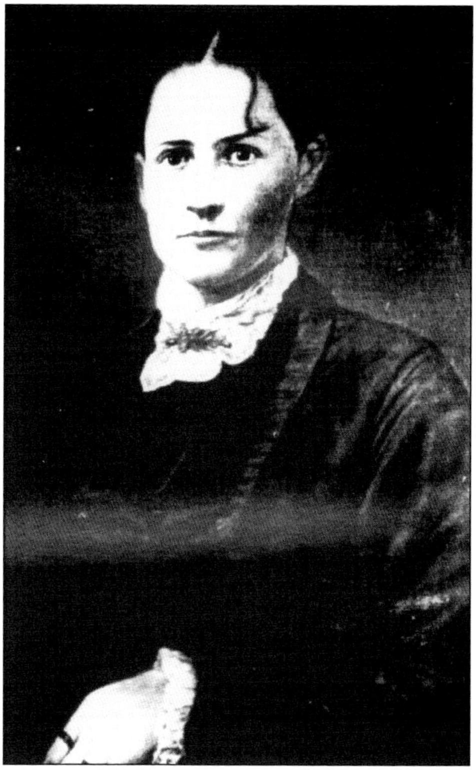

This portrait of Charity Steddom was painted by noted Quaker artist and Lebanon resident Marcus Mote. Painting primarily portraits and religious scenes, the works of Mote are highly collectible and sought after by enthusiasts of early Ohio artists. Unfortunately no portrait or photograph of the famous artist is available. (Courtesy of WCHS Museum.)

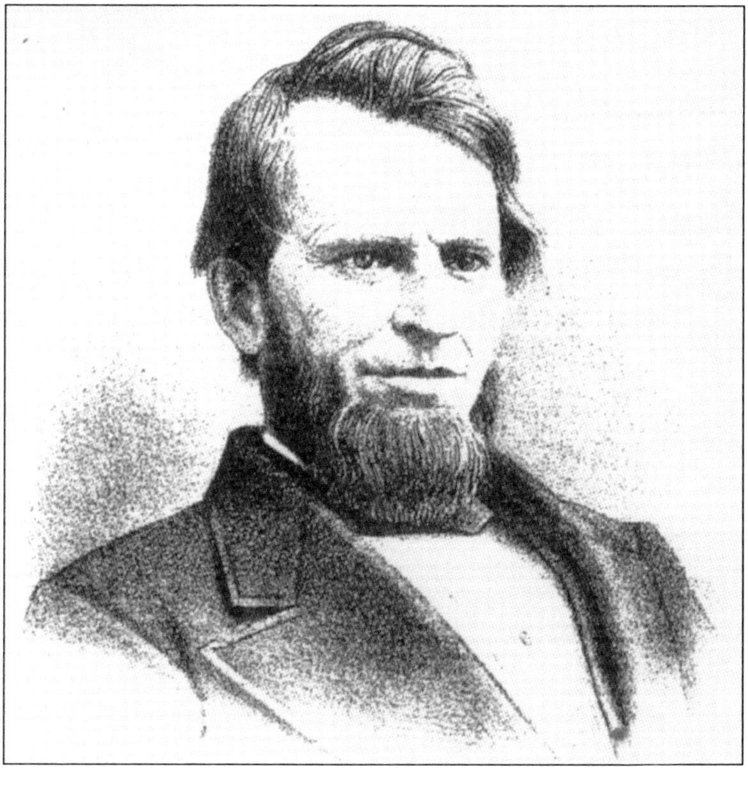

Alfred Holbrook is remembered in Lebanon as being the foremost educator of his time. For over 30 years, Holbrook presided over and administered one of the most unique educational institutions in the Midwest. He did this without accepting any type of government or private funding. (Courtesy of WCHS Museum.)

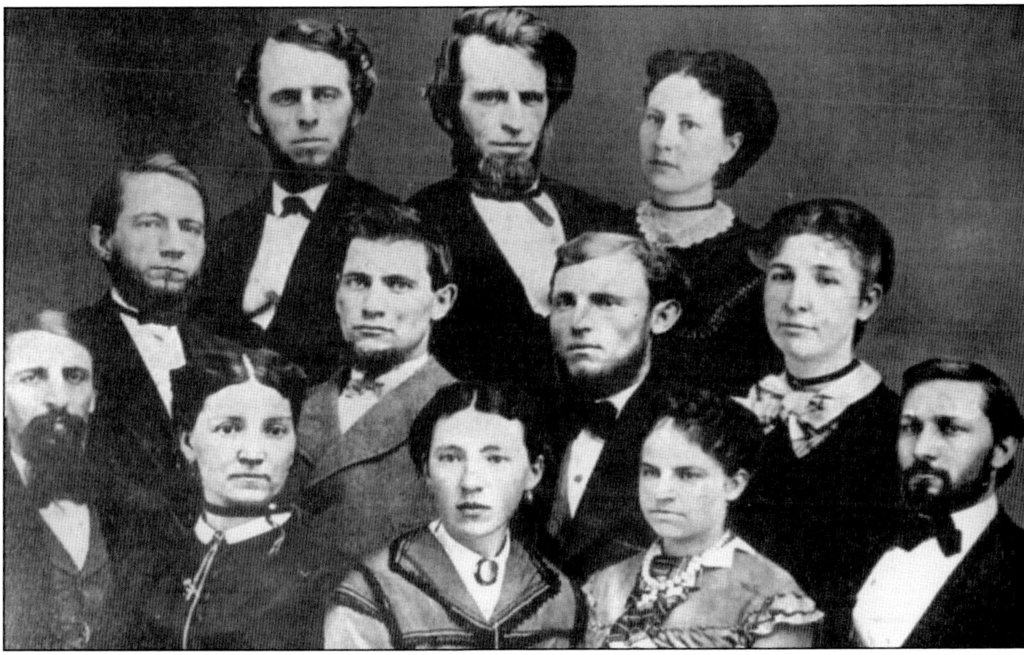

This rare image shows a young Alfred Holbrook (third row, center) with his family. The other family member are, from left to right, (first row) Josiah Holbrook, Elise Aubert, Elsie Kriegler, Irene Holbrook, and W. B. Durie; (second row) H. N. Carrer, J. Fraise Richard, J. Lee Gamble, and Sarah J. Porter; (third row) R. H. Holbrook, Alfred Holbrook, and Georgie Leonard. (Courtesy of WCHS Museum.)

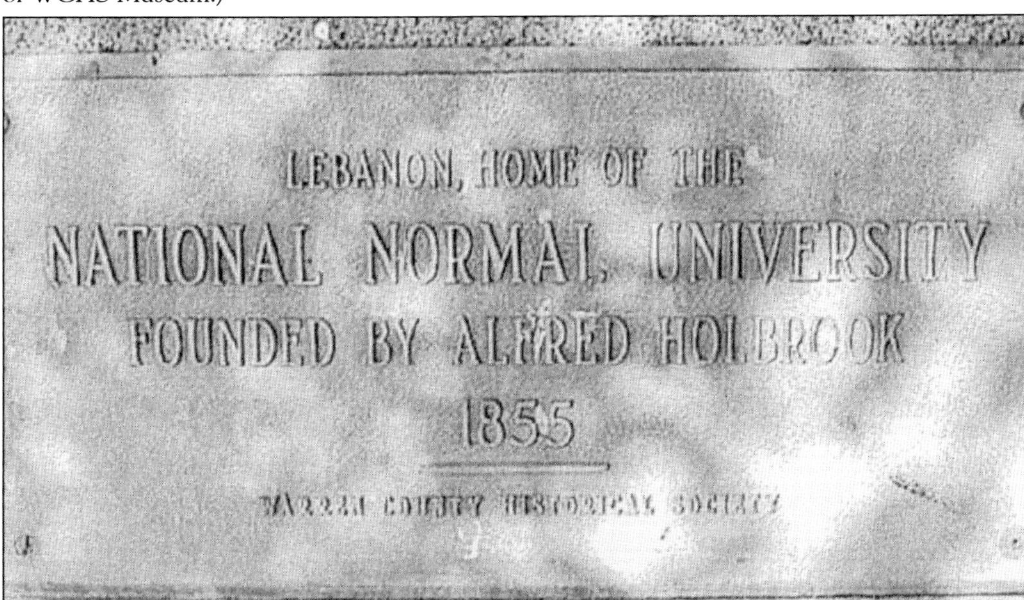

This 1950s image shows the dedication of the marker commemorating the historical significance of National Normal University. The college campus had all but disappeared by this time, so the marker was placed in what is now Gazebo Park in the center of town instead of the college's true location in the northeast section of Lebanon. (Courtesy of WCHS Museum.)